Behind the Scenes of
OTTO
PREMINGER

Also by Willi Frischauer

Behind the Scenes of
OTTO PREMINGER

AN UNAUTHORIZED BIOGRAPHY

by Willi Frischauer

WILLIAM MORROW & COMPANY, INC.
NEW YORK   1974

Contents

Illustrations

Acknowledgements

Most of the volumes listed in the bibliography contain references to Otto Preminger which throw a light on his attitudes. Though many of the facts were known to me, I have quoted from them whenever they contributed new details. The material about Preminger and his work generated by professional publicists is overwhelming and repetitive, and regurgitates facts and fiction with equal *élan*. Where possible, I have simply disregarded the falsehoods and given the facts as I knew and saw them.

Preminger's New York office has provided me with much of the published stories about him, good or bad; Otto's family, staff, associates and friends have talked freely – with his approval. I am grateful for the patience with which they submitted to my questioning.

Well-known show business figures and technicians who talked to me, unless quoted by name, insisted on anonymity because, while highly critical, even contemptuous of Preminger, they were yet reluctant to criticise him openly and spoil their chances of working for him again, which is not surprising in the current state of the film industry.

My friend Pem, who did not live to see the publication of this volume, helped with general information. Ted Purdy's advice, as always, has been invaluable. Gil Pearson has typed the manuscript beautifully, and my wife, as usual, has borne a greater share of the work than is apparent. I owe her a great deal.

WILLI FRISCHAUER
London 1973

9

Introduction

In Vienna in the late 'twenties and early 'thirties – as in most cities and at all times – the practitioners of the theatre and the press jostled each other in the narrow circle of an 'intellectual élite'. It was impossible not to meet. Otto Preminger and I were almost of the same age, both sons of lawyers. As I first remember him, he was an actor and precocious theatre Direktor, a term embracing artistic as well as business management, already bald and looking and acting older than his twenty-five years. (Was Otto ever young? He must have been for, as it turned out, we went to the same school.) His great talent combined with his father's wealth and prominence to give him a secure place in the Vienna establishment. At that time I was a precocious young editor, looking younger than my age, working for my uncle who owned the newspaper. I knew Otto's father well and covered at least one of the spectacular court appearances of this brilliant lawyer. Otto's younger brother Ingo also became a friend.

In those early days Otto and I shared many private preoccupations (but, as far as I remember, never the same women). Though not a show business reporter or theatre critic, I frequently wrote about him because Otto made news as regularly as I reported the events of the day. He left Vienna for Hollywood in 1935 almost precisely at the time I transferred my activities to London but we kept in touch and met whenever we were in the same country or capital. The grapevine which carried information about compatriots in exile kept me informed about his progress or set-backs but the war was not conducive to personal contact across the Atlantic. When I toyed with the idea of emigrating to the

United States he responded promptly to my request for support: 'I shall be very happy to give you the affidavit you require,' he wrote.

After the war we met with increasing regularity as Otto's ventures took him more frequently to Europe. In an honorary capacity I helped with the promotion of Jean Seberg, his new discovery from Marshalltown, Iowa, who became the star of his ill-starred film *St Joan* which was shot in London. I was his guest during the production of many of his films and, though he never made any demands ('Join me,' he would say, 'I don't care whether you write or what you write!'), wrote about them as often as I could.

In this way I saw him at work probably more frequently than most (except his small permanent staff) and under vastly different conditions – *St Joan* in London, *Bonjour Tristesse* in the South of France, *Exodus* in Israel, *Advise and Consent* in Washington (I happened to be in New York at the time and was carried to Washington on the magic carpet of a movie budget). I visited the set (a hospital) when he made *Bunny Lake is Missing* with Carol Lynley in London, was standing in the wings in Vienna watching *The Cardinal* come to life, and back in New York for *Such Good Friends* . . .

Vivid in my mind are some of his first encounters with budding young actresses whom he made into stars and, in the passage of time, I talked to many actors and actresses he directed and to the man who directed him – Billy Wilder – in the remarkable part of a Nazi camp commandant in *Stalag 17*. There was no dividing line between our professional and private meetings – Otto likes an audience when conducting his affairs (except when money is mentioned), and I have sat in on all manner of business conversations. I met his three wives, the second only fleetingly. From visit to visit over the past decade, I saw his twins grow up – they are the same age as my grandson. I was his 'mouthpiece' when he revealed the secret of his eldest son, Erik, whose mother was Gypsy Rose Lee.

By force of professional habit, I collected material about Otto through all those years – perhaps I felt that I might one day decide to record his varied and hectic life between hard covers. It was because they thought of me as his friend that my publishers suggested I write his biography. It seemed a rewarding assignment and I accepted the proposition. But I am no Boswell and friendship is not the ideal point of departure for a biographer. On the contrary, when the biographer appears on the scene, the friend must take his leave.

One does not observe a friend with a critical eye – I like my friends not because of their virtues but despite their faults. One does not – I do not – analyse a friend but take him as he is, and Otto was always very easy to take. Loyal to old cronies to the point of sentimentality, he is extravagantly generous, singularly unpompous, instantly accessible and as free with his time as with his money, never, apparently, operating in compartments and mixing associates from different spheres of his life which suggests an honest man who need not adjust to the company he keeps.

This is the Otto Preminger I knew as a friend for forty years or more but the pattern changed as soon as I began to work on his biography: 'I shall do my best to help you in every way possible and look forward to seeing you in New York,' he wrote. But as soon as I arrived, I was unceremoniously transported into his professional orbit which is crowded by people who are either in his pay or dependent on his goodwill. The master manager of public opinion reared his gleaming bald and forbidding dome and his benevolent smile only thinly disguised the menace below. It was probably my imagination but even his stereotype 'Write what you like about me' evoked an echo – '. . . at your peril!'

From now on the Hollywood code of ethics governed our association. Variations in temper and decibels controlled by a virtuoso of these basic elements in a movie-maker's armoury came out of the old magician's bag. Thunder claps marked every divergence of view and, sometimes, even perfect agreement. Almost in the same breath it was back to the mollifying: 'Watch me, observe me! Write what you like!' No longer an old friend but an old pro who knows his subject already fairly well, this is what I did. To discard the blinkers of friendship was all I needed to get the picture.

I

'Paranoic, You Are Not!'

Behind the gleaming black wooden wall with his name in startingly tiny and austere lettering, design Saul Bass, Otto Preminger's office on the top floor of the Columbia Building at 711, Fifth Avenue, New York, is bright and stagey as if dreamed up by a movie architect.

Not a sound from the cubicles of the staff. The door at the end of the corridor opens to a large room with an outsize marble-topped desk behind which Preminger sits and talks simultaneously to three visitors and aides in the comfortable leather chairs facing him. The walls are covered with some of his fine collection of paintings, many of them abstracts – a Dubuffet, a Sutherland, a Hartnung, a Klee, two Diego Riveras and a Sam Francis.

The telephone rings and OP, as the staff call him (or 'Big O' or Ottocrat, one of the countless puns his name inspires) barks into the receiver: 'This is the worst contract I have ever signed!' His expression is angry. The next sentence comes out a few decibels louder: 'I only agreed because I wanted to make this thing!'

The voice at the other end chatters away as if trying to stem the tidal wave: 'This is an outrage!' Preminger shouts. 'It means the agent is getting more than I!' The receiver comes down with a bang. Preminger's head sways from side to side, the eyes roll until a smile appears on his ample lips which his tongue moistens in a circular movement. Looking across the table, he winks as if to say: 'An impressive performance, eh?'

The project under discussion was his next venture, a realistic fictionalised two-hour television film based on the treason trial of Julius and Ethel Rosenberg for the American

Broadcasting Company. Because the Rosenbergs' name was not to be mentioned on television, the plan was for a cinema version with no holds barred to be shot simultaneously.

The first American civilians to be executed for treason, were the Rosenbergs guilty beyond the shadow of a doubt? Preminger has been planning for some years to tackle the 1951 trial and was groping for a twist to make it newsworthy. He persuaded the great trial lawyer Louis Nizer to write the script with the proposed title: 'Open Question'.

Negotiations about a few points were still in the balance but the announcement of the Nizer-Preminger project made a big impact. It was in character for Preminger who specialises in controversial subjects way ahead of timid showbiz escapism, if not of public opinion.

He has caught the headlines – and earned a reputation for devil-may-care defiance of convention – with *The Moon is Blue* which broke the film taboo on words like 'virgin' and 'seduce'; with *The Man with the Golden Arm*, first movie to deal with the drug scene; with *Anatomy of a Murder* which put rape on the screen. He raised some dust with the homosexual implications in *Advise and Consent*, with the Jewish problem (*Exodus*) and the black-white clash in the deep South (*Hurry Sundown*), though the finished product did not always match the boldness of the decision, and the bark of the moralists was often worse than the bite of the producer.

Emerging from his office, Otto Preminger scans Fifth Avenue for a taxi. He is dressed in the latest fashion – Cardin suit with flared trousers which are held up by a hipster belt as low as the gently swelling waistline permits. Kipper-tie from Bonwit Teller and buckled shoes. Against the rain, a tight-waisted raincoat, no hat on the bald head which, like Yul Brynner's, has become a trademark. Way beyond the age of a raver, he manages to look discreetly elegant in his mod gear.

No need to battle for the cab-driver's attention. In New

York it is the cab drivers who hail him: 'Hi, Otto . . .!' Four stop to compete for his custom: 'How's things, Otto,' asks the driver who has caught the precious quarry. 'Fine, everything's fine!' Otto reassures his fan.

Otto Preminger has produced and/or directed thirty-five major American films, roughly one for every year since he arrived in the United States from Vienna. In a notoriously rapacious industry which makes mincemeat of men and their reputations, he has survived longer and better than most. He has directed successful plays on Broadway and, as an actor, has portrayed ruthless Nazis with remarkable fidelity on screen and stage.

Show business has earned him some five or six million dollars and, while spending lavishly, he has yet vastly increased his fortune by shrewd investment. His art treasures have multiplied in value and he owns an elaborately luxurious New York town house with private cinema. No car, though – except the small fleet he hires for himself, his wife and his staff.

For his immense popularity he has a simple explanation: 'It's television,' he says. And personality, one might add. He was a guest star on the 'Batman' show (to please his children) and on 'Laugh-In'. In the last few years he has become a much sought-after guest on talk shows, always good for a laugh or a provocative remark. He deploys his limited English vocabulary with great strategic skill and the few verbal tanks under his command often bulldoze better equipped but less aggressive opponents.

One day, with Darryl Zanuck and Elia Kazan, he appears on a pre-recorded David Frost Show and raises a big laugh at the expense of James Mason. When Zanuck mentions one Mason film that Mason would like to forget, Preminger interjects: 'You mean Mason wants to forget only one of his films?'

The following day he appears live on ABC's Dick Cavett Show to plug the Rosenberg project for the same company.

Cavett cannot resist the stereotype joke about Preminger's bald head which evokes an expression of tolerant ennui. Exchanging pleasantries with fellow guest Anne Baxter, Otto knowledgeably recalls how he met her grandfather, the late Frank Lloyd Wright, America's leading architect of his time.

The third member of Cavett's cast that evening is a young American girl student just back from an encounter with the Chinese Premier Chou En Lai of which she gives a fascinating account. In Preminger it stirs an interest deeply submerged beneath his celluloid preoccupations and seems to bring home to him the triviality of the showbiz chatter which is his metier. During the next few days, he returns to the girl in every other conversation.

After a visit to Baton Rouge, Louisiana, where Otto Preminger's big film unit was on location with *Hurry Sundown* – the locals on edge about the black-and-white theme, the temperature in the nerve-testing hundreds – Rex Reed, movie reporter and critic, wrote a piece for the *New York Times* which added up to a stinging attack on the film's producer-director.

Reed quoted Michael Caine, the English star, talking about Preminger: 'He loves to embarrass actors in front of other people to tear down their egos. He's only happy if everybody else is miserable. Still, if you can keep his paranoia from beating you down, you can learn a lot from this guy.'

When he read in cold print what he may or may not have said in the boiling cauldron of Baton Rouge, Michael Caine sat down and penned a cable to Preminger: 'Dear Otto. I have looked up the word in the dictionary,' it said. 'Paranoic, you are not.'

The dozen or so tables immediately by the entrance in New York's Twenty-One Club are a club within a club. Admission is by public prominence only, preferably in show business, and tables are eagerly sought by those who like to be seen as much as the club likes to show them off. Among them Otto Preminger is a regular.

We dined there one evening in August 1971 while he was shooting *Such Good Friends* at locations in New York. Otto felt thoroughly at home: 'This is the place I came to straight from the boat when I first arrived in the United States on 21 October 1935,' he said. He nodded in the direction of a youthfully old gentleman a few tables further on: 'That's Prince Obolensky,' he said, 'the man who permitted me to stay on at the St Regis Hotel in the early forties when I told him that I could not afford to pay.' The man at the next table started talking to Preminger – in New York a well-known personality is fair game for approach by anyone.

Formalities observed all round – including a little banter with the head waiter who happens to be Viennese – we concentrated on the subject that interested me most: Otto Preminger. A gossip rather than a conversationalist, he promptly launched out on some highly amusing but wickedly derogatory stories about a fellow film producer of European origin.

Chuckles thickened his accent. He mentioned the name of a car which I had never heard before and which sounded like 'Stutzburger' – it turned out to be 'Stutz Bearcat'.

'What was that you just said?' I asked innocently. Otto broke off his monologue. His shiny pate reddened down to his collar. The jugular vein on his massive neck swelled alarmingly. His guffaws turned into a splutter which contorted his speech even further. As far as I could make out, he was reproaching me for having interrupted his train of thought.

Necks at nearby tables were craned to watch the imminent explosion. They saw the famous face distorted with rage – about nothing. He seemed to be as near apoplexy as I had ever seen anyone. Was it an act in the good old Hollywood tradition or was it a genuine outburst? To my layman's mind it seemed so bewildering; I never even reproached myself for bringing on this extraordinary behaviour.

In a minute it was all over. Regaining his composure and speaking in a voice near to a whisper, Otto said: 'Let's talk about something else!'

Preminger's explosions are almost legendary. Every other actor or technician has his own store of stories about them. On the set, when he directs, it is not the temperamental star who throws the tantrums but the producer-director himself. Since death has gathered in the most turbulent of the species, Otto Preminger has graduated to his position as the film industry's undisputed top screamer.

In an English television programme in the summer of 1971 the urbane David Niven, gentleman of the screen, mentioned the late Michael Curtiz (real name: Kertesz), Hollywood's most tempestuous director in recent memory. Struggling for a graphic word-picture of the Curtiz manner, Niven finally explained: 'Compared with Curtiz, Otto Preminger is as gentle as a choirboy.'

The brand of roughhouse Preminger practices follows the old Hollywood formula: 'When in difficulty, shout, scream, go mad, try to terrify the people around you!' Bob Thomas, in his biography of Columbia boss Harry Cohn, quotes an exchange between Cohn and an associate: 'Harry, why are you so rough on the people who work for you?' Harry Cohn: 'I am the king here. Whoever eats my bread sings my song.'

Alfred Hitchcock who brings British sang-froid to film making was quoted as saying that 'Actors are cattle', but put out an amended version. What he meant to say was, 'actors should be treated like cattle'.

Nat Rudich, Preminger's right-hand man for nearly a decade and the most frequent butt of his outbursts, recalls an incident in his work with Piscator, the German *avant-garde* director who ran a theatre and actors' school in New York. After watching Rudich directing in a school production,

Piscator told him: 'You are a very good director except for one thing . . .'

'What?'

'You do not yell. Even if it is not necessary – always yell.'

Hit by Preminger's barrack-room voice, Nat Rudich takes comfort from the memory of Piscator's Prussian practices but there are many who have not taken these outbursts so philosophically.

Lana Turner is still angry though it is years since their much-publicised quarrel about her clothes. Preminger had a slanging match with the late Randolph Churchill, bullied little Jean Seberg in St Tropez, rowed with Lee J. Cobb in Jerusalem and with David Niven in the Bois de Boulogne. He had a violent clash with agent Irving Lazar in the Twenty-One (and a bloody head to show for it), outraged the Jewish Congress in Brussels and sued an American TV company – over a principle, the mutilation of one of his films – and Faye Dunnaway over a contract. A former Austrian Minster of Education fell victim to his anger, and he was so rude to Rex Reed on a TV show that some of his remarks had to be 'bleeped' out.

In the trade he is known as a teaser, a taunter, a tester of other people's endurance. Jokes at their expense and his heavy humour strike some as plain insulting. Others are so accustomed to it that they hardly notice. One of his former aides swears that the whole scenario is a piece of play-acting to assure Preminger and his work maximum attention. Others have seen him embarrassed and contrite after an uncontrollable outburst. His wife, Hope, on some of these occasions, looks as if she wished the ground would open up and swallow her.

Writers, in turn, can be pretty poisonous when he is their subject. One wrote that, whereas others have a Fan Club, Preminger has a Foes Club; another described him as the man who drinks actors' blood instead of Bloody Marys – and more in the same vein.

Yet, some of his best-publicised rows were worthy battles with censors and busy-body organisations which he has spiritedly defied to his own advantage and that of the film industry. Whoever his opponent, he calms down as quickly as he flares up but has a habit of spreading niggling little tales about his adversaries which drum in his version of the conflict. With his legal bent he constructs contingency plans for every eventuality which he hoards in his mind and for which he lays some foundation. They make him a difficult man to argue with. He may not always be right but he sees to it that he cannot easily be proved wrong.

Since it is usually he who starts a quarrel, he is always ready to make it up. That is why, when all is said and done there is no major studio boss who will not work with him and only a few supersensitive actors and technicians so genuinely terrified of him that they will not knock at his door for a job in his next picture. He has had his failures, but they have not deterred distributors from underwriting his next production.

Neither is he as dependent on cooperation as other producers. He is at his best as an impresario who can put a project together with the flimsiest ingredients. His greatest asset in a notoriously unreliable industry is that he can be relied upon to keep expenditure rigorously within the agreed budget, to overcome obstacles which bedevil other producers and directors, to complete his picture on time and conjure up some crowd-pulling stunt to chisel his name and that of his film into public consciousness.

'Otto Preminger', says Darryl Zanuck, 'is a very good and very talented director. But he makes either a great or a crazy picture! Never in-between!' Preminger himself pretends that he never looks back on a film once he has finished it – and some of his films certainly do not bear looking back upon. His memory is altogether highly idiosyncratic and selective.

He rejects the so-called Hollywood label for himself and generally but is yet the prototype of the proverbial Hollywood executive, probably the last of the breed, with Hollywood's peculiar brand of egocentricity, megalomania, hang-ups, prejudices, constricted view of the world and indifference to things non-Hollywood which is characteristic of this vanishing race. While he does not live in Hollywood – few film men do nowadays – he carries the flimsy Hollywood atmosphere with him like an astronaut who has descended from outer space in a cocoon of weightlessness.

Professionally he is being observed and studied by experts everywhere. Aspiring young scholars from emergent African countries are among those who clamour for permission to watch him at work. They are allowed to lend a hand and, not infrequently, feel the lash of his tongue. Preminger films have been featured in retrospectives in several countries.

The subject of a book published in France which analyses his earlier films, and of hundreds of magazine features, studies, pamphlets and publicity handouts, Preminger is reticent about his personal life, the complications, the difficulties, the conflicts, but they are part of his life-cycle which ought to be seen in the context of his career.

Privately, he is sailing in calmer waters now. His twelve-year-old twins Mark and Vicky, children of his third wife, came late in his life and he is making up for the delay with tender affection which is touching to watch. Almost as moving – his discovery of his grown-up son whose mother was Gypsy Rose Lee, Queen of Strippers.

Among his most cherished memories are encounters with several Presidents of the United States. The most recent invitation to a White House party reached the Premingers six weeks after President Nixon's inauguration. Otto found it on his desk side by side with a letter from ex-Vice President Hubert Humphrey thanking him for his work on behalf of the Democrats. Preminger called his wife Hope: 'Somebody must be making a joke,' he told her. 'Why should Nixon ask us? I voted for Lyndon Johnson but it took him four years to invite us . . .'

'Yes, but President Nixon is much more desperate for friends,' was Hope Preminger's very Preminger-like reply.

It is the kind of remark Otto Preminger loves to quote. He is more honest about himself than his publicists who polish away at the rough edges of his personality and, in the good old Hollywood style, cover it with a gloss of sycophancy until the most basic ingredients become distorted.

How many Hollywood personalities have long since forgotten their real names? For how many – like Otto Preminger – it must be difficult to remember when and where they were born.

II

Tales of Vienna

'Preminger: I cannot remember dates and years... There
are only three dates I am sure of. On the twenty-first of
October, 1935, I arrived in this country from Vienna. On
the third of October, 1960, my children were born. And
on the fifth of December, 1906, I was born.'

New Yorker, 19 February 1966

In the first week of December 1970 Otto Preminger received
a letter from Vienna with the official seal of the Danube city:

'As Mayor of your Vaterstadt [native city] as well as in
my own name,' it read, 'I congratulate you wholeheartedly
and with genuine esteem on the occasion of your sixty-fifth
birthday. The greetings of your old home country go out to
the successful film director who has prevailed and maintained
himself in the United States in the face of the strongest
competition. Apart from your tremendous gifts, you owe
these not least to the training which you received in Vienna
and which have enhanced your inborn artistic qualities . . .'

The letter was signed 'Marek'. The Mayor of Vienna, now
retired, has a distinguished record as an anti-Nazi: 'I did not
even reply,' Otto Preminger said contemptuously.

It was not the first honour Vienna had conferred on him
in the last decade. In 1961 the Austrian President awarded
him the Cross of Honour for Science and Art, and in 1971
he was given the Gold Medal of Honour of the City of
Vienna by the Lord Mayor who, like everybody else, took
it for granted that Preminger was born in the old Danube
city.

The warm feelings which these honours reflected were not
reciprocated. On the contrary. Otto Preminger hates Vienna.
He told me that he could not forget that so many people he

knew and valued were murdered in the Nazi period: 'I could not imagine ever living again in Vienna,' he said. Talking to Viennese in their own language made him feel they might do it all over again.

The Mayor's good wishes have at least jolted Preminger's poor memory for dates, even for one of the three dates he was sure of. The year of his birth was not, as he thought and said on previous occasions, 1906 but 1905. It upset the apple-cart of the various anniversary celebrations planned for his sixty-fifth birthday in 1971. 1905 or 1906 – does it matter? In the Hollywood world of make-believe where publicity handouts take precedence over real life, such incidentals as birth date and family background tend to become blurred. One could no longer even be sure *where* Otto Preminger was born . . .

His father, Dr Markus Preminger, was one of Vienna's top lawyers in the inter-war years. A man with a sharp mind and acid wit, he was a shrewd debater and forceful advocate in court. Although he had a fine command of the German language he spoke it with the faint but unmistakable and persistent accents of the eastern outposts of the multi-national Habsburg monarchy. Markus Preminger was born in 1877, at Czernovic, Galicia, a province of old Austria which, in the turbulent history of eastern Europe, came in turn under Polish and Rumanian sovereignty and has now ended up inside Soviet Russia.

The son of poor, underprivileged Jewish parents, Markus was a gifted boy. He went from high school to university (law school) – higher education in these parts meant German education – and graduated *magna cum laude*, which was the highest distinction and earned him the diamond-studded ring of honour the 'benevolent' Emperor Francis Joseph bestowed on the year's outstanding scholar. His brilliant record enabled him to overcome the chief obstacle – an insidious and pervasive antisemitism – which frustrated the ambitions of even the ablest Jews.

For the brilliant young graduate there was a promising position in government service. Markus Preminger joined the legal administration and became an investigating magistrate, was promoted to the bench, but switched to the public prosecutor's department. When he married at the age of twenty-six his prospects, unlike those of other local Jews, were bright.

Two years later, on 5 December 1905, he wife Josefa gave birth to a boy, Otto Ludwig, a strong, healthy, handsome baby with a fluff of fair hair, finely chiselled features and small bright eyes which looked enquiringly into the world. For six years, little Otto was the proverbial apple of his father's eye, yet when his brother Ingo was born in 1911 he welcomed the new arrival without jealousy. As Ingo grew up, Otto watched over him with protective affection.

The Preminger boys enjoyed a stable and loving family life. They were as yet totally unaware of the political storms blowing up over their heads and threatening their whole existence. Eastern Europe was the world's danger zone. New nationalisms were growing and antagonisms brewing. Two Balkan wars aggravated tension and under the rickety umbrella of the Habsburg empire Slav and Teuton lived in uneasy proximity.

Galicians and Transylvanians, like Bohemians, Moravians, Serbs and Croats, strained at the leash of the Habsburg overlords and clamoured for self-determination and national independence. A harassed but obdurate German-speaking civil service and judiciary struggled to keep them in check.

Markus Preminger had little sympathy for the new national trends. His loyalty was to the old Emperor whom he represented in court, a picture of authority, with a sonorous, modulated voice. If he looked beyond his immediate sphere of office, it was not to some future new state but to the glittering and romantic capital of the empire: Vienna.

With his outstanding gifts, he would have made it to the Danube city in time, but history speeded up his progress.

The shots of Sarajevo changed the face of Europe. The Slav who assassinated the heir to the Habsburg throne provoked the first world conflagration.

Coming to the aid of the Serbs against Austria and her German ally, Czarist armies pushed into eastern Europe within weeks of the outbreak of the 1914 war. For a loyal monarchist, a judge and a Jew at that, it was no longer safe to remain in Czernovic which was within the range of the Russian guns. Though it was another two years before the Russians occupied the city, the exodus of the Jews which had been under way for some time swelled into a mass movement towards Austria.

With the Russians *ante portas*, Dr Markus Preminger arranged for his transfer. With his wife, nine-year-old Otto and three-year-old Ingo, he went to Graz, capital of the province of Styria, which was grappling with the problem of recalcitrant, nationalistic Serbs and Croats. Installed in the Graz Law Courts, Dr Preminger became an expert on the nationality tangle which tied up the Habsburg monarchy and eventually strangled it to death.

Otto joined the Volksschule (junior school) but, in this intensely Catholic and Germanic town, the boy from Czernovic was a stranger and, even worse, a Jew. As immigrants, 'Galician Jews' bore the brunt of antisemitism and the very term was bandied about as an insult. No wonder, local boys did not take kindly to Otto. One day, on his way home from school, he was waylaid, insulted and beaten up.

His injuries were not severe, the pain abated but the scars the incident left on his mind never disappeared. He did not tell his parents – to this day he is not sure what stopped him. He was humiliated – was he ashamed of being a Jew? Did he want to spare his parents the same humiliation?

The traumatic effect was such that, for over fifty years, he kept the secret of that day. It was news to his wife when she learned of it in 1971, and his brother Ingo had never heard about it until I related it to him – he was too young to know at the time. Not until quite recently could Preminger get himself to talk about it.

His fervent Judaism, his aversion to Vienna – since the 1938 Nazi invasion more and more identified with the anti-semitic little gangsters who attacked him – date back to this experience.

In contrast to his father who sought refuge in Vienna where he made his fortune (and his brother who loves Austria where he bought a house in 1970) Otto, from earliest youth, if perhaps subconsciously, was only waiting for an opportunity to get away.

His father's big time started as soon as he was posted to Vienna and joined the imperial army's legal division. Dr Markus Preminger played a prominent part in the trials of defectors, secessionists and opponents of the Habsburg hege-mony which marked the monarchy's decline. A determined defender of the *status quo*, he became a stern prosecutor of all who tried to stab the multi-national country in the back while it was fighting for its life.

He was appointed Prosecutor General. Few Jews held higher office in Austria's Catholic-orientated hierarchy. Who knows how much further he might have gone had he agreed to abandon his Jewish faith. The family say that it was strongly suggested to him but he refused to convert.

As it was, Dr Preminger figured in some of the period's most spectacular court scenes. He led the prosecution of Dr Kramarz (which in German rhymes with 'arse'), Bohemian member of the Austrian parliament, who was indicted for plotting the breakaway of Bohemia from the monarchy. The verbal duel between public prosecutor and Kramarz in court was a forensic occasion. Facing the dock, Dr Preminger stemmed the flow of Kramarz's inflammatory rhetoric:

'You ought to be ashamed,' he said with an icy voice, 'right into the last syllable of your name!' The phrase is still quoted as a unique example of courtroom invective. Dr

Kramarz was sentenced to death but not executed. With Thomas Garrique Masaryk, he became the founder of Czechoslovakia.

Otto was sent to the Piaristengymnasium, the Catholic high school (with a liberal sprinkling of other denominations) within walking distance of the family apartment in the Strozzigasse in Vienna's Eighth district. Another pupil, two years ahead of Otto, was Walter Slezak (son of the great Viennese heroic tenor) who, like Otto, was to make a career for himself in Hollywood and on Broadway. The two did not meet at the time and compared notes only many years later. (Two or three years behind them, I attended the same school.)

There was a war on but it needed more than a war to interfere with Vienna's addiction to the arts. The Burgtheater (Court or National Theatre) and the State Opera competed for the minds and hearts of the young. Actors and singers were worshipped with a fervour which only film stars and pop singers commanded a generation or two later.

To visit the Burgtheater – more so than the Opera – was part of the education of a teenager from a middle-class home. To see the new plays and attend new productions was an integral part of social life. Otto managed to get to the theatre rather more frequently than other boys – too young perhaps to get the full flavour or be infected by his elder brother's enthusiasm, Ingo nevertheless tagged along.

Goethe, Schiller, Lessing, the German classics, shared the repertoire with Ibsen, Shakespeare and the whole repertory of established playwrights. The acting was conservative, speech declamatory, the atmosphere dignified, almost awe-inspiring. The venerable figures on stage in this cathedral of a theatre fascinated Otto and transported him into their world of fantasy. The theatre filled his young life. Playing truant from school for weeks on end, he and his class-mates congregated at the public library where they monopolised volumes of famous plays.

Otto was no more than eleven or twelve years old when they organised themselves into a cast each with a part to read aloud. He played, or rather spoke, many of the leading roles: Wilhelm Tell threatening the tyrant with a menacing monologue, the handsome Mortimer infatuated with Schiller's *Maria Stuart* (Mary Queen of Scots) or, again, Mark Antony intoning his rousing funeral oration with a perfectly articulated 'Mitbürger, Römer, Freunde, hört mich an!' ('Friends, Romans, Countrymen, lend me your ears!'). Preminger looks back on these public library readings as his first venture into the performing arts.

His father was in the thick of the dying monarchy's dissentions and quarrels in which insults were freely traded across the national divisions. Once war ended in defeat for Austria and new states grew from the ruins of the Habsburg empire, Dr Markus Preminger was furiously criticised by Czech and other neo-nationalists. He shrugged off these attacks: 'When you are in public life', he later told his son, 'you must learn to take it!'

When talking about his own reaction to bad reviews or criticism in the press, Otto Preminger often quotes his father and adds proudly: 'I have never ever complained to a newspaper.' He wants to suggest that, like his father, he can take it. But he is human and occasionally hits back hard – in private or in public – at those who attack him where it hurts. He can also be as compassionate as his father was with him. Dr Markus Preminger never punished his son, even covered up for him when he missed school without good excuse.

Dr Markus Preminger left government service and started his own law firm. He was as effective as an advocate as he had been as a prosecutor and prospered quickly. Some of Austria's richest men became his clients. He represented banks and industrial combines. The family moved from the eighth district to an apartment (Mahlerstrasse 9) in the more fashionable inner city. Ingo went to a different school but the brothers remained close.

They were close but different. Ingo played football, ice hockey, loved all sport. Not Otto. Otto learned great monologues, sometimes whole scenes from famous plays by heart. He wrote poetry. Ballads, romantic and heroic. None of them has survived and neither he nor Ingo can remember any of his 'immortal' verse.

Vienna was the ideal city for a youngster hooked on the stage. A well-built, good-looking student could easily insinuate himself into crowd scenes in one of the leading theatres – no pay, no unions, just fun. Otto did even better and managed to get a part (Lysander in *A Midsummer Night's Dream*) at the open-air theatre in the Burggarten, the grounds of the old imperial palace.

Papa Preminger at first looked indulgently upon his son's artistic excursions. So far so good! Young people should be romantic and adventurous, and this was surely a passing phase. For a prominent Viennese lawyer it was one thing to love the theatre and applaud the performers. For a member of his family to think seriously about making the stage his career was an entirely different matter.

It was Dr Preminger's dear wish that the boy should follow in his footsteps, become a lawyer and join the firm. Otto was still at high school when the family realised that this was a forlorn hope. His announcement that he was determined to be an actor, though not entirely unexpected, caused quiet consternation. No rows, no scenes but sad disappointment. Whatever Otto's ultimate ambition, Dr Preminger insisted that he should complete high school, go on to university, study law and graduate; for a young man with his background a degree was the accepted thing. If, at the end of it, he still wanted to be an actor, very well!

There was no question of defying father – the thought never occurred to Otto. But the reluctant scholar and aspiring young Thespian was anxious to put the years ahead to good use and not waste the time entirely with futile law studies. Matriculation was just around the corner and the long summer vacation before his first term at university was a good opportunity to step out on 'the boards that mean the world' (a typical German paraphrase for the stage).

III

The Magician's Disciple

A rare artistic event, a great social occasion, a red-letter day
in the history of the Vienna theatre. The début of 'The
Players of the Theatre in the Josefstadt under the Direction
of Max Reinhardt'. On the first of April 1924 the old house,
recently refurbished, glittered in tastefully opulent garb. The
huge, retractable chandelier, a symphony of glass and light,
hovered over the élite of Vienna's wealthy patrons of the arts·
A delightful décor, new ideas, acting of great quality.

Max Reinhardt opened the first Vienna theatre he could
call his own with Carlo Goldoni's *Servant of Two Masters* in
the classic Comedia dell'Arte style. The audience was literally
drawn into the action, the curtain not lowered during inter-
missions and scene changes were carried out by young
apprentice actors in period costumes. One of the proud
scene shifters on this great day: nineteen-year-old Otto
Preminger.

'Reinhardt! Reinhardt!' The audience clamoured for the
man responsible for this splendid evening.

Max Reinhardt. So great, so quickly and sadly forgotten –
except by connoisseurs of the German theatre and devotees
of the Salzburg Festival. Even those who remember him tend
to think vaguely of a 'Cecil B. de Mille of the Stage', more
concerned with appearance than with content. But his con-
temporaries celebrated him as 'The Magician of the
Theatre', the greatest showman of his time. He, more
modestly, described himself as a 'middleman between dream
and reality'.

When young Otto Preminger first became aware of Max
Reinhardt and long before he came face to face with him,
the 'magician', though still a giant of the profession, was past

34

his zenith. But the story of his life and work which filled newspapers and magazines was an inspiration for budding actors and directors.

Otto lapped up everything he read and heard about him. Sensitive artist! Pioneer of the modern theatre! Imaginative showman! Even a youngster less alert and dedicated would have been fired by the ideas of such a genius.

Was it instinct or – stretching imagination a little – did he, Otto Preminger, not have some things in common with Max Reinhardt? Son of an impecunious father, Max Goldmann (Reinhardt was the stage name he adopted later) had his roots in one of the non-German parts of the Habsburg monarchy to which Vienna's intellectual and artistic life owed the flavour of so much Jewish brain and talent.

Born in 1873 in Pressburg ('Poszony' when it belonged to the Hungarians, 'Bratislava' when it came under Czech rule), he grew up in Baden, a little spa only a stone's throw from Vienna. His first acting engagement was in Salzburg, the Mozart city to which he later returned with some of his greatest productions.

In Berlin, at the beginning of the century, Reinhardt took over the Deutsches Theater, threw conventions overboard, introduced revolving stages, sometimes operating three at the same time, broke up the proscenium, let the action spill over into the audience and moved the audience closer to the performers. Rapid changes, scenes fusing and dissolving – he liberated the old format, even presented some of his shows in the circus and in exhibition halls. One of his productions employed a cast of two thousand.

Wherever Reinhardt was mentioned – and he was frequently discussed within Otto's hearing – the talk was of his delicate touch and sensitive approach to individual actors from whom he extracted great performances. Intense, serene, quietly spoken, he allowed some talents to blossom unaided but with others patiently, almost hypnotically, explained each move, playing out a scene to show exactly what he

35

wanted. (Preminger, too, likes to demonstrate for his actors, if not always as tenderly as the old master.)

In Reinhardt's repertoire, classics alternated with contemporary plays. Old chestnuts were revived with musical and dancing interludes. Not content with available plays he commissioned works as vehicles for his own interpretation, among them *The Miracle*, a great spectacle, which has been described as a religious pantomime and was first shown in Vienna.

Reinhardt took the play to London where it was enthusiastically received: the star was Lady Diana Manners, the Duke of Rutland's beautiful daughter who married Alfred Duff Cooper. One of the smaller parts was taken by Ernst Lubitsch who went on to become one of Hollywood's most ingenious directors. During his stay in London with *The Miracle*, Max Reinhardt married Else Heims, the actress. The company went on to New York and Hollywood where the Reinhardt production was hailed as a great theatrical event.

Shortly after the war Reinhardt took over a second theatre in Berlin, drawing hundreds of thousands to his spectaculars – *Orestes*, *Lysistrata*, *Antigone*, *Julius Caesar*, *Othello*, *Danton*, *The White Saviour* (by Gerhard Hauptmann). Tremendous popular successes but often fiercely attacked by some critics. He was accused of 'murdering culture', of 'showbiz' tactics, though the word was not as yet in use at the time.

Dispirited, he turned his back on Berlin: 'We have deprived ourselves of the most magnificent talent of the German theatre,' moaned one of the culprits in the wave of self-criticism which followed his departure. Reinhardt returned to his native Austria, his eyes on Salzburg where his acting career had started over a quarter of a century earlier.

Otto Preminger was barely fifteen when he first heard the news: 'Max Reinhardt', someone said, 'wants to turn Salzburg into a festival city.' The idea had cropped up years earlier but it was Max Reinhardt's drive and imagination which made it possible, so soon after the war, to launch an artistic project of this magnitude.

With more faith than funds and without a theatre to call his own, he persuaded Hugo von Hoffmansthal to adapt *Everyman* from the English and turn it into a modern morality play. On 22 August 1920 it was first staged in a public square in Salzburg against the imposing backdrop of the old College Church. It became an annual event and, with Max Reinhardt attracting theatre lovers from all over the world, the star attraction of the Salzburg Festival.

In Vienna Reinhardt found a home for some of his productions at the exquisite little Redouten Theatre within the precincts of the old imperial palace. For decades the Burgtheater had to fear no rival, not on its Viennese home ground. Now, suddenly, the name of Reinhardt was once more on all lips. The more adventurous and progressive fans were dazzled by his modern, ingenious, personal approach.

Otto Preminger is not certain when and how the idea of him joining Reinhardt first originated. He was not aware of Reinhardt's attempts to raise big sums for a theatre of his own but they were no secret to his father whose clients were some of Austria's wealthiest men.

Money-wise, this was a fantastic period. A few years after the 1914–1918 war Vienna, like Berlin, was in the throes of an unprecedented run-away inflation. There was so much paper money about with so little real value that people papered the walls of their lavatories with one-million-kronen notes. While the giddy drop of the currency spelled impoverishment and starvation to thousands, a handful of clever operators with international connections exploited the situation and made huge profits on the London and New York money markets.

The undisputed champion of Vienna's 'inflation profiteers' was Camillo Castiglioni, a banker of Italian antecedents, who played the markets so brilliantly that he amassed a big real-money fortune. In the most hackneyed style of the proverbial 'angel', he not only had a surfeit of money but also a wife who fancied herself as an actress. It was no coincidence at all that Max Reinhardt's attention was drawn to this highly propitious combination of immense wealth married to theatrical ambition.

Castiglioni no sooner heard of Max Reinhardt's search for capital when he offered to finance his theatre provided there were parts for Iphigenie Buchmann, who happend to be Madame Castiglioni. When it came to realising his artistic ambitions, no sacrifice was too great for Max Reinhardt. What could he not accomplish with Castiglioni's backing!

Although her Hollywood career in the mid-thirties lasted barely three years, Louise Rainer, the sensitive actress, is well remembered as the star of *The Good Earth* (with Paul Muni) and *The Great Ziefeld*, both of which earned her Academy Awards in Hollywood. She lives quietly in London, the wife of an eminent publisher.

Among the paintings in their London mews house, Mrs Knittel, as she has been since 1944 (she was previously Mrs Clifford Odets), her favourite is a memento of her work with Max Reinhardt in Vienna. It is by Johann Fischbach, a nineteenth-century Austrian artist, and depicts a colourful group of travelling players with horse-drawn caravan, stage props, dogs and all. This motley group was the first ensemble of the Theater in der Josefstadt which was inaugurated with a piece, 'Consecration of the House', specially written for the occasion by Ludwig van Beethoven.

A very Austrian theatre, the Josefstadt carried on into the twentieth century when it came into the hands of Josef Jarno, a fine theatre man whose wife Hansi Niese was Vienna's foremost musical comedienne. It was Jarno's Josefstadt which Max Reinhardt wanted as his Vienna base. With finance largely provided by Camillo Castiglioni, he bought Jarno out; clients of Dr Markus Preminger were among his other rich supporters.

The great stars of the German stage assembled under the Reinhardt colours. Eugen Klopfer, Fritz Kortner, Alexander Moissi (the inspired Triestine), Else Lehmann, Helene Thimig and three male members of her family joined the new theatre. Louise Rainer was among the talented newcomers who became members of the exclusive company.

The rush for places even on the fringe of the Reinhardt ensemble turned into a stampede. Except for Madame Castiglioni, it needed more than money and influence to catch the magician's eye. Talent was the only sesame which opened the stage door of the old theatre which was rebuilt, redecorated, reborn in the image of its new master.

'Otto Ludwig' – as many friends and colleagues called young Preminger – went for an audition. Confident of his own ability, he appeared before Reinhardt, spoke his lines with conviction, if without the benefit of professional voice training. Reinhardt sensed the spark, the personality of the raw recruit. Otto Ludwig Preminger was accepted as an apprentice and only a few months separated him from his first appearance as a Reinhardt player, albeit as a silent scene shifter, which coincided with the Josefstadt début of the great man himself.

The players of the Theater in der Josefstadt under the direction of Max Reinhardt went from triumph to triumph but for the ambitious young Preminger the few walk-on parts which were the best he could get were a sorry anti-climax: 'I got bored,' he recalled. He was impatient, determined to get ahead, Reinhardt or no Reinhardt, to put it bluntly.

His other career – as a law student – required little effort. Studying in Austria in the early twenties was a casual affair for those who simply wanted a degree but had no intention of practising in adult life what they learned at university. Attendance at lectures was not strictly obligatory and students could pursue other interests and yet comply with minimum requirements. Besides, there were the long summer vacations.

Otto Preminger duly enrolled in the law faculty, then turned to his real love, the theatre. Even with the Reinhardt background, theatre managers in Vienna did not exactly fall over themselves to offer him star parts, neither did he really expect them to. He was prepared to learn the hard way which took him to the German theatre in Prague, capital of the new Czechoslovakia.

Though for a young actor it was a move in the best tradition of the theatre, his new job could not be counted among the plums of the profession nor, in the prevailing circumstances, was it helpful to Dr Markus Preminger to have a son performing in some distant theatre. So as not to embarrass his famous father, Prague's new player took the stage name of 'Otto Pretori'. He was given the odd part but there were no great prospects for him here either.

He still sported a head of fair hair with a parting but his hairline was receding fast which made him look much older than he was. Another couple of years and, save for a fringe along a line from ear to ear, he was virtually bald: 'It worried him,' Ingo Preminger said when we discussed it. 'Someone told him he ought to shave all his hair off or at least cut it very short – and it would grow. It was a silly superstition but Otto did cut it off. It never came back again!'

At twenty, Otto was at the Schauspielhaus in Zürich, Switzerland, playing 'younger leads'. Occasionally he wore a wig but his acting career was coming to an end and he did not allow his lack of hirsute splendour to worry him much longer – not until the fringe started to turn grey did he shave it off completely. By that time he was in New York where his gleaming bald pate assured him instant recognition.

In his early twenties – this was about the time I first met him – Otto Ludwig was a very presentable young man with alert eyes which x-rayed pretty young girls and with the habit of following up quickly what he so avidly reconnoitred. He already emanated the sexuality which made him attractive to many women and which he retained when, with age coarsening his features, he could no longer, not with the best will, be described as handsome.

A third 'foreign' engagement took Otto Pretori to the German theatre in the small Czech town of Aussig (Usti), this time as director. Klabund's *Chalk Circle* was the first play entrusted to him. His career as an actor was over.

Presently, the stage had to share his attention with the university. Final exams were looming up and required an extra effort. He was not yet twenty-one when he graduated and became Otto Preminger, Doctor at Law, or, as they put it in Vienna, Dr Otto Preminger.

IV

Boss Otto

There are the born 'Number Twos', the best of whom become *éminences grises* behind great men; and there are the storming spirits who feel inhibited by restraint from above and claw their way to the top where they can best serve their own cause. Though as yet some way from reaching his destination, the top was Otto Preminger's natural habitat. He made an early and valiant attempt – nay, two – to be his own master even before the shine of the school benches had faded from the seat of his pants.

Almost immediately after graduation, he and another ambitious young man put their heads together and came up with a plan for a new theatre in Vienna. Rolf Jahn was married to the very wealthy (and, incidentally, very attractive) Marita Strelen who was happy to invest in her husband's theatrical ventures. Otto, as we know, was the son of a very wealthy father who would not dream of investing money in the theatre. Still, Otto's talent and Rolf's money soon added up to an intimate little theatre in Vienna's Inner City. Joint managers: Jahn and Preminger.

They called the theatre 'Die Komödie', suggesting not the English 'comedy' but the basic meaning of the Italian 'commedia' which is 'the play'. For Preminger it was an important phase in his theatrical education, a most useful exercise in stage control, artistic and managerial, which often go together in the European theatre. It was a hint of the future when, combining artistic and commercial ability, he became one of America's foremost producer directors.

Perhaps I ought to have said that there are also top dogs who operate well in harness – like those hardy huskies who pull the sleighs of Arctic explorers – while others are not temperamentally suited to run shoulder to shoulder with a partner. By nature Otto Preminger was a loner but the trait did not develop fully until later in his life.

Though distinguished by a few first-class productions, the Jahn-Preminger double act at Die Komödie was a short-lived experiment. After less than a year, Otto broke loose and headed for another partnership on a larger scale or, at any rate, on a larger stage. He took over a suburban theatre of veritable Reinhardtian proportions and named it 'Neues Wiener Schauspielhaus'. His new partner was a well-established actor by the name of Jakob Feldhammer whose sister happened to be married to a German industrialist (name of Hoechst) for whom the money needed to run a theatre in Vienna was very small change indeed.

Soon the word was passed from dressing-room to dressing-room in German theatres. As a contemporary theatrical agent put it to one of the actors on his books: 'A new theatre is opening up in Vienna. They want young, gifted but unknown actors. They want to do classical plays and modern plays. They have great plans for the future, lots of money and an artistic manager with a Reinhardt background!'

The siren call reached one Gerhard Hinze who was young, gifted and unknown and playing minor character parts on the German provincial stage. He applied for a job at the Schauspielhaus: 'They did not offer a lot of money,' said Gerhard Hinze who now calls himself Gerrard Heinz (like one of the fifty-seven varieties) and is a highly successful character actor in England. 'This is a private theatre,' he was told, 'we receive no subsidies but we want to do something very special with young actors all sharing in the experiment.'

'Being young and stupid, I believed them,' Hinze-Heinz said forty years later.

His first encounter with Otto Preminger was on stage when they were rehearsing a Frank Wedekind play. The young director seemed competent but rather aloof. According to Heinz, his ideas ran along currently fashionable lines, pepping up productions with song and music (à la Brecht's *Dreigroschenoper*). It was a fashion which owed much to Max Reinhardt.

Watching the Preminger–Feldhammer team at work, the staff concluded that they were not getting on too well with each other. Preminger was creative and anxious to modernise; Feldhammer just wanted to play every part himself. The two men were not very well suited.

A succession of indifferent, pedestrian productions was the inevitable result. The atmosphere was not conducive to great artistic accomplishments. The actors felt neglected – people were not even properly introduced to each other. Preminger was only interested in perfection – at any price – and plain rude with people who did not live up to his standards. The younger members of the ensemble never really got to know him and wrote him off as arrogant and remote: 'There was no row,' Heinz said. 'People were just getting angrier and angrier!'

People have been getting angrier and angrier with Preminger for years as stories about his behaviour multiplied. But many of them were coloured by hindsight. Some simply began to identify Preminger with the 'heavies' he played on stage and screen, particularly the Nazi types. Since he took the part of the brutal Nazi prison commandant in Billy Wilder's *Stalag 17* it has pursued him into private life. His detractors say that he was so convincing in the part because he played himself.

At the Schauspielhaus, in spite of his egocentric partner, Preminger continued to take artistic risks. From Berlin he imported a highly successful political drama *Brülle China!* (Roar China) but Vienna, rather parochial in outlook, was not really interested in China's troubles. The excellent Preminger production was not a success. He next engaged Oscar Homolka (who went on to make an international name for himself), hoping for great things but there were difficulties – with Homolka, not with Preminger – and the result was another disaster.

Big dreams of classical successes dissolved into cream puff productions like *Die Sachertorte* (the famous Viennese chocolate cake) which Preminger directed and turned into a smash hit. It saved the theatre financially but did not do much for his reputation. A similar production was called *Vienna, as it Cries and Laughs*. The season was at an end. So was the Preminger-Feldhammer partnership and the Neues Wiener Schauspielhaus.

At the respectable age of twenty-five and with two useful if not entirely satisfying entrepreneurial partnerships behind him, Otto Preminger examined the theatrical scene in Vienna. His eyes, not surprisingly, came to rest on the Josefstadt. With one expensive production after another, Reinhardt was keeping his theatre in the limelight of public interest – but not out of the red. His brother Edmund passed round the hat for contributions. Max spent the shekels as quickly as Edmund gathered them in.

Reinhardt was shielded, over-protected against the outside world by a big and snobbish coterie. An exception was his friend and artistic adviser, a gifted and lovable man who was proud of his Galician origin and who, mocking anti-semitic prejudices, invariably introduced himself to high and low as 'Rudolf Kommer – from Czernovic!' (Alexander Woollcott's *While Rome Burns* has a whole chapter devoted to Kommer, and he is the principal character in Sam Behrman's novel, *The Burning Glass*.)

Kommer's friend and master Max Reinhardt lived in princely splendour. With Camillo Castiglioni's money, he bought Leopoldskron, for centuries the magnificent ancient seat of the Archbishops of Salzburg, furnished it in grand style and held court there with his wife, the actress Else Heims.

Chandeliers – Reinhardt had a thing about them – illuminated the palatial rooms with hundreds of candles. Along the drive, guests passed through a lane of liveried footmen holding torches aloft ('What a pity', Castiglioni was supposed to have remarked, 'that the electricity should fail!' but this tale was spread to ridicule Reinhardt's wealthy sponsor).

Well in his fifties, the master himself was looking for triumphs farther afield. The Americans were planning to make a film of *The Miracle*, and he travelled hopefully to Hollywood which was rapidly becoming the Mecca of showmanship. He was well received in the States but Hollywood, not greatly concerned with sensitivities, let him cool his heels before shelving the project. Disillusioned and defected, Reinhardt returned to Europe and not until he went to the States as a refugee from the Nazis did he make a film in Hollywood.

In Vienna, what Reinhardt needed was an assistant of Preminger's qualifications which embraced all sectors of the business – with the emphasis on business. And Preminger could not do much better than resume the association which he had severed, perhaps a little impatiently, in the early days of his career.

The Reinhardt management welcomed him back with open arms but in the Josefstadt's assembly of outstanding and rather self-centred stars, the youthful ex-co-director of two undistinguished theatrical enterprises could not command a great deal of special attention. Neither were his duties very well defined. For one thing, the master himself was not much in evidence. The day-to-day running of the theatre was in the hands of Emil Geyer, a practised but not particularly inspired manager.

Without any specific brief, Preminger kept busy with rehearsals, negotiated with actors, dealt with scripts and stage instructions – Reinhardt wrote a page of instructions for every page of dialogue, and volumes of them turned up among the belongings left behind by Marilyn Monroe, of all people.

There was one more acting assignment for him. In a new

production of *The Miracle* Reinhardt asked him to take the part of a silent friar. In brown habit, hood and sandals and carrying a candle, Preminger headed the procession of monks but his real job was to keep his fellow friars – less experienced crowd players – in their right places. Throughout his apprenticeship, Otto Ludwig behaved with tact and circumspection and became completely integrated in the distinguished ensemble.

Looking as mature as his bald head, acting as mature as he looked, he was associated with artistes whose names filled a roll of honour of the German theatre. The dreamily tender Elisabeth Bergner wafted in and out; then there was the dark and very beautiful Lilly Darvas, wife of playwright Ferencz Molnar whose work already commanded top rates in American magazines.

Oskar Karlweis (long before his spell in Hollywood), Peter Lorre (the murderer in the highly successful film *M*), also *en route* to Hollywood and internationally renowned; Alexander Moissi and the lovable Hans Moser, a Viennese W. C. Fields were some of the names that stand out – time was not yet when every Austrian and German performer with hopes of the big time in America boldly stuck the Reinhardt label on his artistic baggage whether or not he ever walked on in a theatre under Max Reinhardt's control.

Preminger worked, watched, learned and waited. Where else was there so much scope? In the repertoire Marcel Achard ('Will you Play with Me?') followed Molnar ('Liliom'), Molière, G. B. Shaw and contemporary Germans, long since forgotten. Classics and operettas alternated with stimulating speed.

More than a year passed before the novice director got his hands on a play, *Voruntersuchung* (a judicial process best described as preliminary criminal investigation). The subject was well suited to Preminger's legal background. The author was Max Alsberg, a well-known Berlin criminal lawyer. Forty years later, the memory inspired Preminger to persuade Louis Nizer, another criminal lawyer, to write the script for his television film about the Rosenberg trial.

Emil Geyer gave his junior colleague a free hand. Watching him at work, he had little qualms about the outcome. Was Preminger as confident? He already affected the air of unconcern which he still likes to project although, as an act, it ranks far below his performances on stage or screen. The furrowed brow, the occasional twitch, the clenched fist were unmistakable signs of tension. Not surprising! This was an important test. He was anxious to prove himself to himself as much as to others, wanted to be worthy of the Reinhardt label and begin to coin a Preminger label.

The premiere was on 20 January 1931, a very cold night, but the reception the players received in the theatre was warm enough. As the action developed there was much applause, culminating at the end in an ovation for author, performers and director. There were twenty-one curtain calls. The play turned up in the Reinhardt repertoire intermittently well over a hundred times – consecutive performances of the same play were not the practice.

In the following weeks Preminger devoted much of his time to the 'Reinhardt Seminar', the school for actors founded by his chief and housed with grandiose snob appeal in the Schönbrunn Castle Theatre – where there was Reinhardt, there was a castle. He lectured, demonstrated, discussed problems of production and direction with students who responded to the young instructor with the old head.

Many of his pupils became friends in later life. None of them came closer to him than Maximilian Schulze, a young German actor whom he promoted from the Seminar to the Josefstadt. Schulze, who later became Slater and an American citizen, joined Preminger in the early fifties as casting and dialogue director on all his independent productions.

Already Preminger had a tendency to shout but it certainly did not worry Schulze-Slater: 'I have never been afraid of

OP,' he says. 'I think he is basically a gentle, sentimental soft touch who screams to hide his soft spots . . . *Wenn nicht im Zorn* [when not in a fit of anger] he is a generous man, a gentleman!'

With the *Voruntersuchung* success to his credit, Preminger was not long kept waiting for his next assignment as a director. The second play allocated to him was called *Reporter* – it triggers off memories and associations in several directions. Better known by its original title, *Front Page*, it was an American play by Charles McArthur and Ben Hecht (who later said that there was a holiday in his heart every time a Palestinian Jew killed an English soldier).

The German translation was by Rudolf Lothar who, in the passage of time, succeeded Otto at the Josefstadt. One of the principal parts was taken by the talented young Paula Wessely whom Preminger introduced as a serious actress and whose subsequent personal fate preoccupied him for a long time because in the Austrian Nazi period she became fiercely anti-Jewish.

But, perhaps most important, Preminger gave the part of Peggy Malloy to a tall, provocatively sexy minor actress by the name of Marion Mill. And thereby hangs a tale.

V

Marlene—No! Marion—Yes!

There was considerable excitement in the paternal home of the Premingers in Vienna. As brother Ingo told me, Otto brought home a stunning girl about the same age as he, a tall, lithe young German actress with fair hair and high cheek bones. Her name was Marlene Dietrich. With Margo Lyon, also from Berlin, the little-known Marlene was sharing the lead in the Mischa Spolianski revue *Es Liegt in der Luft* (It's in the Air) which was showing in Vienna.

Otto said he was considering Marlene for a part with the Komödie's road company: 'She was very attractive,' Ingo recalled. Otto, too, thought she was gorgeous – but not right for the part. He turned her down. Just as well for Marlene. Another director, Josef von Sternberg, saw her and promptly offered her a part. Had Preminger engaged her, she would not have been free to become Lola in the *Blue Angel* which Sternberg directed and which put her on the road to one of the most fabulous careers in show business. For that, in a negative sort of way, Otto Preminger can take credit.

There was another girl who was appearing in a small revue, *Snake in Paradise*, in a suburb of Vienna. Like Marlene, she was lithe but dark-haired with a round face and a retroussé nose. She was Hungarian. Her name was Marion Mill. Instead of Marlene, Otto Preminger took her on – and not only for the road company.

Marion Mill has since written her autobiography (*All I Want is Everything*, MacFadden Books, New York, 1957) and published various versions of her life story in Europe. In the German magazine *Hör Zu!* she introduced herself as a baroness who grew up in a castle.

In the days of the Habsburgs when Marion was born,

Hungary produced as many barons and baronesses as gypsies or rabbits. If a Hungarian baron had twelve children, they all became barons by birthright and their off-spring, however numerous, again were entitled to call themselves barons. Not a few others inserted a little 'von' or, more elegantly, 'de' between their first and their family name – one more baronial family entering the fray but not the Almanach de Gotha. It would not be very rewarding to examine Marion's claim too closely.

In Vienna where the 'Baroness' lived, she was, we are told, in trouble with a theatrical producer – in the German version he somehow becomes the owner of a bar which seems just as likely. Whoever he was, he threatened to sue Marion for breach of contract. A terrible predicament! A friend suggested she ought to seek advice from a man with both legal and theatrical experience, the erudite, charming and compassionate Dr Otto Ludwig Preminger.

Otto was at the peak of his masculine form. His success with Vienna's golden girls was phenomenal. No need for him to lure them to his casting couch (throughout his career he has refused to mix pleasure with business). They flocked into his arms which were strong and wide enough to embrace them all.

It was at this point that he found himself in his office face to face with the delectable Marion Mill: 'Take a seat!' In her unmistakable Hungarian accent she asked him for sympathy, advice and help:

'Why don't we discuss it over dinner?' Otto suggested. They had dinner and talked. Their conversation soon went beyond Marion's legal problems. She told him that she was married – married when she was very young – now she was seeking a divorce. Otto's protective instincts were roused. He helped to solve her problem, saw her again and started giving her private tuition to improve her accent.

Soon there was more to it than legal advice and voice training: 'My love for him came like lightning and was as

51

intense,' Marion wrote. 'Everything that happened before our meeting lost all significance for me.'

Otto was also very much in love. He and Marion were inseparable. First at the Schauspielhaus, then at the Josefstadt she was a permanent fixture in the Preminger circle. A great many people thought they were already married.

1932 turned out to be a fateful year for Otto. It was not only his affair with Marion which was different from all that went before. He was also about to make his début as a film director.

The first of the Preminger films remains a shadowy enterprise. As he put it, a rich man offered to finance a film directed by Dr Otto Ludwig Preminger. As far as he or anybody else remembers, he was an industrialist from Graz by the name of Hass. Allianz-Film of Vienna undertook the project. The prospective director was not very sure of himself: 'I could hardly read or write at the time,' Preminger said later, 'let alone direct a film!'

An able screenwriter, Siegfried Bernfeld (now of New York and Twentieth Century Fox) turned a true life story into a script. Walter Landauer (half of the Ravicz and Landauer double-piano act) was the musical director. Peter Herz wrote the lyrics for the musical interludes and Otto's friend Ernst Häussermann, a future Director of the Burgtheater, also had a hand in it.

Preminger engaged Hansi Niese for the star part and gave the juvenile lead to Attila Hörbiger who was as Teutonic as his first name, and who eventually married Paula Wessely and became a rabid Nazi.

The story? It tells of an Austrian soldier returning to Vienna after the first world war, of a woman who thought he was her son, of trouble with the law, half tragic, half comic, not good, not bad. 'I prefer to forget it,' Preminger said, but the French dug it up when they arranged a retrospective showing of Preminger films and screened it forty years after it was made. The world premiere was scheduled for 28 March 1932. The film's title, most appropriately, *Die Grosse Liebe* (The Great Love).

Otto Preminger was not the only one in love. Max Reinhardt, too, was planning to marry for a second time and took Latvian nationality because Latvia, a European 'Reno', was the only country to grant a legal divorce even against the will of one partner of the marriage. He divorced Else Heims without her consent and married Helene Thimig, of a famous Vienna theatre family.

Now it was Preminger's turn to go to the registry office. He himself is too discreet to discuss the marriage but Ingo has no such inhibitions. He vividly remembers how dismayed the family were when it dawned on them that Otto had decided to marry Marion.

There was nothing wrong with a young Hungarian actress trying to make the grade in Vienna. But the Premingers had their own ideas of a future daughter-in-law and, while religion did not play a great part in their lives and they did not go to synagogue more than once a year – Otto hardly ever – they, like Jewish parents everywhere, would have preferred their son to marry a girl of their persuasion and from outside the theatrical profession. That Otto's future wife was still married did not help matters.

'Bigamy' was much in Otto's mind. Not that he had any intention of asking Marion to marry him before her divorce was through. *Bigamy* was the title of a play he was directing and it was touch and go what would be first – Marion's divorce or Otto's 'Bigamy'. As it happened the divorce became final while Otto was still busy rehearsing. On 3 August 1932 he took an hour off and went to the Rathaus (Town Hall) where he and Marion were married. Then he went back to the Josefstadt to continue with the rehearsal.

Ferencz Molnar was one of their friends who were surprised: 'How did it come about?' he asked Marion. She told him of her visit to Preminger's office and of their first dinner: 'Typical!' Molnar said. 'Preminger asked you to have one meal with him – not three hundred and sixty-five. He asked you to sit down for a moment – not for his whole life!'

Marion revelled in the part of a rising young theatre director's wife and played it with great allure. That summer in Salzburg she and Otto were Max Reinhardt's guests at Leopoldskron. She was enchanted by the grandeur, more than a hundred candle-lit rooms, the magnificent interior decoration equal to the most spectacular stage sets. The stage was much on Marion's mind: 'Why don't you give me a part?' she asked her host. 'If I did,' was Max Reinhardt's ambiguous reply, 'we would not remain friends.'

It was an embarrassing question which might have strained Max Reinhardt's friendship with Otto Preminger – if they had been friends. Relations between them were never easy. Reinhardt had a high opinion of the younger man's ability. Excellent director. Good administrator. Fine teacher. Collaboration was harmonious but tenuous, since Reinhardt was already withdrawing from active control.

The two had nothing in common except the theatre, and even so . . . Reinhardt, shy, introspective, with a small, impenetrable circle of friends, a thinker, philosopher of the theatre, his approach to authors and their work intellectual. Preminger, already an extrovert, youthfully brash, volatile, sociable, a public rather than a private man, doer rather than thinker, was propelled by instinct as much as by theory. Professionally, their different attitudes stimulated discussion. Privately, they had little to say to each other.

Marion Mill's part in the Preminger production of *Reporter* the previous year was the beginning and the end of her as a Max Reinhardt player. With 1932 moving to a close, it was all but the end of Max Reinhardt as a theatre manager. The Nazis saw to that. A great phase in the history of the German theatre died with German democracy. The Nazis used the arts for cheap and nasty propaganda to which, shamefully, many German actors lent their name.

Max Reinhardt was in Oxford when Hitler came to power

in January 1933. Had the Gestapo caught up with him in Berlin, it would have been the concentration camp for the magician of the German theatre who happened to be a Jew. From Oxford he wrote a naïve letter to the Nazi government saying that, even if permitted (as if this was even remotely likely), he could not work where he was merely tolerated: 'To have contributed to the national assets with the strength of my life', he wrote, 'softens the bitterness of my farewell . . .'

He returned to Austria and Leopoldskron where he lived in the style to which he was accustomed, making only the occasional 'guest appearance' in Vienna. The day to day affairs of the theatre which he had founded held no interest for him. The Josefstadt needed a vigorous new man at the helm. Emil Geyer hardly filled the bill and Castiglioni, as rich as ever – and with a wife still stage-struck – offered Preminger the same financial support he had given Max Reinhardt. New agreements were quickly drawn up. The same year that Hitler took over Germany, Otto Ludwig Preminger took over the Josefstadt.

It was a triumph of youth which was not as yet in fashion. While the Burgtheater vegetated under the direction of a middle-aged German manager, the Josefstadt under the youthful Preminger sparkled in the reflected glory of Max Reinhardt's reputation. Any other theatre would soon have become a Preminger theatre. The ghost of Reinhardt was not easily exorcised.

Preminger tried. He did not look for easy successes. His repertoire was a measure of his ambition – Goethe's *Faust*, Schiller's *Maria Stuart*, Cocteau's *La Voix Humaine*, Pirandello's *Six Characters in Search of an Author*, Sacha Guitry, Karl Zuckmeyer, Jacques Duval, Hans Jaray, the gifted young playwright-performer in the manner of Noël Coward, the great Hungarian crowd pullers . . .

One of the plays Preminger introduced to the repertoire was Duschinski's *Makart*, about the nineteenth-century painter who created a style of fashion and women for ever associated with Vienna. A huge gilded frame surrounded the stage, and Preminger designed each scene to look like a work from Makart's brush. A great deal of work went into the production. With the first night almost at hand, descendants of Makart turned up at the theatre with a posse of lawyers who threatened legal action because, according to them, the play libelled the painter and reflecced adversely on them.

A few years on and Preminger would have sent them packing or fought them to a finish. In these early days he thought it best to heal the wounded pride of the complainants with the balm of a modest cash payment. Minor changes were made, legal action was averted and the play went on as scheduled.

Plus ça change . . . The inevitable Iphigenie Buchmann-Castiglioni, the theatre's meal ticket, turned up in the Preminger production of *Christiano between Heaven and Hell,* and Louise Rainer appeared under his auspices in Sidney S. Kingsley's *Men in White*: 'Not a hint of trouble,' she told me when I talked to her in London. It went so smoothly in fact that she could not even remember whether Preminger himself directed the play: 'Yes, there was talk of Preminger being excitable and inconsiderate . . . I personally never experienced anything of the kind,' she said.

Looking back on the Josefstadt's rich repertoire of 1934, who would believe that this was the year Vienna went through two bloody revolutions? In February the Socialists rose against the authoritarian Catholic regime and there was a massacre in the streets before the government prevailed. In July the illegal Nazis staged a putsch to force Austria into an Anschluss (union with Germany). They murdered Austria's diminutive Chancellor Engelbert Dollfuss. The country was an armed camp. In the Josefstadt, as in other theatres, the shows went on.

One of the plays Preminger produced and directed was *Libel* by Edward Wooll which he himself translated from the

English. The German title was *Sensationsprozess*, a dramatic piece about a British politician unmasked as an impostor and war-time murderer. It was a fine production which I vividly remember. For Vienna's theatrical *wunderkind* it turned out to be more than another play in his repertoire. As we shall presently see, it became a link between Vienna and New York, a bridge across the Atlantic.

There was one more outstanding occasion before Preminger crossed that bridge. In the summer of 1935 he abruptly left the chief executive's suite at the Josefstadt – abruptly as the general public saw it. There was no shortage of candidates for his succession. The theatre's future was not at risk – under his management it was making money but, whoever would run the show, could still depend on Castiglioni's subsidy.

Ernst Lothar, an author of considerable standing whose brother was also a prominent playwright, was appointed to the vacant throne of Reinhardt, Geyer and Preminger. He was so delighted with this opportunity that he offered his predecessor a very special send-off – one big final production under the Preminger aegis. This is how, on 4 October 1935, the Josefstadt became the centre of tense and frantic activity outside as well as inside.

Police took up positions at strategic points in the streets. A small army of plain-clothes detectives was at action stations, some mingling with the crowds. The stalls were stiff with champions of the authoritarian Catholic regime, men in dinner jackets, women in evening gowns: no opponent of the régime could get anywhere near.

As the principal guest arrived, the audience rose to its feet. It was one of the rare evenings when Dollfuss's successor Chancellor Kurt von Schuschnigg, denounced as an Austro-Fascist, threatened with death by the Nazis, showed his face in public. Another guest of honour was Cardinal Theodor Innitzer, Archbishop of Vienna. How piquant! If only Otto Preminger could have looked ahead and seen himself in Vienna thirty years later! The Catholic establishment was present in full force bidding to be entertained by the Preminger production.

The play which drew them to the Josefstadt was an American one, Emmett Lavery's *The First Legion* – God's own warriors. The cast included Albert Bassermann, an aristocrat of the stage, Attila Hörbiger – few Preminger plays without him – Max Reinhardt's brother-in-law Hans Thimig and Anton Edthofer, a polished Frederick March type.

Welded together by the confident director, the all-star ensemble earned the applause which acknowledged the performance – a less committed audience would have been as enthusiastic. Exhilarated, if a little solemn, Preminger joined the performers on stage to accept the plaudits. He bowed and waved gently – waved goodbye to the audience, the Josefstadt, Vienna.

Another fortnight and he was gone. What had happened?

VI

Hollywood Calling

The late Gilbert Miller, resourceful, imaginative New York impresario and theatrical producer with a penchant for Europe – England mainly but also Paris, Berlin and Vienna – kept an eye on Reinhardt productions whether directed by the master himself or by one of his fledglings. In the Josefstadt he was a familar figure in the stalls. He had been watching Otto Preminger's progress for some time.

Passing through Vienna while *Sensationsprozess* was still on repertoire, he saw Preminger and asked casually: 'How about directing the play for me in New York?' It was not a definite offer nor was it said lightly. Perhaps he was not as yet prepared to back his judgment with a great deal of money but there may well come a time when the young Austrian might wish to spread his wings and would need support.

New York! In the restricted, claustrophobic atmosphere of Vienna New York had a magic ring, sounded grand, desirable, tempting. In Vienna, the Nazis were already knocking – pounding! – at the door and trying to break it down. New York was like a safe haven – they were still talking about the streets of New York being paved with gold. Gilbert Miller's idea settled in Otto Preminger's mind like a seed that needed only a little moisture to make it grow.

For foreign managers, producers, agents, middlemen scouring Europe in search of talent to supply America's insatiable entertainment industry, Vienna was an important stop-over. Danube city, Beethoven, Mozart, Strauss, Lehar (Jeanette MacDonald in *The Merry Widow*), Richard Tauber, Sachertorte, whipped cream, wine, women, song. High-powered scouts who had their eyes on him would almost, a little extravagantly, add Preminger to the list.

59

Half a dozen of them have since claimed credit for bringing Preminger to the notice of the great Joe Schenck who had Hollywood in the palm of his podgy hand. Schenck was the man who told Darryl F. Zanuck: 'Write your own ticket' and pressed a 100,000 dollar cheque on him to seal the deal which created Twentieth Century Fox.

Preminger did not know any of this and had only the vaguest idea of Schenck's standing when an agent took him to meet the visitor from the legendary film capital at his Vienna hotel. What he saw was one of the ugliest men who ever lived but one who, in the words of a friend, struck those who knew him really well as 'one of the most attractive, charming people'.

'I've heard great things about you,' Schenck told Preminger. 'I hear you are a very good director. Why don't you come to Hollywood?'

The question sounded like a command. Authoritative but paternal. Inspiring confidence. Schenck instructed his European representative to 'bring Preminger over'. Free passage, naturally; first-class accommodation, matter of course; a contract, certainly (though nothing extravagant). In the first instance, a visit to look around, see how he liked it and how it liked him . . .

The secret yearning for America was no longer a secret. The Nazis, Preminger said later, had nothing to do with it but this is what most people said who were leaving at that time and it was something he would probably not have spelled out even to himself. Marion, perhaps more than he, was restless for new pastures. Novelty. Adventure. Excitement. Fabulous Hollywood. Unlimited budgets. Opportunity. Five-star stars.

Was there nothing to keep him in Vienna? Otto Preminger tells of a fantastic invitation that nearly stopped him in his tracks. The Minister of Education offered him the plum of Vienna's theatrical posts – Director-Manager of the Burgtheater. What was the Minister's name? I asked. 'Not the

Minister, actually,' Preminger replied. 'Sektionschef Perntner.' Perntner was the head of the Austrian State Theatre Administration which controlled Burgtheater and Opera.

According to Otto, it was all fixed when, at the final interview, the Minister – no, Sektionschef Perntner – suggested a minor formality. Would Preminger adopt the Catholic faith? A dramatic coincidence – it was the same thing that had happened to his father twenty years earlier. Of course, he refused. Of course, he did not get the job. No documentary evidence exists about the intended appointment or the insidious condition attached to it but, then, this is not the kind of conversation of which an official would make a record.

No other candidate seemed suitable, so the incumbent head of the Burgtheater remained in his job. Preminger consoles himself with the thought that, had he become Burgtheaterdirektor at the age of twenty-eight, he would have been in Vienna until Hitler arrived three years later.

As it was, he informed Reinhardt and Castiglioni that he wanted to quit the Josefstadt, the sooner the better. Reinhardt himself was sold on Hollywood and did not try to stop Preminger. No obstacle was put in his way. It was agreed that he should stay on for a few more months until a successor was found and do two or three more plays. Then he was free to go.

The Gilbert Miller offer took on a new hue: 'I could come to New York on my way to Hollywood,' Preminger suggested. Miller jumped at this arrangement. The proposition, Preminger recalled a little unkindly, was so acceptable to Miller because someone else was paying the fare.

One of Preminger's parting shots at the Josefstadt was a light, a very light, musical comedy, *The King with the Umbrella* by Ralph Benatzky which did not greatly tax his resources. It was a delightful and successful production. Almost in the same vein was a very indigenous cameo set in the milieu of a Viennese magistrate's court.

In these weeks and months, the outgoing Josefstadt manager concentrated on learning English, a more intricate exercise than he had expected. He never really learned it properly. His detractors say he lacked professional voice training which helps most actors to master foreign languages. Others, putting the cart before the horse, suggest that he nursed his atrocious accent so as to qualify as an actor of Nazi parts. Nonsense! He just does not have the gift but makes up for it with his intelligent use of the English language.

From the very beginning he handled it with confidence and aplomb. He had translated *Libel* while still practising his 'cat' and 'mat', and only just proceeding to the first few basic English sentences. The prospect of operating in the unfamiliar medium held no terror for him.

Preminger's departure from Vienna was fixed for October. Gilbert Miller kept in touch. It was up to him to get a cast together in New York and some of the stars who appeared in the London production of *Libel* were an obvious choice. With flattering confidence in the young director he had recruited, he fixed the date for the New York opening of the show for the end of December. That would leave Preminger three months to pull the play into shape.

'Meet you on the *Normandie!*' Gilbert Miller signalled. Arrangements were for him and Preminger to cross the Atlantic together on the French liner which was due to leave from Le Havre in mid-October. After three months in New York, next stop would be Hollywood.

Exciting as the prospect was, the hopeful traveller was not prepared to pull up his roots altogether. Marion was staying behind in their Vienna apartment to await his advice before starting to wind up their affairs. The separation would be brief – no problem in a sophisticated marriage like theirs.

For the first stage of the trip, the road to Paris, Otto found a congenial companion, film producer Sam Spiegel, a man with big ideas as yet unrealised – and years from *The Bridge on the River Kwai* which made him wealthier than most of his fellow producers on either side of the Atlantic. Spiegel offered Otto a lift in his limousine.

Though with an utterly different approach to life the two fledglings leaving their Vienna nests for Paris were very much birds of a feather, their dreams of success underwritten by arrogant self-confidence. They were both talented, talked the same language. Preminger was better known with solid achievements to his credit. Spiegel knew more about films – and the world. In Paris, their ways parted. Preminger went on to Le Havre where he met up with Gilbert Miller. With his American protector watching over him, the *Normandie* carried him towards the United States.

The first impression of New York was so powerful that Preminger has been struggling for words to describe it ever since. The best he could offer – in a conversation with a tape recorder – was the kind of comment he would ruthlessly strike out if a writer put it into the mouth of a character in a Preminger film: 'The skyline!' he said. 'The Statue of Liberty!' The subject is so emotional that he cannot think of anything else to say. He did not exactly kneel down and kiss the ground when he set foot on the pier (that was left to another Viennese showman who found refuge in New York); 'I was overwhelmed,' is all Preminger remembers of the great moment.

His eminent companion steered him quickly past the customs officers. As a temporary visitor there was no problem with the immigration officials. Had the October sun not been shining so brightly that morning – Preminger did not as yet know that New York can ring the changes of the four seasons within a single day – one would have said that he arrived under a very good star. The date, one of the few Otto is certain of, was 21 October 1935.

Without much further ado, Gilbert Miller took his protégé straight from the docks to lunch. Under the impact of so many new impressions, it was difficult to keep track of the route through the canyons of Manhattan which led to a narrow street off Fifth Avenue. A few steps down and Otto found himself in a quietly elegant New York lunch and dinner club: 'This is the Twenty-One,' Gilbert Miller explained.

On 21 October into the Twenty-One. No wonder the name imprinted itself on Preminger's mind and he became a regular customer. He has remained loyal to the club throughout the years that have gone by. Sentimental and generous as he is, he takes friends and acquaintances on their first visit to New York to lunch or dinner – at the Twenty-One. To this day, he jumps down the throat of anyone who dares to voice the gentlest criticism of the club's culinary offerings.

Few cities can be as cold, hard, indifferent and inhospitable to impecunious strangers as New York where loneliness is an endemic social disease. Few cities offer an embrace as stimulating and captivating as New York reserves for the prosperous and well-appointed newcomer particularly when a friend helps him on to the social roundabout of the upper crust. A personable, educated, well-heeled European of Otto Preminger's background had Park Avenue as well as Broadway roll out its most colourful welcome mat for him.

He stepped straight into Gilbert Miller's magic social circle making friends as he went. His days were spent in the familiar atmosphere of the theatre where the cast made him welcome. Now he was overwhelmed with their indulgence for his imperfect English, characteristic in a city of some four or five million 'foreigners' – Americans, that is, of non-English origin.

His intimate knowledge of the play got him over all language difficulties. New York's brisker pace appealed to him – he never really liked Vienna's gemütlich-leisurely approach. The adrenalin was flowing as never before. His mind was made up. This is where he wanted to stay.

Marion received his signal with joy, packed her things,

Henry Fonda and Joan Crawford in *Daisy Kenyon*

The Moon is Blue: Maggie MacNamara and Preminger

Kim Novak and Preminger on set: *The Man with the Golden Arm*

closed down the apartment in Vienna and caught the next boat to New York. Otto was on the pier to meet her. He took up position at the customs post for arrivals with names beginning with 'P'. Passengers were pouring from the ship and drifting to their places in the alphabetical queues. There were quite a number of 'Ps' – no Marion.

It was some time before Otto spotted her a little further down the line behind the 'M' sign. She was travelling not as Mrs Preminger but as 'Marion Mill'. Actress in her own right? Premature Women's Lib? Not proud of the Preminger label? Otto was perplexed but pleased to see her and did not pursue the matter. Thirty-five years later I was caught up in the tangle of Marion's names.

By that time she and Otto had long been divorced and she was married to her second husband, Mr Albert Meyer, a wealthy New York industrialist. In the New York telephone directory she was still listed as 'Marion Mill Preminger'.

'It causes confusion,' Otto told her. Messages intended for her came to his house and parcels for the current Mrs Preminger ended up in the apartment of Marion Mill Preminger who was really Mrs Meyer. In 1971, her entry was still under 'Preminger'.

'Marion,' I asked her over the telephone, our first contact since 1935, could I come and talk to you? I am writing a book about Otto.'

'Preminger?' the still familiar voice came over the line, a little less Hungarian-accented than I remembered it. 'I have forgotten him. I do not remember he ever existed. I do not want to hear his name . . .'

'You have written about him in your book . . .'

'That was years ago. I repudiate the book!'

'But you are still calling yourself Preminger?'

'I want you to know that I am "Your Excellency" now . . . I am Consul-General of Gabon!'

'Congratulations!' I just managed to say before she replaced the receiver. (Gabon which Marion Mill Preminger

Meyer now represents in New York is, of course, the former French colony in equatorial Africa where Schweitzer lived and worked.)

In 1935, when Marion Mill and Otto Preminger were reunited in New York, a few years of hectic social life together were still ahead of them. Before the year was out they were bound for Hollywood.

VII

Preminger - or Something

'Nobody gave Otto Preminger a start;
he gave himself a start!'

DARRYL F. ZANUCK

'Joe Schenck was the financial man,' Darryl F. Zanuck
explained to me. 'I remember he wired me – this fellow,
Preminger or something, he could be of use to you. Joe ran
the business, I ran the production. It was for me to decide
whether I want to use Preminger . . .'

In pursuit of Preminger's early American trail, I went no
further than two floors up from my apartment in the Plaza
Hotel, New York, to Darryl Zanuck's permanent suite. The
ageing ex-Tsar of Hollywood, with cigar dangling from his
lips but without his polo mallet for once, was wearing a blue
white-spotted dressing-gown over no pyjamas, and light
pig-skin slippers. Crossing his big sitting-room I had to tread
carefully to avoid stepping on his two delightful miniature
terriers? – poodles? chihuahuas? – who were yapping round
my ankles.

'Preminger? Now let me think!' Zanuck searched his
memory. To him young Preminger was just one of the
foreigners who were working for him. Hungarian Mike
Curtiz, German Ernst Lubitsch . . . 'I got on well with the
foreigners.' But, then, most of the founder members of
Hollywood were 'foreigners' and, like Preminger, had their
roots in Eastern Europe. Zanuck himself was from Nebraska.

In 1935 it was still the Hollywood of the big razzmattazz.
Dazzling the newcomer. Big thinking, big money, big names.
Joe Schenck was a splendid host. He installed the Premingers
in the Beverly Hills Hotel and threw a huge party for them.

Schenck entertained, everybody was there: 'That's Thalberg
. . .' 'Meet Mary Pickford . . .' '. . . Gary Cooper'.

There were scores of other parties. Once Preminger's name
was on the list of socially desirables, the invitations poured
in. Figures he had only seen flashing across the screen in
Vienna took on shape. He met Garbo, he met Chaplin who,
incidentally, had visited Vienna only a few months earlier
on his European tour.

Joe Schenck watched over Otto like a guardian angel,
more than that: 'He told me he had no son,' Preminger
recalled, 'and that his house was open to me at any time –
there would always be an extra plate for me at his table.'
It was reassuring for a newcomer to the tough reality behind
Hollywood's sunny smile to have such a fatherly friend.

But where the social round ended – if this was to be more
than an instructive visit – Zanuck was the man who decided
Preminger's fate: 'I asked him to stay, watch and learn,'
Zanuck recalled. The all-expenses-paid visit became an
engagement: 'We did not pay him much to begin with,' said
the man who fixed his salary.

Preminger hung around the lots, dropped into studios and
studied the method of directors and the manner of stars. He
noted details of lighting and camera angles and went through
a practical training course which taught him a great deal
about the technicalities of film making.

Six, seven, eight months went by. He was waiting for a
call. At long last it came. Zanuck summoned him and asked:
'Are you ready to make a film . . .?'

'I am,' Preminger said quickly.

Zanuck does not remember much more of this phase. In
the Preminger version of what happened next, the conversation continued. Zanuck went on: 'I have this son-of-a-bitch
under contract and don't want to lose any more money on
him . . .'

The son-of-a-bitch turned out to be Lawrence Tibbett, a
fine singer whose Fox contract for two films was worth

200,000 dollars. The first was a total flop and now there was one more to go: 'You can practise on him,' Zanuck told Preminger.

It was not an auspicious beginning. The script was no great shakes either. Preminger studied it page for page, line for line, word for word. He pondered the construction, swtiched scenes and polished points – his sense of drama and construction, possibly his strongest asset, was already well developed.

Not that the story gave much scope for individual treatment – a concert pianist, his publicity man making life difficult, retirement to a farm, a young society girl invading his rustic privacy and, predictably, ending up as his wife. Songs, comic interludes . . . The ready-made cast, provided by the studio, included Wendy Barrie, Arthur Treacher (now Merv Griffin's 'second banana') and Gregory Ratoff, a rotund, amiable and wise Russian who had made a name for himself in Berlin in the early twenties and soon became a Preminger intimate.

Nobody could make a masterpiece of these ingredients but Preminger did well. So well that he was quickly given a second assignment. The next script arrived ready with title: 'Danger, Love at Work'.

'I want Simone Simone to play Toni Pemberton!' Zanuck told Preminger, introducing him to his new French find.

The story revolved around the Pemberton family who were completely off their heads except for Toni who was at least near normal. Preminger tested Simone. The confrontation of the French girl and the Austrian director was a comic treat for all who could see the joke. Simone Simone was prattling away in her French accented pidgin English, Preminger listening with growing despair. His English was not so good either but, then, he was the director and did not have a speaking part.

'She can't do it!' he told Zanuck, who accepted the

position and switched Simone to another film. She made her Hollywood début in *Girls' Dormitory* which also introduced Tyrone Power to the screen. In her place, Ann Sothern was assigned to the Preminger production.

It was a much trickier job, a much bigger cast, a much longer movie. The novice-director made a first-class job of it. Darryl Zanuck congratulated him and passed on the glad tidings that Fox had found a new young talent. Preminger was certain to make it three in a row.

He might have done it, had it not been for Robert Louis Stevenson. Stevenson, a tower of British literature, wrote *Treasure Island* and *Dr Jekyll and Mr Hyde*, classics which have flowered in modern garb and become part of international lingua franca. In Hollywood in 1937, Otto Preminger was sent the script of *Kidnapped*, a film based on a Stevenson novel: 'Stevenson?' he asked. 'Never heard of him!'

A very Scottish tale, written in 1886, *Kidnapped* was all about the Highlands and horses and a little boy. All Preminger knew about the Scots was that they wore kilts. Unlike other Hollywood directors who cheerfully tackle subjects of which they are utterly ignorant, he shook his head sadly: 'I don't understand it!' He was going to turn the assignment down.

'You are signing your professional death warrant!' he was told by old Hollywood hands. This sort of thing was not done, Gregory Ratoff warned him. For a director at the beginning of his career to turn down a major film was madness. Preminger decided to bow to the judgment of his friends, and what ensued explains why ever since he has not been over-receptive to advice.

He tackled the strange subject and the strange cast among them Freddie Bartholomew, one of Hollywood's child prodigies. It was a hard slog. Each day's shooting meant hacking a path through the dark undergrowth with the most un-Scottish of all directors groping for verisimilitude in a milieu that was utterly alien to him. Each evening Darryl

Zanuck watched the rushes. One week later – the inevitable crisis.

'Why didn't you have the boy speak to the dog as the script called for?' Zanuck asked after viewing the day's work. He seemed to be missing a scene of personal appeal.

'But this is not in the script?' Preminger replied.

'You think I don't know my own script?' Zanuck hissed back.

Preminger was right, Zanuck was wrong but for practical purposes and in Hollywood of all places this was neither here nor there. Zanuck, who made his name writing scripts for Rin Tin Tin, had a soft spot for dogs. Maybe he was angry because he did not want this young man suggesting that he did not know the script. Preminger never made it to the Highlands: 'Next day,' he recalled, 'I was on the back lot.' *Kidnapped* was completed by Alfred Werker.

No other script came along. No other offer of a film. Nothing happened, nothing the discarded director could put his finger on. Invitations to parties and dinners continued to arrive but the subject of work whenever it was raised drew blank faces.

The Hollywood freeze defined the hottest sun. It gripped by stealth. If only somebody had told Preminger 'You are finished!' it might almost have been a relief. It was like being a leper without knowing it. How long before he recognised himself as the fool who dared to cross swords with Zanuck, disappointed Zanuck, defied Zanuck or whatever . . .

Death sentence was pronounced with the callous ritual which I used to think of as invention of a sadistic scriptwriter – one day, when Preminger arrived at the studio, his desk was gone. In Hollywood terms, this made him a nonpersonality. Naturally he did not go back to the deskless office: 'You are not coming in,' one of the minor executives told him with pernicious logic; 'you are breaking your contract!'

Only Joe Schenck could help to resolve the ridiculous situation. 'Mr Schenck is out of town!' 'Mr Schenck is in conference!' 'Mr Schenck is not available!' 'Mr Schenck will call you back!' Preminger called in vain. There was no place at Schenck's table for him now.

A few more months of his contract remained. He had no choice but to hang on. Not given to idling or lazing, he enrolled for a drama course at the University of California to improve his English but gave a false name to hide his shame. It was a self-defeating precaution. His identity was promptly discovered, he was thought to be spying and was sent packing. Did the Zanuck curse reach even to the UCLA?

Hope was running out. There seemed no chance of getting back into films. At least there was still the theatre! Preminger scoured the literary landscape for something to produce or direct – anything. He read books, scripts, treatments, plays. One property seemed only to require a top-class actress to make it a potential smash. The unemployed director clung to it with his whole strength. How about Louise Rainer, the Reinhardt star of Old Vienna?

Relations between Louise Rainer and Hollywood were the opposite of the Preminger situation. Hollywood loved Louise but Louise did not reciprocate. She was at the peak of success but could not bear the city, the outlook, the people. She was at the brink of a personal crisis. Preminger wanted in, she wanted out.

'Otto Ludwig came to see me about some play or other . . .' Louise Rainer-Knittel said vaguely 'All I remember is that I did not want to do it.'

Their common background did not bring them close. Louise, sensitive, vulnerable, with her hopelessly idealistic views; Preminger, pragmatic, tough-skinned – there was no *rapport* between them. She studied his face: 'Some people are what they look like,' she said. 'What did he look like?'

The frustrations of the past weeks and months showed.

The forehead was knitted, the furrows were deepening. Determination to fight back was written all over him: 'He looked like a man with a certain amount of hardness,' Louise said. 'A man who wants to get what he wants to get!'

He did not get what he wanted. Louise Rainer declined. The rebuff, as other Hollywood snubs, cut deeply. Though he never lost his bland air, Preminger was a disappointed and bitter man. By contrast, Max Reinhardt who came to the United States not much later was fêted and celebrated on all sides. Otto's former chief was brought to America by the ubiquitous Meyer Weisgal, a leading fund-raiser for Jewish causes and eventually head of the Weizmann Institute in Rehovah, Israel – in years to come Weisgal played a big role in Preminger's life. Reinhardt in the meantime made a movie of *A Midsummer Night's Dream* with two new stars: Olivia de Havilland and Mickey Rooney. The old master started a Max Reinhardt School for actors.

He never recaptured his prominence. Louise Rainer was one of the ex-Reinhardt players who visited their mentor regularly in the modest Hollywood home in which he settled down but Otto Preminger hardly ever saw him again. In all the tens of thousands of words that he has spoken about his own past, he has paid scant tribute to the man under whose banner he sailed for so long.

The tragic situation which developed in Austria did not allow Preminger to dwell on his own predicament. Though not unexpected, when it arose it came as a great shock. Without any foreboding, he despatched a cable with fond wishes to his mother in Vienna – the following day was her birthday. The cable never reached her. That day, 11 March 1938, Hitler invaded Austria.

Otto Preminger was frantic. His parents were in terrible danger. A prominent Jew in Nazi hands meant the concentration camp. Otto telephoned friends here, there, everywhere. It was of no avail. At this vast distance there was little he could do to help.

He did not know how desperately close the old couple came to disaster. That fateful morning, as the *Wehrmacht* was marching on Austria's capital, Dr Markus Preminger and his wife caught the first train out of Vienna. They travelled hopefully but not far. Storm Troopers were on guard at the frontier and turned them back.

Trapped in Vienna with swastika flags going up around them and threatened with imminent arrest, Dr Preminger racked his brain for a way out. Happily, he was a man with many friends, and one of them was Otto Skubl, Vienna's Police President, a supporter of the Catholic regime: 'I'll get you on a plane to Switzerland,' he promised Dr Preminger. He was as good as his word. The police president's *laissez passer* saw the couple through safely. As his parents flew to Switzerland, Otto's brother Ingo escaped to Czechoslovakia. After a brief Odyssey the whole family reached the United States, entering on visitors' visas.

They were safe and reunited, but the future was precarious. The visitors' visa did not entitle them to remain indefinitely. They still needed help. Otto cast round for people who might be willing to intervene on their behalf. Strictly speaking, to remain in America, they needed immigration visas and even if they could get on the crowded quota it meant leaving the country and re-entering as immigrants. They were old and tired and still shaken . . .

Otto took his problem to Tallulah Bankhead who, like other prominent Americans in those days, rose magnificently to the occasion. To help Hitler's victims was a point of honour and Tallulah was in a better position than most. Her father and uncle were in Congress and were powerful men in Washington – she called them and they responded. US authorities, as ready to help as individual Americans, were preparing for special Bills to be introduced in Congress to overcome all bureaucratic obstacles: 'Give me your homeless . . .!'

One such Bill enabled Dr Markus Preminger and his wife

to dispense with the rigmarole of leaving and returning with the right piece of paper. The Premingers were accepted as immigrants. Otto took out his first papers and the whole family was on the way to American citizenship.

Washington was characteristically generous. Hollywood, with the exception of Tallulah Bankhead, was characteristically unfeeling. Professionally, young Preminger – not all that young any more at thirty-three – was at a dead end. To hell with Hitler! To hell with his enemies in Hollywood. Before 1938 was much older he turned his back on them and headed for New York.

VIII

From Hollywood - *Outward Bound*

'Look,' said Preminger with quiet authority,
'I'm in charge now.'
Laurette by MARGUERITE COURTNEY

In the evening of her career Laurette Taylor faced problems
as big as Preminger's at the beginning of his, except that they
were of her own making. She was fifty-four, a critical age for
an actress however inspired, her triumphs were far behind
her and jobs difficult to come by. When Preminger mentioned her name to Gilbert Miller, the old showman raised
a warning finger:

'Laurette was a great actress – once,' he murmured. Now
she had a drink problem. She was unsure of herself. Her
memory was not as good as it used to be. She could be very
awkward. Only Hartley was keeping her going – J. Hartley
Manners, her second husband. 'And look what's happened
now . . .!'

What had happened was that, just when he needed it
most, New York offered a chance to Otto Preminger. Would
he like to direct a play on Broadway? Would he! After the
desolate, arid months in Hollywood, he was raring to go.
The play was a rivival of Sutton Vane's *Outward Bound*, an
eerie fantasy about a shipload of people who discover that
they are dead and bound for eternity.

It was really a matter of taking over from another director,
veteran Broadway producer William A. Brady told Preminger. That was all right by him. Rehearsals were already
in progress, the cast standing by – including Laurette Taylor
who was seeking a comeback after lean and tormenting
years. Yes, she could be difficult . . . That's how this emergency had arisen. Bramwell Fletcher was directing and taking

a leading part but Laurette was not happy about being directed from the stage.

Her's was a key part, Mrs Midgit, the dowdy, self-effacing little Cockney charwoman who recognises a drunken and useless fellow passenger as her son but asks for nothing more than to be near him, earns the respect of the passengers, and, when the Examiner of the Great Beyond grants her wish, gasps contentedly: 'It's 'Eaven, that's what it is, 'Eaven!'

Bill Brady tried to reassure Preminger. He did have some grim experiences with Laurette but this time his own wife, Grace George, was standing by to step in if anything went wrong and take Laurette's part.

Preminger knew and liked the play. As for Laurette – he would have done battle with a dragon to get back into the theatre. The challenge of the intricate situation became an added stimulus.

It was worse than he expected. Meeting Laurette Taylor, he realised at once that there was something seriously wrong. She was suspicious and deeply disturbed, more than could be explained by the pressures of a comeback. He took her out to lunch and decided to be brutally frank and tell her what Gilbert Miller and Bill Brady had told him.

She was equally frank with him: 'Grace is sitting at the back of the theatre,' she told him, 'and I know why! They don't expect me to go through with this. It's disgraceful, humiliating!' Having an understudy breathing down her neck was disconcerting. Laurette was convinced the producer only wanted to exploit her name for the publicity and then quickly replace her with Grace George.

Laurette's daughter, Marguerite Courtney, who wrote her mother's biography, takes up the story. She says that Preminger turned to her mother and said: 'I assure you that no one will play your part but you. I will see to that. No one will study your lines. There will be no understudy. But if I do this for you, you must come through for me!'

He said he would send Grace George away and give her,

Laurette, all the cuts and changes: 'Take them home and do not return until you know your lines – whether it is a few days or two weeks.' As Marguerite Courtney adds: 'In three days she was back, letter perfect! It was a psychological boost of inestimable importance.' Preminger saved the self-respect of a fine actress who went on to help Tennessee Williams towards his first great success.

Gently, with infinite care, he guided his star – one might almost call her his patient. They discussed every aspect of the play and her own performance. Though their backgrounds were so different, their views on acting were amazingly similar. She would not tolerate incompetent partners: 'She could be sharp about other actors' weaknesses,' Preminger said. That applied also to Preminger. 'She was not in any sense a mild woman!' Nor was Preminger a mild man.

During rehearsals her voice rang out gaily: 'M'sieur Printemps' – her name for Preminger. He amused her. She imitated his heavy accent and the way he wiggled his fingers over his head when he was excited. He treated her thoughtfully, never warned her not to drink, never exhorted her to be good: 'I knew she would not allow it.' Watching her and listening to her unexpected phrasing was a great joy to him.

It did not mean that he was soft with her or the rest of the cast. He called them for rehearsal on opening day and kept them in the theatre until late in the afternoon: 'Nobody has ever asked me to do that!' Laurette protested. Preminger, all sweetness: 'I think it is better if we do it this way.' Laurette never had a chance to become depressed and take to the bottle.

Her performance that evening was magnificent. She made the play her own and her role the star part. There were twenty-two curtain calls. The press was enthusiastic and Laurette's comeback made emotional news. Some of the glory, less than he deserved, rubbed off on Preminger without whom she might never have made it.

Outward Bound ran into 1939. In January the company received an invitation to present the play at President Roosevelt's birthday celebrations. It was Mrs Roosevelt's own choice. After the performance the cast would take supper with her and her husband at the White House. Otto Preminger was going to meet the President of the United States.

The supper party was an informal affair. The President asked Laurette Taylor to sit by his side – there was no seating plan. Preminger found a place at the same table: 'Laurette was pale and excited, like a child,' he remembered. 'She scarcely took her eyes off Roosevelt.' Neither did he. Preminger was as excited as Laurette.

Roosevelt's charisma was inescapable and overawed his guest. As after his arrival in New York three years earlier, Preminger could not find words adequate to describe his impression of the President. A man who really cared, he thought. Roosevelt impressed him more than any other person except Nehru, whom he met years later. The President was well briefed about him – it might be a politician's trick but the subtle flattery was no less pleasing for that.

The fleeting encounter still exercises Preminger's mind. Probably from a sense of modesty, he is casual about his salvage operation on Laurette Taylor to which he owed the invitation to the White House. It was not an isolated incident. This hard man is very good at helping lame dogs over stiles.

Two years after *Outward Bound* he was engaged to direct *My Dear Children*, a light comedy by Catherine Turney and Jerry Horwin. The star of the show – another comeback after twenty-nine years absence from the stage – John Barrymore, harassed by personal problems, pursued by creditors and evidently on the decline. Preminger handled him as gently as Laurette Taylor.

Let Barrymore have his say about that. When the applause died down at the end of a successful first night, he stepped to the footlights and addressed the audience: 'The credit is due to Otto Preminger,' he said, 'who has been a demon of tolerance and a tower of patience!'

Otto also earned the gratitude of Tala Birell, a ravishingly beautiful girl and a friend from his Vienna days, whom he gave a part in the play. *My Dear Children* had a long run. For John Barrymore, when it closed, it was the final curtain.

The tinsel of these years, as so much in show business, was deceptive. For people working only in the theatre, Preminger said, it was almost impossible to make a living. But, though his income was inadequate, he could not change his standard of living – that would have given the game away.

To keep himself busy while assignments were few and far between he held classes on directing and producing at Yale University taking what comfort he could from his status as titular professor. In New York he kept in touch with the profession which meant frequenting the right places. It was important to be seen but it was also comforting to move in luxurious surroundings and enjoy the company of beautiful women, particularly if they were available.

And where better to do just that than at the Monte Carlo, a club on Fifty-Fourth Street, run by Felix Ferry, a Rumanian? The club boasted all the ingredients that appealed to Preminger, and still do. He and Felix Ferry were close friends – all his life Otto had a thing about night-club owners.

The Monte Carlo was the ideal retreat for big business operators and showbiz personalities: 'One of the regulars I met there,' Otto told me, 'was Aristotle Onassis. I did not know he was such a rich man.'

Otto and Ari talked, came to like each other. Onassis was attracted by the glamour of show business: 'Very able, interesting man,' Onassis remarked when I mentioned Preminger. 'Charming man,' Preminger said about Onassis. 'Charming man' or 'nice man' are accolades Preminger confers on every other person he mentions (sometimes adding: '. . . with white hair' or some such distinguishing mark).

Like many a theatrical man of standing, Otto Preminger occupied a suite at a Manhattan luxury hotel, the St Regis. In his memory, this period survives as the proverbial 'bad patch' story without which the career of American millionaires is not complete. As Otto tells it, there came a time when his funds were no longer equal to his weekly hotel bill. He went to see Prince Obolensky who managed the hotel for the owner, Vincent Astor, and told him: 'I am afraid, I can't pay!'

A hotelier of sound judgment, Prince Obolensky was unperturbed. This young man was not a bad risk. His difficulties were obviously temporary. The hotel was not very full: 'Stay on and pay when you can,' he told Preminger. But the princely manager had to draw the line somewhere: 'Do not ask for room service!' he added.

'We had a roof over our heads,' Preminger said, 'but if we wanted a bite or coffee, we had to go out!'

Otto could have asked his father for help. Dr Markus Preminger had brought a nice nest-egg with him from Switzerland (where many prosperous Austrians kept secret accounts). The younger Preminger would not think of it: 'I was not sure whether I could ever pay him back,' he said, and added a perfect non-sequitur: 'I was quite certain things would look up before long.'

A solid establishment figure, Dr Markus Preminger could not reconcile himself to his son's uncertain existence: 'I shall buy a farm and all of us – including you and Ingo – can live there quietly to the end of our days.' Otto was moved, and so was Ingo. But farmers . . .? The Premingers were not cut out for the life.

Otto struggled on but it required some odd transactions to keep going. He had an Oldsmobile on order – 500 dollars down, 700 or 800 to pay on delivery. It was fortunate that compatriots from Europe were arriving, mostly refugees from Hitler, some quite well off. An old friend from Vienna, George Marton, the eminent literary agent, celebrated a happy reunion with Otto. They were so close that Preminger had no need to hide his problems:

'I have this car on order,' he told Marton, 'but I can't afford the amount due on delivery . . . Will you take it over and give me the 500 I have already paid. I need the money!' The deal was done.

Though few others were aware of the precarious situation, Marion did not take kindly to this life. Poverty did not suit either of them and keeping up pretences was a nerve-racking business. Relations between husband and wife suffered. They drifted apart but, as with their financial position, outsiders had no inkling of their marital difficulties.

Both were pastmasters in the art of making friends; Marion, snobbishly, seeking out celebrities like Albert Einstein and Sinclair Lewis, Otto preferring relaxation in the company of lesser mortals like Felix Ferry and other chums from the Europe of his youth.

Soon, they could no longer hide that their marriage was breaking up. Marion overhead two perfect strangers talking: 'The Premingers are divorcing,' one of them told the other. And it became true.

There was no question of who was the guilty party, at least in law, certainly none when it came to accepting the blame. What followed was the usual protracted and unpleasant negotiations about alimony which seem inseparable from American divorce proceedings.

By the time the lawyers reached a conclusion, Preminger's income was considerable. He was compelled to pay his ex-wife a large percentage of his earnings – until her re-marriage. Fortified by her share in Otto's growing success, Marion Mill Preminger became a staunch follower of the late Dr Albert Schweitzer, the good Samaritan of Lambarene in equatorial Africa who enjoyed the support of many philanthropists. Their money supplied hospital beds, medical equipment and medicine for sick, poverty-stricken natives. In Hollywood it was whispered that a considerable part of this charitable activity was financed with Otto Preminger's money. Quite untrue, of course.

Even without Schweitzer, Marion Mill Preminger occupied the gossip columns whom she supplied with a string of things supposed to have been said about her. Sample crop from the *New York Herald Tribune*:

'Do you know that Winchell once said my voice was so sexy it was strictly for adults?'

'Do you know, Salvador Dali once said I had the world's most beautiful skeleton?'

'Do you know I was called the most photographed woman in Vienna, the best dressed woman in Vienna, and the most photographed woman in Europe?'

'Do you know I'm known as the girl with the million dollar smile?'

Frankly, I didn't. Neither did Otto Preminger.

IX

A 'Nazi' Star is Born

Empty stalls except for a few desultory figures in the dark. A hollow echo mocking exchanges on stage and throwing back the harsh accents of the director whose voice cut into the somnambulant atmosphere of the rehearsal. That afternoon – we are in the late summer of 1939 – Clare Boothe Luce, trim and elegant, strolled into the theatre to watch her play taking shape.

Getting Otto L. Preminger to direct *Margin for Error* was not a bad idea. Who better to handle a play whose central theme was a clash between Mo Finkelstein and Karl Baumer: Jewish-American policeman versus brutish Nazi Consul who terrorises his staff and his wife and is finally found murdered.

With Europe at war against Hitler, it was an apposite subject. The characters were cleverly drawn. Finkelstein was melancholy and subtly comic. Directing Sam Levene in the part, Otto Preminger, supplementing his inadequate English with dramatic gestures, acted out each move and each posture.

Returning for another look at the rehearsals a week later, the author was struck by the startling switch of mood when Preminger turned his attention to Finkelstein's Nazi antagonist. He was completely transformed, even more in his element than with the Jewish policeman.

As if possessed by the Furor Teutonicus, he breathed life into the character and impressed the man at the receiving end of his instructions, the Viennese actor Rudolf Forster, cast as the Nazi consul. Stiff-necked and bald and really getting under the skin of the part, Preminger looked far more Germanic than the languid, almost gentle Rudolf Forster.

As he rapped out each sentence, the voice became harder still. The tone did not change when he switched from the lines to his own interpolations. Preminger and Baumer seemed to be one and the same person. Was he play-acting? Did it come naturally? 'There's a Nazi for you!' Clare Boothe Luce thought to herself.

Only a few days remained before the opening in Washington. The cast was in fine shape. In spite of the play's subject, the war in Europe seemed a long way away. There were no problems. No problems – except Rudolf Forster. The Austrian actor had come to New York to be with Elenore von Mendelsohn. Now their affair was at an end, he found the lure of Austria, the mountains of Salzburg and his little house in Bad Aussee irresistible.

One morning Forster was gone. A farewell note to Preminger said briefly that he was going home 'to join Adolf'. By that time he was on his way via Japan and Russia, which were not as yet in the war.

For one of the principal characters to drop out on the eve of opening was a blow enough to shatter any playwright. Not Clare Boothe Luce. What she had been turning over in her mind was suddenly a practical proposition. In manner, even in appearance, who really fitted her conception of the Nazi character she had created? Who was far more suitable than the departed Rudolf Forster? It was quite obvious: 'You take the part,' she told Preminger.

It was a tempting suggestion. Preminger's protestations were formal and brief: 'All right!' he agreed. 'I shall play the part in Washington . . .' If the reviews were favourable he would carry on when the play transferred to Broadway. Otherwise another actor would have to be found. The reviews were excellent. The play was a success. *Margin for Error* settled in at the Plymouth Theatre, New York, for a long run.

The public queued to see Otto Preminger strutting across the stage as a hateful Nazi, and show business joined in the chorus of praise for a most realistic performance. Before long, the character – and the performer – goose-stepped right on to Hollywood.

For Preminger the road back into films was paved by Nunnally Johnson, who saw *Margin for Error* and was impressed. He went backstage to congratulate Otto: 'We are just casting a movie for which I've written the script,' he told him. It was *The Pied Piper* which Fox was making with Monty Woolley (best remembered as *The Man Who Came to Dinner*): 'There's a part in it which is not unlike Karl Baumer . . .'

Hollywood called again. Nunnally Johnson asked Preminger to join the cast and, though he wanted to direct and not act and was not happy to go back to Twentieth Century Fox of evil memory, he could not very well refuse – he needed the money. At least Darryl Zanuck would not be there. (Zanuck, 'Hollywood Colonel' by order of General George C. Marshall, was in London organising army training films and eager to see action, crossed the English Channel with a British commando unit on a mission to blow up a radar centre in occupied France.)

In Zanuck's absence the man in charge was his executive assistant William Goetz, son-in-law of Metro's Louis B. Mayer. Bill Goetz signed the contract and Preminger picked up a handsome cheque for a few day's work. It was good to have a foot in the door again.

He took an apartment in Hollywood and was prepared to bide his time. He did not have to wait long before the telephone rang: 'This is the Charles Feldman Agency . . . Ned Martin to speak to you!'

Preminger's agent was on the line to pass on a new offer. Twentieth Century Fox were making *Margin for Error* – they wanted him to take the part he had created on the stage: 'They are offering big money!'

The exact amount has never been disclosed but it was certainly well over 50,000 dollars. If Ned Martin expected

Preminger to jump at the chance, he was in for a shock: 'I'll take the part under one condition,' Preminger countered. 'I directed the play in New York. I want to direct the film here!'

It was a gamble and needed strong nerves. Preminger is a gambler and there is nothing wrong with his nerve. Yet, had he been able to see Ned Martin's face at that moment, he would not have rated his prospects very highly. The note of futility in the voice which came over the line was unmistakable: 'I'll talk to the studio,' Martin told Preminger. It sounded like a hopeless mission.

The agent was not far wrong. Within hours he had the studio's answer. The curse of Zanuck was still upon Preminger. Even with the witch doctor thousands of miles away, the answer was the same as half a dozen years earlier: 'No, no, no!' Or rather: 'Acting – yes. Directing – never!'

The agent pressed: 'Take the part! Take the money!' Now it was Otto's turn to say: 'No!' No amount of pleading would shift him. Acting was good enough for others: 'I love actors,' he says (echoing Max Reinhardt). But he did not want to be restricted to acting all his life. Nor was he giving up. Persistence is one of the secrets of success – Preminger was nothing if not persistent.

There had to be a way! There was bound to be a formula to enable him to get what he wanted. Slowly the outline of a deal began to take shape in his mind. Deciding to go straight to the top, he called Bill Goetz: 'I'll take the part if you let me direct,' he said, and before Goetz could answer he added quickly: 'I don't want to be paid as a director. Just give me one week – if you are not satisfied with my work, another director can take over and I shall play the part of Baumer to the very best of my ability.'

Bill Goetz agreed to think it over: 'I'll let you know.' It no longer looked so utterly hopeless but Preminger was tense and agitated as he waited for the verdict. The days dragged on, the uncertainty became almost unbearable. It seemed an eternity before Bill Goetz came back to him. Over the telephone he said simply: 'It's a deal!'

The victory came too late to leave much time for celebrations. There were a hundred things to do. For the time being he was on probation: one week to show what he was worth. First the script. Reading it page by page, Preminger grew more and more apprehensive. It was not a good script – there has yet to be a script he will accept as it stands. He must work on it. He could not as yet analyse it . . . Later he explained quite cogently that he could only direct a picture if the script was 'filtered through my brain' scene by scene, sentence by sentence, word by word.

His English may not have been of the highest order but he knew how to build up a situation, create tension and keep the action moving. He only needed a congenial writer willing to accept his direction – the director directing the writer long before it was the turn of the actors.

But this was not the moment to dicker – about anything. Clutching at his provisional assignment Preminger did not even dare to tell the studio what he thought of the script. In this shape, he was convinced, *Margin for Error* was doomed. There was only one solution – he had to take a risk and commission a completely new script to be written on his own account.

It so happened that Samuel Fuller, an excellent writer who was then a serving soldier, was on leave in Hollywood and not averse to earning a few extra dollars. He agreed to help out for a moderate amount and for a few hectic weeks the odd couple – the director on probation and the writer on leave – worked together. They produced a corker.

The cast loved the script. Joan Bennett as the long-suffering wife played opposite Preminger's Karl Baumer. Milton Berle was the Jewish police officer, and a German, Carl Esmond, took another leading role. Otto worked day and night, acting, revising, directing. The first few days' rushes proved his point. At week's end there was no thought of replacing him with another director.

Billy Wilder, who has a corner in Preminger stories, watched him at work as actor and director, concluding each successful scene with his stentorian: 'Cut! Print! Very good!' When it came to his own death scene, with him as a corpse – and as director – things did not work out. He made the cast go through the scene over and over again, fourteen, fifteen, sixteen times. At long last it clicked. Preminger, the corpse on the floor, raised his head and shouted: 'Cut!' Print!' After a brief pause he could not resist adding: 'Very good!'

Margin for Error was a highly commended motion picture which earned Preminger a double fee, as actor and director. His real reward was a long-term contract as actor, director and producer. It put him in the big league and he could well afford the status symbols of success in Hollywood. The house in Bel Air, the valuable paintings – perhaps he was mortgaging his future but the future looked good enough. His triumph was short-lived.

A hero from the wars returning, Darryl Zanuck was not pleased to see Preminger installed at his studio. How dare this man whom he had sent packing years earlier sneak back while he was away fighting (or at least filming) for his country? Preminger says that the boss instantly banished him to the 'B' picture unit – worse than Siberia! Zanuck does not admit that he was vindictive: 'I think we paid Otto $750 a week, which was a lot,' he said blandly when we discussed this period at Twentieth Century Fox. 'I myself received only $2000 for being the boss of the whole damn job!'

Zanuck explained the structure to me: 'We had a DFZ unit, my own outfit' (DFZ are his initials). 'Then we had another unit under Bryan Foy which made 'B' pictures.' With some thirty writers and twenty directors, Foy produced films with low budgets of around half a million dollars each, chicken-feed: 'Foy was very good on melodramatic subjects,' Zanuck said. 'The delicate subtle thing was out of his range. With Preminger it was rather the other way round.'

Banishment to the 'B' lot did not cramp Preminger's style. There were compensations. In that year his final citizenship papers came through and he swore allegiance to his new country – the United States could not have wished for a more loyal and devoted subject. Almost symbolically, at the very moment when he hoisted the Stars and Stripes, a bond with his Austrian past was broken. Max Reinhardt, lonely and almost forgotten, died as the result of an accident while walking his dog in Fire Island. War reports drowned the news.

In some ways, though, Hollywood was very much like home. The Austrian and German film colony grew and stuck together. Curfew and other restrictions on aliens did not damp their spirits. They were a convivial lot. Among the actors were the talented Walter Slezak and the less talented but better looking Paul von Heinried, adopted son of an Austrian baroness who bequeathed him the aristocratic 'von'. The writing brigade included Billy Wilder whose ingenious, fertile mind constantly conjured up amusing situations, Walter Reisch, a Viennese with a penchant for romantic subjects, and George Froschel, best known for his Oscar-winning *Mrs Miniver*. Preminger saw a great deal of fellow directors William Dierterle, Fritz Lang, Ernst Lubitsch . . .

There were several others who congregated in each others' apartments and in restaurants, mostly peddling nostalgia. They were brilliant, inventive, witty and destined to add a flavour of their own to Hollywood film making. One of them who prefers to remain anonymous reminisced about Preminger in this period:

'I don't want to split on Otto after all these years,' he said. 'But his amorous excursions brightened our table talk. We could see it coming on. There was this glint in his eye. He smacked his lips as if to take a bite at a Vienna pastry – only in his case it was a girl. Next he would turn up with some delicious young creature!'

'Girls?' Preminger himself said to me. 'Between marriages, of course!'

His reputation for sexual appetite and prowess which had followed him from Vienna was enhanced when he was seen with some of Hollywood's prettiest faces and best figures. To escape the pressures and frustrations, he slipped away for long weekends in the company of some very slim, very tall, very long-legged and very willing partner – they all had to be slim, tall, long-legged and willing. Since he hated being alone, he could be a little indiscriminate in his choice – some of the pretty girls turned out to be pretty dumb, which is the occupational hazard of an amorous man with a big turnover.

On occasions he even welcomed these empty-headed beauties because they gave him time to think out his own problems in the intervals. The trouble was that there were too many would-be actresses hoping to get a part in one of his films and others who just wanted to bask in a film producer's reflected glory to impress their agent and their girl friends. Discretion on his part would have been the worst possible service he could do them.

When his companion for the night or the weekend was herself well known, as happened not infrequently, Otto was scrupulously discreet. There were rumours galore linking his name with Hollywood headliners but by the time the whisper got around, the affair was usually long over.

One girl he met towards the end of 1943 was different. Not a hint, not a whisper suggested the identity of his latest paramour, an attractive, clever and notoriously famous young woman: Gypsy Rose Lee (real name: Louise Hovick), the undisputed 'Queen of Strippers'. Preminger was captivated the moment he saw her.

Statuesque but with an animal grace, Gypsy at thirty was ravishing – with or without clothes. Basically they had little in common, the very European theatrical producer and the very American trouper from Seattle who was almost literally born on stage and left vaudeville to become the greatest burlesque star of all time. Like everybody else who met her, Preminger was fascinated by her intelligence, her quick wit, her range of interests unusual for someone without formal education.

Just parted from her second husband, actor Alexander Kirkland, Gypsy was as free and uninhibited as Preminger himself. They were kindred spirits enjoying sex as much as talk. Their love affair was intense but brief and not even intimate friends could guess that the link between them would be strong and permanent – beyond Gypsy Rose Lee's death.

Let us pursue the sequel to their love story through the eyes of the child that Gypsy Rose Lee bore Otto Ludwig Preminger . . .

X

Gypsy's Son, Otto's Child

'To ERIK, my son,
So he'll stop asking so many questions.'
Gypsy, A Memoir by GYPSY ROSE LEE

The baby was born in New York City where Gypsy Rose Lee
had a town house. The date was 11 December 1944. She
called him Erik and registered him as 'Kirkland' which was
still her legal name. The baby boy was only a few months old
when his mother first took him along on her tours across the
United States from city to city.

His world was a rugged landscape of props, trunks, clothes
but his mother's affection for him was strong and possessive.
While she was on stage, he slept peacefully in his cot in a
corner of her dressing-room. Music-halls and night-clubs,
some posh, some sleazy, where Gypsy was the star attraction,
were his natural environment. Superannuated comics patted
his head, dizzy stage blondes pinched his cheeks and gave him
their widest smiles.

Though little Erik never performed, he was as much a
trouper at five or six as his mother was when she was his age.
If he thought of it at all, he took it that his father was
Alexander Kirkland from whom his mother was divorced
(though they continued on friendly terms) and she did not
disabuse him of the notion. When Otto Preminger became
aware of the boy's existence, he went to see Gypsy and
offered to provide for him.

She would not hear of it: 'She just wanted the baby,'
Preminger said. 'She was a very independent, sophisticated
woman, way ahead of her time!' Neither did she want the
boy to know of their association: 'Promise that you will not

93

tell him,' she implored the father of her child. Preminger promised. Gypsy was well off and quite capable of looking after the boy. Besides, she told Preminger, she was about to be married again. That year Erik acquired a stepfather, Julio de Diego, a Spanish painter.

It did not change the course of his life: 'When we were in New York,' Erik recalled, 'I went to school – the Professional Children's School.' His periods at school were intermittent and brief. 'More often I took lessons by mail.' What he learned without the benefit of teachers was the rudiments of show business and life, literally, in the raw.

A photograph in *Life* Magazine dating back to 1949 shows Erik, aged five, sitting by the side of the Minneapolis censor watching Gypsy perform – disrobe, that is – and smiling proudly: 'That's my mommy! Can your mommy do that?' he asks the censor. The censor gave the act his blessing. Said Erik: 'From the time I was seven or eight, I worked backstage, helping with Mother's changes, taking down the scenery and that sort of thing. I was a general stage manager.'

It was all routine for the boy who took the professional hazards on the night-club belt in his stride – the Mafia, the gangsters, the hidden menace of the protection rackets: 'Sometimes it was a little tense,' he told me recently, amused at the memory.

'On one occasion, we were at a night-club in Buffalo, N.Y., which was run by the Mafia. The owner was broke – my mother was not the only one he could not pay. I could see the hoods in the audience with their broads, waiting, watching . . . Mother had a healthy respect for dangerous characters. She went upstairs and left me to pack up. Nobody bothered me, and I just went on with the work. By the time everything was stored away, it was one-thirty a.m. We got out.'

For six to eight months in the year we were on the road, travelling in a convoy of limousines, accompanied by two

Afghan hounds, seven cats, and an assortment of exotic birds, with trunks, suitcases and scenery.

'I knew nothing else,' Erik went on, 'and was never able to get a sense of proportion about this kind of life, the publicity, the money, the travelling. I was right in the middle of it. It was quite normal to me. Always in night-clubs. Lots of newspaper people around. Interviews, photographs, applause . . .

'In the late 'fifties Mother stopped travelling and we settled down in our town house at East Sixty-Third Street, New York.' Erik went to Riverdale County School, Gypsy started writing, first a popular thriller (*The G-String Murders*) then her autobiography, which she dedicated to Erik – 'so he'll stop asking so many questions'. She did not mention her Hollywood encounter with Otto Preminger.

Presently, she became a stage figure; *Gypsy*, the show based on her life, was launched on Broadway. Sandra Church played the name part, Ethel Merman was Gypsy's mother: 'I only remember her vaguely – my grandmother,' Erik said, 'but as Mother described her she must have been an extra-ordinary woman.'

In the first-night audience, sprinkled with show-biz per-sonalities, was Otto Preminger. He did not recognise the boy sitting in an aisle seat in the second row. For Erik it was a tremendous occasion: 'A shiver ran down my spine. It was so exciting to watch this play about Mother and live through her whole life . . .' There was Gypsy at seventeen, a star for Billy Minsky, a top-liner in Ziegfeld's Follies, admired by Damon Runyon, celebrated by Walter Winchell – and Jean Cocteau who saw her shedding her clothes and exclaimed: 'How vital!' In the film of the same name, Natalie Wood played Gypsy.

Gypsy herself no longer stripped for a living – she had no need to. She did a television show and summer stock work and Erik went with her – Detroit, Warren . . . 'Oh, so many places,' he said. He was having fun, drew his friends from among show people rather than schoolmates. Plenty of girls: 'I had a good time.'

'In 1961 Mother grew tired of New York and moved to California. I was in my last year in high school, had a girl friend and did not want to go. We had a row and I stayed behind in New York.'

Gypsy's house was divided into several apartments one of which Erik occupied. As soon as his mother left, his girl friend moved in. He could have done with a father like Otto. Erik was heading for trouble: 'I did not do my work,' Erik said. 'I was extravagant. Mother was worried but I was not really concerned about the future. I did not know what I wanted to do. Nothing really.'

He was rootless, restless. His closest friend was Boyd Bennett who had been living in the basement of their house for many years: 'The only real friend I ever had,' Erik said to me. The only one he would talk to and with whom he would discuss his problems: 'For some time I had my doubts whether Kirkland was really my father . . .' Kirkland was in Palm Beach running an art gallery. He and Erik did not get on. Whenever they met they quarrelled. It upset Erik. He poured out his heart to Boyd Bennett: 'Don't worry,' Boyd burst out, 'Kirkland isn't your father, anyway.'

Then, who the hell was? Bewildered and angry, Erik called his mother in California and asked her point-blank. She tried to pacify him: 'Of course, Kirkland is your father.' Erik did not believe her. When she flew into New York, he badgered her again. At long last she admitted: 'It's true – Kirkland is not your father.'

'Then who is . . . ?'

'If I tell you, will you promise to keep it to yourself? Will you promise not to contact the man?'

'I promise!'

'It's Otto Preminger . . .'

Said Erik, recalling the dramatic moment: 'I did not know

Preminger directing *The Man with the Golden Arm*

Preminger with Jean Seberg: *Saint Joan*

very much about Otto. Though I was tempted, I did not contact him. I kept my promise.'

He was still unsettled and unsure what to do with his life: 'I went to college – Columbia University.' After two semesters he dropped out: 'I took a job with a jeweller in the Village,' – Greenwich Village, New York. He did not keep it long: 'I drifted. I washed dishes, worked as a cook, lived wherever it was convenient to lie down.' Not surprisingly, his mother was unhappy about his way of life and reproached him bitterly. He would not listen or mend his ways. There were more quarrels and finally a break.

They were no longer on speaking terms: 'I was very independent,' Erik said, 'and had a wonderful time.'

The newspapers celebrated Otto Preminger as a great director and producer. Young Erik hardly thought of him, and Preminger had no idea what had become of his son. For Erik, the wonderful time was turning scour: 'After a while I had a couple of frightening experiences down in the Village,' he told me. 'Two very bad trips . . . Mother got in touch with me and asked me to come to California. I went and stayed for three months but I was bored.' Again, he could not decide what to do. On an impulse he joined the army.

Basic training in California, School of Army Security Agency in Massachusetts, no security clearance, posted to Texas, then overseas. With the 24th US Infantry Division, Pte Erik Kirkland was flown to Augsburg, Germany, then moved to Munich. He rather liked army life, did not mind the discipline, however sharp the contrast with the life he left behind. He was settling down.

It was at this stage that a letter reached Otto Preminger at his New York offices in Fifth Avenue: 'You would probably wish to know,' it said, 'that Erik is aware that you are his father . . .' For Otto it was exciting news. Though he was happy with his third wife and the fond father of a very pretty girl and a highly intelligent boy, twins born in 1961, the thought of his grown-up son was a pleasurable sensation. Feeling bound by his old promise to Gypsy, he wrote to ask her permission to contact – their son. It came by return of post.

Erik continues the story: 'Otto wrote me a delightful letter . . . He had always wanted to get in touch with me but my mother would not have it . . . He was anxious to meet me as soon as possible . . .'

Otto Preminger was due to fly to Europe to promote his latest film, *Hurry Sundown*, a controversial epic with a racial background set in the Deep South. London and Paris were the main stations on his itinerary. His suggestion was that he and Erik meet in Paris. He would be staying at the Plaza Athenée and was looking forward to seeing Erik there. Erik wrote back to explain that he was engaged to a girl called Barbara Ann van Natten, an airline hostess: 'Bring her along!' said Otto who is always free with his invitations.

In Augsburg Pte Erik Kirkland asked for a few days leave. He exchanged his uniform for a dapper civvie suit and travelled to Paris. With a pounding heart, he presented himself at Otto's apartment at the Plaza Athenée: 'It was awesome, kind of strange,' he recalled, 'to meet someone who is your father but is a total stranger.' He was aware that his father did not know him either. An awful thought bothered him: 'What if he does not like me?' He tried to be as pleasant as he could.

When Otto Preminger first set eyes on his grown-up son it was impossible to overlook the distinct family resemblance. Though the eyes reflected Gypsy's charm, Erik looked very much like Ingo. The face thinner than Otto's, the nose as prominent as those of other Premingers. Graceful movements and a pleasant manner but a streak of independence not far below the surface.

First impressions are often crucial. Otto Preminger liked the young man instinctively and very definitely: 'Let's go out and talk,' he said. For hours they walked the wintry streets of Paris. Erik told his father everything about himself, holding nothing back. What a relief to be able to talk like that. He felt that Otto understood. The rays of sympathy emanating from the older man were strong and warming.

'Barbara and I intend to get married in March,' Erik told Otto. Barbara joined them and the family in the making spent a few pleasant days together in Paris: 'I don't want to start running your life for you,' Otto said. 'When you are discharged from the army, you can come and work for me – if you want to. Whatever you decide, I hope we see a lot of each other!'

By the time Erik and Barbara were married in Augsburg in March 1967, Preminger was back in the United States. Little Christopher, their baby, was born in April of the following year. It thrilled the new grandfather. Erik Kirkland joined the Preminger outfit straight from the army and spent most of his time watching Otto at close quarters, listening to his conversations, following the negotiations with authors, agents, actors, technicians, distributors. His own show-biz background helped him to grow naturally into the organisation.

It was at this stage that I first met him. 'I'll tell you a secret,' Otto whispered one day as we were leaving his New York office: 'This boy is my son!' He sounded pleased with himself.

'Who is the mother?' I asked.

'I have promised not to say . . .'

I met Erik again in New York and London but did not press Otto for further information.

His period of training over, Erik became casting director and story editor, looking out for subjects and performers for his father's projects, a basic ingredient which can make or break a motion picture before the first foot of film is shot. Intense and hard-working, his rhythm became synchronised with his father's: perpetual motion and incessant telephoning. He was rapidly developing into a solid executive.

Without a deliberate effort he was also, by way of cross-fertilisation, making an important contribution by exposing his father – sometimes stuffy and old-fashioned despite appearances – to a sharp breeze of new-generation thinking. If Otto wanted to bridge the generation gap, Erik was a most knowledgeable guide. Inevitably, a little healthy tension between them generated electricity. Among Otto's docile and terror-stricken associates, Erik was the only one who could talk back at him with impunity. Preminger could only profit from friendly dissent in his own circle.

In 1970 Gypsy Rose Lee died in Hollywood. Her death enabled Otto to put the family house in order: 'I want to adopt you formally,' he told Erik. They were so close that an official seal seemed hardly necessary, but Erik was delighted. Otto wanted him to take his name. The legal arrangements for adoption were put in hand.

There was no longer any reason for secrecy. In London early in February 1971, Preminger asked me to join him and a few friends for drinks at his apartment at the Dorchester Hotel. He was his usual expansive self, taunting his guests and pumping them for information, dropping hints and amusing everybody with studied indiscretions: 'Within a few weeks,' he said eventually, 'Erik's adoption will become official. He will take my name. He will be Erik Preminger!'

To the others it came as a surprise that Otto had a grown-up son. For me it was a signal to ask him once more: 'And who is the mother?'

With a tell-tale sideways glance, Otto surveyed his audience. He was obviously about to spring a surprise. It was difficult to escape the impression that he wanted the world to know. As casually as he could he answered: 'Gypsy Rose Lee.'

'Can I make this public?' I asked.

'Sure, why not!'

So I did (via the London *Daily Express*). For days after the wires were busy relaying this titillating showbiz scoop round the world.

When Otto's twins were told that Erik was their brother – well, half-brother – Mark and Vicky chirped in chorus: 'Welcome to the family!' What pleased them most was that they were now 'uncle' and 'aunt' of Erik's three-year-old son. Erik himself was relieved that he could now openly acknowledge his father for whose accomplishments he had a great respect.

A reporter asked him whether he thought Otto Preminger really loved his mother: 'I don't know,' he replied. He never asked his father. They did not discuss such aspects of the past, just accepted each other. But Erik Preminger has been studying his father's life and work way back to the early forties when Otto Preminger clawed his way to the top in Hollywood.

XI

Success with *Laura*

Interviewer: 'What particularly interested you about
Laura?'
Preminger: 'The gimmick!'

Going back to 1943 and Otto Preminger's meeting with
Gypsy Rose Lee, it happened to be a period in which he was
equally engaged with another woman – *Laura*. Arriving at
his office at Twentieth Century Fox one morning in the
autumn of that year, he found two scripts on his desk. He
was not particularly thrilled at the sight. Directors in the
Bryan Foy unit were not often allocated subjects to rouse
the enthusiasm of a discriminating movie maker. With two
subjects, Preminger would at least have a choice.

He pushed the scripts aside with a contemptuous gesture,
part of his repertoire to this day, picked them up like a cat
playing with a mouse, then went through the routine a
second time. Even a brief glance at one of them tentatively
entitled 'Army Wives' confirmed his instinctive reaction.
Perhaps the other one offered a glimmer of hope.

The moment he started to read it his mood changed. The
story was based on a novel by Vera Caspary and, though
the outline does not sound so compelling, it generated
curiosity and suspense. Reading on, Preminger became
quickly involved with the principal characters, the handsome
Laura Hunt, who is thought to have been murdered, her
neurotic and frustrated friend Waldo Lydecker and the very
masculine Detective Mark McPherson. Laura turns out to
be alive and is suspected of the murder of the girl who was
killed in her place by mistake until the dashing detective
saves her in the nick of time from being done to death
after all.

A great deal of work remained to be done on the script. Preminger threw himself into it with gusto. In the final version, the story was narrated by Lydecker with Detective McPherson taking up the thrilling tale and acting it out to the surprise climax. Pleased with his own effort, Preminger took the finished script to Brynie Foy . . .

What followed was a real-life plot of intrigue, subterfuge and falsehood typical of Hollywood, which is etched deeply into Preminger's mind – it might have scarred a lesser man for life. Instead he proved himself no mean combatant in the traditional Hollywood catch-as-catch-can style.

Nowadays he recalls the story behind the story with glee. In the summer of 1971 we were at his New York house watching television. On the screen: Otto Preminger recounting some of the details to David Frost. Also on the show: Darryl Zanuck, starting out as the villain of the piece but ending up as the shrewd, flexible and perceptive top executive.

Reclining on his famous undulating couch each section of which can be raised or lowered independently to fit the body and the mood, Otto listened to himself and elucidated many points for my benefit. As it emerged from our session, the battle over *Laura* was almost as entertaining as the film.

Otto took up the story at the stage where the script was with Foy. A few days elapsed before the 'B' chief called him to his office: 'The script isn't very good,' Foy said. 'I don't think you can do it!'

Preminger: 'Did you read it?'

'No, but David read it.' David Stevenson was Foy's assistant.

Preminger's gall was rising: 'Look here,' he said acidly, moving in with the kind of argument to which Hollywood is most susceptible, 'David gets 75 dollars a week; I get 1500 dollars.' (When he told the story to Mel Gussow, author of the Zanuck biography, the figure he gave was 1000 dollars but this is neither here nor there.) 'So I think that maybe you should read it yourself.'

According to Preminger, Foy was on to him the following day: 'I have read it. David is right. It's a lousy script!'

'Bryan,' Preminger countered, 'I would like to give the script to Zanuck . . .'

'You know how Zanuck feels about you. It's suicide. He will throw you out . . .!'

'I'll take the risk.'

Preminger was confident. The first round had gone to him. Before the day was much older the script was on the way to Zanuck.

The scene shifts to Zanuck's big office in the executive suite with Bryan Foy and Otto Preminger appearing before him to hear his verdict. Now it was Zanuck's turn to perform the Hollywood *paso doble*: 'You don't like the script?' he asked Foy.

'No,' was Foy's answer.

'And why not?'

Foy was taken aback. If he thought he had been reading Zanuck's mind and helping him to stop Preminger he soon knew better. He mumbled and stuttered. Quite obviously, he had not read the script. 'Zanuck let him hang himself,' recalled Preminger, smacking his lips with *Schadenfreude*, that descriptive German word for pleasure at other people's misfortune.

Now Zanuck moved in for the kill: 'Well, I like the script,' he told Foy, 'and I'm going to do it in my unit.' Foy was left red-faced and out on a limb. Preminger was elevated to the DFZ unit and 'A' pictures.

Relations between Zanuck and Preminger were by no means fully restored. Zanuck called him to his house in Palm Springs: 'I was ushered to the swimming pool,' Preminger recalled, 'where Zanuck was sitting with his back to me. He was still mad at me, didn't get up or even turn around . . .'

Zanuck told him: 'The other things you have prepared

are no good. But the Laura story I like. You can go ahead and produce it but as long as I'm here you will never direct!'

Preminger had made it – at least part of the way. Dearly as he wanted to direct, he was happy that he was at least allowed to produce a major picture. He had won a battle but the war was not over yet. He wanted Lewis Milestone to direct *Laura* but Milestone turned it down and, with questionable logic, told Zanuck that Preminger himself ought to direct. Zanuck said: 'No!' The script went from one director to another. None of them wanted to take it on. At long last it came to Rouben Mamoulian who snapped it up: 'He needed the money,' is Otto's charitable explanation. The fee was in the neighbourhood of 70,000 dollars.

There was no love between the two men. They would not speak to each other – or rather, Mamoulian would not speak to Preminger. The delicate process of casting became a nightmare. Jennifer Jones was offered the part of Laura. She politely refused. Preminger suggested Gene Tierney who was doing very well on Broadway – the suggestion was kept in cold storage.

When Preminger went to Los Angeles with a party of friends to see Noël Coward's *Blithe Spirit* he was struck by the performance of Clifton Webb whom he had not seen before: 'That's the man to play Waldo Lydecker,' he decided. Back in Hollywood he told Zanuck; Zanuck called Rufus LeMaire, the casting director who had joined Fox from Metro. Preminger asked LeMaire: 'Can you arrange a screen test for Clifton Webb?'

'No need for a test, Rufus replied. 'Clifton Webb made a test at Metro's which I can get.' He was another one who thought he was doing what Zanuck wanted.

Nothing happened until Preminger met Clifton Webb and told him: 'I'm waiting for your test!'

Webb shook his head: 'What test? I've never made a test at Metro's.'

The stage was set for another of those dramatic confrontations off stage. Preminger was getting very adept at this sort of thing. It happened at the studio's executive luncheon table where the combatants foregathered at mealtimes, Darryl Zanuck presiding. This time it was the casting director's turn to stand in the dock.

Sweetly, with the guile of a public prosecutor luring the defendant into a trap, Preminger asked: 'When are we going to see the Clifton Webb test?' Pause. Pointedly: 'Tomorrow?' 'Sure!'

Preminger pounced: 'You are lying!' he shouted. 'Clifton Webb never faced a camera at Metro.' Collapse of stout party.

Darryl Zanuck agreed to have a test made but all was not well. Clifton Webb would not come to the studio. They could film him on stage doing his bit in *Blithe Spirit*, he said.

'I am not filming the damned play,' Zanuck snapped back. 'He must come and do a scene from the script!'

Confident of his own prowess as a Hollywood warrior, Preminger took on Zanuck himself, if only surreptitiously. Without bothering to ask for permission, he arranged for Clifton Webb to be filmed on stage during his big monologue. It was an impressive performance. The opposition was fighting a rearguard action: 'Webb looks effeminate,' some said. 'His voice does not sound right,' said others. Preminger persevered, Clifton Webb was signed, Gene Tierney was brought from New York, Dana Andrews was cast as Detective McPherson.

They were still haggling over the script ('A police story without a police station – impossible!'), the locale, the costumes, everything. The producer was the *bête noire*: 'Mamoulian started the picture,' said Preminger, 'but he treated me as though I was not alive. I was the producer but he did not want any part of me.' Preminger was not welcome on the set: 'He threw me out!'

The budget was kept tight and the amount allocated for the musical score was small. Preminger was assigned a young composer, David Raksin, who suggested that a Gershwin tune be adapted as the main motif. The rights were not available, and Raksin was experimenting with a tune of his own. He played it for Preminger, who knew nothing about music but knew what he liked. He liked Raksin's composition.

This is how the *Laura* score came about. Raksin wrote several more scores for Preminger pictures – the young, comparatively unknown musician was prepared to work with the producer-director throughout the shooting, while top ranking composers would simply write their piece and turn to other ventures.

In the meantime, Mamoulian was shooting away. 'When the rushes came, they were terrible,' Preminger recalled with a triumphant 'I told you so!' ring in his voice even after all these years. He had nothing to shout about at the time. Whatever was wrong or said to be wrong, he was blamed. Clifton Webb was no good: Preminger's fault. Gene Tierney inadequate: who suggested her in the first place? Dana Andrews: no sex appeal!

Back from New York, Darryl Zanuck quizzed the producer: 'What's wrong with the picture?' Preminger acted out his answer: 'Why don't you explain that to Rouben?' Zanuck asked.

'Rouben does not listen to me!'

Rouben carried on for a few more days. Zanuck did not like the new rushes any better.

With the blood spilt in the earlier jousts still staining the floor, the cut and thrust – not of the film but of the intrigues – transferred once more to the executive dining-room where so many plots end with heads rolling and new princes being anointed. Zanuck and his entourage were breaking their slim-line bread when the company was startled by one of those brief throw-away sentences in which Hollywood Tsars announce major decisions. Quite casually, Zanuck said: 'I think I'll take Mamoulian off the picture!'

The lunch was over and everybody rose to leave. Walking down the corridor, Tsar Zanuck touched Preminger with his polo stick, the Hollywood equivalent of an English monarch creating a knight, and told him: 'You're on!'

Unmarked by the insidious internecine struggle Preminger went to work with a vengeance. There were rumblings suggesting that Mamoulian was trying to put a spoke in: 'He told the actors that I hated them!' Preminger says.

Mamoulian retaliated with a version of his own. There were conflicts, he said, between him and Preminger who was a comparative newcomer to Hollywood at the time. The studio offered to fire Preminger but knowing that he, Mamoulian, already had a reputation for being difficult, he preferred to bow out gracefully as he was not particularly involved in the film anyway.

Without looking back over his shoulder, Preminger started from the very beginning. It was music to his ears when he heard Clifton Webb's well-modulated voice intoning the narration with which the picture opens:

I shall never forget this weekend – the weekend Laura died . . . A silver sun burned through the sky like a huge magnifying glass . . . It was the hottest Sunday in my recollection. A heavy silence lay on the town. I felt as if I were the only human being left in New York. And in a sense it was true. For with Laura's horrible death I was alone – with only my crowding, poignant memories of her . . .

The production went ahead briskly, Preminger-style. He put the performers through their paces, acted out every part so that there was no question about what was in his mind, and most of them were openly enthusiastic about his firm direction. They became accustomed to the stentorian voice which echoed through the studio. There were no hitches, none that Preminger could see . . . None, until Darryl

Zanuck and his entourage settled down in the studio's screen room to watch the completed picture.

Groans in the dark and a few lightning remarks signalled another storm ahead. Zanuck seemed to be shaking his head. His courtiers made disparaging noises. When the lights went up, Zanuck looked straight through Preminger and said: 'We've missed the bus with this one.' It was like a judge prounouncing sentence of death.

The corpse was too costly to bury without another attempt to revive it. At the post-mortem, the diagnosis was that the ending was wrong. There followed the usual ping-pong of suggestions and counter-suggestions, memoranda sailed backwards and forwards and the outcome was that the objectionable ending was recast and reshot. A fortnight later the film with the new version was put on again for Zanuck's inspection.

It so happened that Walter Winchell was in town as Zanuck's guest. He was watching the screening with a girl-friend from the back row. He and the girl could be heard chuckling and, even before the lights went up at the end, Winchell's staccato voice could be heard: 'Big time, big time, Darryl!' Preminger was jubilant and Winchell continued: 'The end – I don't get it! You're going to change it?'

'Darryl was very flexible, a great executive!' Preminger says now, all the humiliations, indignities and rejections forgotten. What reconciled him to his powerful protagonist was Zanuck's reaction to Winchell's comment. Turning to Preminger, he asked: 'Do you want your old ending back?' Then he added generously: 'If this is a big success, it will be all to Preminger's credit.'

The original ending restored, the film was premiéred. It was highly praised, except for one or two prominent critics who slammed it. In the years that followed when *Laura* was acknowledged as a classic, Preminger drew much comfort from the bad reviews. They have often served him as an illustration of how wrong critics can be. Since then, whenever a critic dislikes one of his films, his rejoinder has been: 'Look what they said about *Laura*!'

Laura was the beginning of Preminger's friendship with Zanuck: 'There's nothing malicious about him,' he told Zanuck's biographer. 'I have a warm feeling for him.' Zanuck reciprocated: 'I hired him, I fired him. I had him as an actor, producer, director. A great talent, but he has to be controlled.' That's exactly what Preminger does not want to be.

The experts made a feast of *Laura*, studied it, analysed it, questioned Preminger about it – without getting much enlightenment from him. While he remembers every foray and exchange in the vicious battle that preceded the shooting and went on to the much-disputed end, he is reticent about the intellectual process behind the direction, if there was one. Having prodded his laggard memory in vain, I was referred to an issue of the attractive silver-bound mag *On Film* whose reporter asked him some idiotic questions about the attitude of the McPherson character to Laura. Preminger replied: 'I couldn't tell you, because I don't remember the film that closely any more . . .'

The success of *Laura* brought Preminger close to the ethereal Gene Tierney with the angelic face and the misty eyes which make her look permanently entranced and entrancing. The gorgeous, exquisitely gowned girl attracted shoals of eligible and non-eligible men. Close as Preminger was to her, there was never any question of him getting too close. Had he been so minded, he would have met formidable competition.

One weekend when Otto and Gene stayed with Charles Feldman, another house guest was the handsome, young John F. Kennedy. It was not the first time that Jack had come to California to court Gene – he was not yet married and she was between marriages.

Being friends of Gene Tierney, the two men from such disparate backgrounds, met several times within her orbit and got on well with each other but in Preminger's mind these early encounters are overshadowed by the rumpus around their meeting when John F. Kennedy was already President of the United States.

My wife and I were Preminger's guests in Washington in 1961 while he was shooting *Advise and Consent* with which he restored Gene Tierney to stardom after her long absence from the screen. Otto was elated when he received a message saying that the President would like him to dine at the White House with any members of the cast he would chose to bring along. The date suggested was a Wednesday.

'Of course!' Preminger replied quickly – too quickly. Looking into his schedule, he found that elaborate arrangements had been made for a major scene to be shot on Wednesday night. He called the President's Press Secretary: 'I am so sorry. It was a mistake. We are working on Wednesday evening.'

'That's all right,' the secretary said. 'Let's make it the next day, Thursday, for lunch.'

'Thank you – that's fine.'

No sooner had Preminger put down the receiver when his own secretary reminded him: 'You are scheduled to address the National Press Club at lunch on Thursday!'

What a quandary! He called the Press Club and explained the position: 'I cannot cancel the President's invitation a second time,' he said. 'I am terribly sorry!'

'Permit us to call the President,' they said.

Press Club and White House sorted out the tangle among themselves and fixed mutually convenient dates. The story leaked out, and *Time* Magazine thought Preminger was so arrogant that the President of the United States had to invite him three times before he accepted.

There was no complication about the offer Preminger received as a reward for the triumph of *Laura* which was a boost to the Zanuck régime. He was given a long-term contract for what he described as 'a fabulous sum'. As usual he was vague and variable about figures. Recently he put the amount at 7500 dollars a week. In an earlier interview with Jacques Lourcelles the figure he gave was 7000 dollars. Whichever it was, it was a warming thought and an enviable augury.

XII

'That Bitch, Jean Simmons'

Now a well-groomed, expensive stallion in the Zanuck stable, Otto Preminger went through his paces in the Hollywood rat race. He was a frequent visitor to Darryl's Palm Beach retreat, was consulted on most matters, read scripts and pronounced on them and joined in the paper chase which sent memoranda fluttering from desk to desk. Searching for useful properties, finding suitable parts for contract artistes, keeping an eye on rival studios became second nature.

Ingo Preminger joined a Hollywood agency: with a brother in the higher echelons of the profession his affairs prospered. Athletic and personable but without Otto's personality, with a quiet voice and pleasant manner, he became known as 'the nice Preminger'. It hurt Otto: 'I am really very nice,' he told a friend.

For Otto, after *Laura*, anticlimax. His next film was *Army Wives*, the script of which had been gathering dust on his shelves. He tried to make the most of it, renamed it *In the Meantime, Darling*, but it remained a trivial marital romp in an American army camp. What did he know of life in the American army? He had never worn a uniform except the Nazi insignia on stage and screen. Only his barrack-square attitude qualified him for the subject.

In Preminger lore the film is largely remembered for his confrontation with Stanley Prager, then a bit player, now a TV and film director, who was at the receiving end of what initiates call the true OP 'shtick'. Facing the camera and the bald Germanic terror, Prager fell completely apart. He was unable to say his lines and do the simple business he was asked to do. He was close to a break-down.

OP got into one of his rages, his face became redder and

redder and he kept shouting: 'Don't you want to do it?' – a somewhat superfluous line because most actors are ready to cut their own throat if so ordered by OP.

Prager just happened to have 'OParalysis'. His hands and knees started to shake, his lips tried to form the line of the dialogue but nothing came out. OP looked like having a stroke any moment, advanced towards the actor, took him by the shoulders in a hard grip, shook him violently, his nose almost rubbing the actor's nose, his bulging eyes close to the other's eyeballs. And then he shouted at the top of his lungs: 'RELAX! RELAX!! RELAX!!!'

Little else came along after this picture and Preminger might have continued to draw his 7000 or 7500 dollars a week for God knows how much longer without doing any productive work, had it not been for a sudden crisis at the studio. Ernst Lubitsch, the subtly-witty ex-German director – the 'Lubitsch touch' was a Hollywood byword – was working on a film called *Royal Scandal*, written by two Hungarians (Lajos Biro and Melchiore Lengyel), adapted by an Austrian and scripted by an American.

A splendid cast had been assembled for this light-hearted glimpse of Russia's Tsarina, Tallulah Bankhead as Katherine II, Anne Baxter as a countess at court and Eva Gabor as one of the other aristocratic ladies. Shooting was about to begin when Lubitsch fell ill. In Zanuck's eyes one foreign director was as good as another. Lubitsch, Preminger – what was the difference? Preminger, currently unemployed, was assigned to *Royal Scandal*.

Bursting with energy, he tore into it, creating tensions which were not conducive to the light-hearted mood the film required. (Anyway, Preminger is emphatic that, though he worked in the wake of Lubitsch, he was never influenced by his style.) On a visit to Hollywood, Anne Baxter's famous grandfather Frank Lloyd Wright came to see her on the set. That day Preminger seemed to be in a foul temper. He put Tallulah twenty-seven times through the same scene. Bored stiff, Frank Lloyd Wright departed...In the end Preminger's professionalism helped him to see the job through. It was not his fault that *Royal Scandal* did not bring the house down.

In a brief interlude he put on grease paint again for a part in a film of his friend Gregory Ratoff. The title: *Where Do We Go From Here?* It was a good question. Somewhat indiscriminately he was made to turn his hand to thrillers, musicals, romances, classics – in this mixed lot only blind sycophants could discern a distinct Preminger style.

He made *Fallen Angel*, a thriller, and *Centennial Summer*, a Jerome Kern musical. Jerome Kern did not live to see the opening of his film, and death presently saddled Preminger with more unfinished business – Lubitsch died before he could complete *That Lady in Ermine*. Preminger took over.

Though he struggled and protested manfully, he was indented to direct the film of Kathleen Winsor's best-selling shocker, *Forever Amber*. 'It's a horrible book,' he told Zanuck. Zanuck replied that he had spent two million dollars on the film already: 'Look,' he told Preminger, 'you're part of the team. Your contract has still six years to go. We are stuck with you, but you are also stuck with us.' Preminger's comment on this shot-gun approach: 'Zanuck had this very persuasive manner, and I finally agreed to do it.'

Having agreed, he wanted Lana Turner for the star part but had to make do with Linda Darnell who belonged to the studio while Lana did not. (Zanuck: 'If you think Lana Turner is right, then we'll dye Linda Darnell's hair blonde, and she'll be exactly like her!') Preminger was grumbling because the studio's reservoir of top-liners was rather shallow.

The film aroused the Catholic 'League of Decency' to protests, and the head of the Legion did not even want to see the picture: 'We banned the book,' he said. 'Why make the picture at all?' Fox countered that six million dollars were invested in the picture . . . Finally some offending passages were cut to appease the Catholics and a foreword about 'the wages of sin' was inserted. Whenever two people kissed, the film was cut before their lips joined. Preminger's first clash with censorship was a defeat, but since it was the studio which caved in and not he, it does not count against him.

Slave-driver Zanuck managed and manœuvred him ruthlessly exploiting his organised mind and skill for the greater glory of Zanuck, if not Preminger. At least he was able to weld an efficient production team together which, like a commando unit, learned to work under fire with verbal bullets whistling around their ears. Shackled to the set throughout the shooting, David Raksin produced some fine well-integrated music. Lyle R. Wheeler, art director, Harry Reynolds, editor, and Charles LeMaire, wardrobe designer, made up the permanent staff.

Preminger was a stern puppet master, vigorously pulling the strings, storming his way through production after production, losing his temper, terrifying one moment, all sweetness the next as if there had never been an unholy row.

Many top stars received acting lessons from him which lacked nothing in realism. Those who came under his direction included Joan Crawford and Henry Fonda in *Daisy Kenyon*, one of the pictures he has completely 'forgotten': 'I don't remember anything about this film,' he said recently. This is a recurring phenomenon.

What he ought to remember was that Walter Winchell to whom he owed the success of *Laura* turned up in *Daisy Kenyon*, this time as a performer – a just reward. Preminger made *The Thirteenth Letter*, another 'forgettable' film except that one of his stars was the late Michael Rennie who, as we shall see, came to play a part in his private life which was not easily forgotten.

Unlike other creative artists with a clear line of development, Preminger insists that he must wipe his mental slate clean away after every film so as not to repeat himself. Not surprisingly, his wilful amnesia only covers with oblivion pictures which are best forgotten. Others, revived on television twenty years after they were made, were not bad at all.

Sudden changes, improvisations, dropping out of and stumbling into jobs was the pattern of life in the movie industry. The bosses shuffled and dealt the cards, and Preminger was just one of the jokers in their pack. Zanuck was about to slip him under the table to a rival mogul with a problem on his hands.

'Otto,' Darryl said, 'I have just had a call from Howard Hughes who wants to borrow you.' Howard Hughes, eccentric multi-millionaire aircraft manufacturer and airline operator, was dabbling in films in a big way. Only a handful of people personally knew the mysterious recluse who would sound utterly unconvincing if he turned up as a fictional character in a Hollywood movie (years later the courts were asked to decide whether he really existed). Though Hughes controlled the rival RKO Studios, Zanuck was not averse to helping his powerful friend: 'I have agreed to release you,' he told Otto.

Preminger related to Jacques Lourcelles one version of what followed: 'When Zanuck told me to go to RKO,' Preminger said, 'I went and was given a script.' Next morning at a quarter to four he telephoned Mr Hughes and told him: 'Howard, I hate your story. Please do not force me to make this film!' Hughes replied: 'My friend, I need you. Come to my studio tomorrow and you will be like Hitler. The studio will be at your disposal and you can engage whom you like. Whatever you wish will be done . . .!'

Some details which Preminger recalled for my benefit make it a much more dramatic story. Having received the script of a thriller entitled 'Murder Story', he was asked to meet the RKO boss: 'You know,' Otto explained to me, 'Hughes was in the habit of driving around in a battered old car at nights. He picked me up and we drove round and round, Hughes wearing creased old clothes and tennis shoes . . .'

Hughes was insistent – as Otto might well have guessed

there was a woman behind it all – and soon spelled it out: 'Jean Simmons, the bitch!' he hissed. 'She has cut her hair short . . .!' Jean and Howard had had a fight – it is not clear whether it was a lovers' tiff or a dispute between studio boss and star – and she apparently took a pair of scissors and snipped away to spite him because he hated short hair. Hughes told Preminger that Jean was on loan to him for a few weeks, and only eighteen days remained: 'I depend on you!' he pleaded.

Here was one of the richest men in the United States virtually at Preminger's feet. Never before had a director been propositioned in such circumstances. Irresistible! Otto succumbed and turned to his brother Ingo. In Salzburg in the summer of 1971 I met Ingo, who takes up the story: 'I did sell Otto a writer for this film,' he said. It was Oscar Millard who was Ingo's client then and was right there in Salzburg with him now working on a film . . .

'My agent approached Otto,' Millard said, bowing with mock-deference in the direction of Ingo. As a result he was summoned by Otto who told him: 'My brother tells me you are a genius – let me see proof!'

Preminger (Otto) engaged Millard and another writer, Frank Nugent, who quickly started on a new script for the Howard Hughes film: 'Relations with Otto steadily deteriorated,' Millard recalled half-jokingly, half-seriously. They settled on a new title, *Angel Face*. Robert Mitchum played opposite Jean Simmons. The production team was RKO rather than Preminger. Well built and well directed, the film became a success.

XIII

Hello Mary, Farewell Hollywood

Hitler's loss was Hollywood's gain. One of the most satisfying successes of the new Americans whom the Nazi terror had driven from Europe belonged to George Marton whose friendship with Otto Preminger had, if anything, been strengthened in their new country. A literary agent of talent and imagination, Marton had some gifted playwrights and script writers under his umbrella, many of them Hungarians, who were responsible for several celebrated Hollywood motion pictures.

He was in New York on 4 December 1951, when the telephone rang in his apartment early in the morning: 'This is Otto,' the familiar voice rasped. Marton was in constant touch with directors and producers but Otto's call was particularly welcome. It was at Otto's house that he had first met Hilda Stone, and Preminger was the first to know that he and Hilda planned to get married – Hilda Marton, incidentally, was Otto's witness when he became a citizen of the United States.

'Will you and Hilda have dinner with me tonight?' Otto asked. Marton seemed to detect an undertone of mystery in the invitation. He accepted gladly: 'Nine-thirty at the Stork Club,' Otto said.

A splendid opportunity to catch up on Preminger's affairs, private and professional, Marton thought. Otto had been away from Hollywood for the better part of a year, devoting himself to the living theatre in New York. With his delicate direction he had made a smash hit of *The Moon is Blue* by F. Hugh Herbert, another American from Vienna. The delightful comedy involving the virginal Patty O'Neil (played by Barbara Bel Geddes), an architect who lures her to his apartment and an elderly bon-vivant (Donald Cook in the part of David Slater) was set for a long run on Broadway.

When George and Hilda Marton joined Preminger at the Stork, there was no time to talk about his stage triumph. Otto was in the company of a tall, elegant woman, no longer in the prime of youth but very attractive with all the attributes of a typical Preminger girl: 'This is Mary,' Otto introduced her.

Marton thought the Stork's owner Sherman Billinsgay was fussing around Otto even more than usual. Bottles of Dom Perignon were standing to attention for the occasion – it obviously was an occasion. After allowing the tension, or rather curiosity, to reach a theatrical climax, Otto came out with his secret: 'Three hours ago,' he said, 'Mary and I were married!'

The surprise was genuine. The Martons knew nothing of the lady who had just become Mrs Preminger. There had been so many girls in Otto's life, most of them looking more or less the same, that even close friends could not possibly remember every single one.

It appeared that Mary had a son from a previous marriage, a hulking big boy whom Otto affectionately called 'Baby' even when Baby's six-foot-two frame dwarfed 'father'. Mary used to be a model who, at some time, had shared an apartment with another equally long-limbed, equally elegant girl by the name of Hope – Hope something or other – whom Otto was to meet before long and come to know rather well.

They were not married long when Otto brought Mary and her son with him on a visit to London, my one and only meeting with them. He was still Baby-ing the young man but relations between him and his second wife seemed already strained. It did not look like a marriage that would last, and there was, perhaps, nothing quite as remarkable about it as the inevitable ending which made such a big splash when it came.

The couple were still in honeymoon mood in New York

when Otto received a call from Hollywood, almost routine in his life, which yet profoundly affected his public image, if not his mental make-up. It was from Otto's old friend Billy Wilder, a fellow European who first made a name for himself in pre-Hitler Berlin in the depression of the late twenties when he was forced to take a job as a 'gigolo' a professional dancing partner of ladies frequenting tea and dinner dances, and published his horrendous experiences in an uproariously funny newspaper series.

Billy Wilder went on to make an impressive German film ('People on Sunday') without professional actors and, as a writer and director in Hollywood, projected wit and social awareness long before such films as *The Lost Weekend* and *Ace in the Hole* put him in a category of his own. After a little long-distance banter, he told Otto that he was preparing a film about a German prisoner-of-war camp. Preminger could guess what Billy expected him to do. 'There's a part which belongs to you,' Billy said. Would he like to play the snarling, sadistic, needless to say, close-cropped German prison commandant?

Yes, he would! Otto went to Hollywood and made the character so life-like and convincing with unadulterated nastiness welling up from a cold heart that he never lived it down. The Nazi character in *Stalag 17* became totally identified with Otto Preminger. Otto Preminger became totally identified with the archetypal Nazi. From then on, were he cast as Romeo, the public could still only see him as a Nazi at his worst. He rivalled Erich von Stroheim as the man people love to hate. As the memory of Stroheim faded, there was only Otto Preminger left to be hated.

Intentionally or not, he began to live up to this impression, instinctively capitalising on his new trade mark. Some thought he was carrying his 'Stalag' qualities too far into his off-screen life but paid and unpaid publicists took up the theme and he provided plenty of incidents to bear them out. After twenty years people are still wondering where the act ended and inclination started. Friends and enemies draw the line at varying points; both cite evidence, however contradicting, to prove their case for or against Preminger.

While he was in Hollywood, the ageing Dr Markus Preminger died suddenly. His death was a shock to his sons, who had remained devoted to him through all the vicissitudes of exile. Their mother never got over the loss. She fell ill and remained an invalid until her death.

Otto Preminger himself, unaware as yet of the monster he had created with his masterly performance in *Stalag 17*, was preoccupied with a more immediate problem. Not long after he surrendered his personal independence in marriage, he decided to become professionally independent. There was nothing now to hold him in Hollywood. He would have no more of the tyranny of the studio bosses. He wanted to be free. Free and independent.

When, in the summer of 1971, the subject of his decision to break away cropped up, he was almost as vehement about the old-style Hollywood as he was about Old Vienna. How dare I call him a Hollywood producer! Hollywood – bah! Hollywood in the early 'fifties which we were discussing was already on the decline and there were very definite reasons for it. Hollywood was beginning to outlive its *raison d'être*.

Technical progress was liberating movie markers from the studios. New light-weight cameras with powerful lenses enabled them to dispense with artificial lighting. Huge, costly sets were outmoded by the fashion for realism. Why mock up houses, streets, cities on big lots when you could take cameras, crews, performers to the real thing. Rome was not built in a day, but with modern communications a film unit could be in Rome within a day – or at any other place the script demanded.

The studio system, old-fashioned and calcified, discouraged initiative and originality. Hollywood tycoons only wanted to repeat successful formulae, and advisers told them only what they wanted to hear – he would be a foolhardy executive who lured his boss into risky adventures. For men with ideas, new ideas, it was impossible to penetrate the thick wall of stereotype which surrounded the decision makers.

There were other factors. The star system was on the verge of collapse, the huge amounts top-liners demanded were crippling the industry. With their minds on dividends, the heads of studios sensed greater profits in the revenue from oil which flowed under their vast lots. The whole arrangement was rotten and deserved to be ended.

What irked Otto Preminger personally was that he had allowed himself to become part of the rotten set-up; that he had tended, almost automatically, to see things the way the bosses wanted him to see them. Come to think of it, the films he had made in Hollywood (with the possible exception of *Laura*) were just what he had been told to do: 'They did not really give me much satisfaction!' he said.

To look at him, Otto Preminger was probably history's most unlikely revolutionary but he had really nothing to lose but the chains which tied him hand and foot. And when it came to blowing up Hollywood, he turned out to be a veritable Guy Fawkes. 'Independence!' became his slogan.

The bosses were aware that a new day was dawning but did not have the gumption either to greet it or resist it. But when anti-trust legislation forced them to sell their theatres, they could no longer hope to hold the march of the independents by denying them outlets. Suddenly, the giants of Hollywood looked weak and vulnerable. It needed only a good push to topple them. Preminger was one of the first to shoulder them aside and strike out on his own.

He did not join battle unprepared. The vehicle to carry him to independence was *The Moon is Blue*. Delighted with the play's success, Hugh Herbert, on Preminger's advice, was refusing offers from the studios and hanging on to the film rights: 'We can do it ourselves, together!' Preminger suggested. 'Let us produce the picture independently . . .!'

He was so enthusiastic and persuasive that Hugh Herbert

agreed. In the event, Preminger set up his own company, Carlyle Productions, with offices in New York. For *The Moon is Blue* he and Hugh Herbert would sign jointly as producers.

Fortified by the play's stage success (and the *Laura* halo around his head), Preminger obtained financial backing from the banks and United Artists agreed to distribute the picture. He was elated but it did not take him long to find out that being an independent producer did not mean being independent. United Artists were not supporting him without reserving certain rights for themselves, largely financial. He seemed to have exchanged one set of bosses for another.

However, when it came to the contract, he insisted on an unusual and novel stipulation – the right to cut and edit the film would be his, and his alone. The clause would enable him to present the picture exactly as he visualised it – cutting and editing are among a director's most significant functions. The new departure enhanced his authority.

Without delay, he started work on the script with Hugh Herbert, an intense routine, day by day, often night by night. He has since followed it with all his pictures. One of his rare excursions into social life at this time was a drive to Hartford, Connecticut, to see the preview of a play directed by Gregory Ratoff, *Nina*, translated from the French and starring Gloria Swanson and David Niven.

Going backstage to congratulate Gregory, he ran into David Niven: 'I liked you very much,' he said, high praise indeed, Niven thought, from a man like Otto who did not mince words. Otto's praise was genuine but calculated. Watching David Niven it had struck him that he would be ideal for the part of Donald Slater in the film version of *The Moon is Blue*.

A few days later he called David Niven to offer him 'the best part in my next picture'. David and his wife Hjordis were beside themselves with excitement: 'Something he has seen in my performance in *Nina* at Hartford,' Niven recalled, 'had persuaded him that I was the actor he wanted.'

'You could first play the part on stage in San Francisco,' Preminger suggested. David Niven agreed. He was impervious to the stories about Otto's methods as a director making the rounds in the profession. There was this occasion in Chicago . . .

Otto was directing a touring company of *The Moon* . . . and the scene in which the older man bursts into the bachelor apartment and knocks out the young architect, a difficult job to perform on stage (much easier in the film). Watching the action, Otto thought there was too much space between the fist of the aggressor and the temple of the victim. It did not look realistic, and he made them repeat it again and again. Getting more and more agitated, he finally shouted, eyes bulging: 'Do it right! Hit him, why don't you hit him right!'

In the next rehearsal the terrified Thespian – terrified of Preminger – obeyed instructions too literally. The young man (Murray Hamilton who, years later, played the father in *The Graduate*) was knocked out cold: 'Oh, my God!' Preminger stammered, losing his composure for once. 'Why did you do that?' 'Because you told me, Sir,' the offending actor replied.

Nothing so dramatic happened to David Niven who took over the part in San Francisco and played it for three months. *The Moon* . . . did well even in competition with Charles Boyer who was playing in an adjacent theatre.

In the meantime, Preminger put up Niven's name to United Artists: 'Niven is washed up!' they told him. 'Get somebody else!'

'But Otto', Niven remarked, 'is an immensely determined individual, and what Otto wants, he usually gets . . . He got me . . . bless him!'

Otto also got William Holden to play the lover – no opposition there from any side. To play the girl, Patty O'Neil, he engaged the slender, sensitive Maggie MacNamara, and the part of Niven's wife went to Dawn Addams. There was always room for a friend – Gregory Ratoff was given the part of a typical New York taxi driver participating in the affairs of his customers, a beautiful cameo.

While working on the script an idea struck Preminger and Herbert whose conversation sometimes lapsed into German: 'Why not make a German version of the film and shoot it at the same time?' Otto suggested. The suggestion was only one short step ahead of execution.

Page by page, the Herbert-Preminger script went to Karl Zuckmayer who had scripted Marlene Dietrich's *Blue Angel* and later wrote *The Devil's General*. For his German version of *The Moon . . .*, entitled 'Jungfrau auf dem Dach' (Virgin on the Roof), Preminger engaged a German cast headed by the good-looking, fair-haired Hardy Kruger and Johanna Matz (in Maggie MacNamara's part). The Gregory Ratoff character? 'I shall dub it myself,' Preminger decided.

He had no trouble getting a production team together – one of the men he engaged was Max Slater with whom he had worked in Vienna and who is still associated with him. To keep the budget low, he set a back-breaking production schedule for both versions: 'Twenty-four days, not a day more!'

As soon as the German cast arrived, rehearsals started and went on for a month, Preminger commuting between the two languages. Once shooting got under way, it went with clockwork precision. Both versions were completed in a record eighteen days.

There was no hitch, not until Preminger directed a crowd-pulling trailer. The idea was for a live giant bear to sit in a movie house between an old lady and 'Prince' Mike Romanoff, the Hollywood restaurateur and darling of the gossip columnists. The old lady was supposed to turn to Romanoff, saying: 'Are you crazy? You can't bring a bear to a movie!' To which the snobbish Mike would answer calmly: 'Why not? He loved the play!'

Preminger did not like Romanoff's amateurish performance and showed him again and again how to do it. Everybody was getting impatient and irritable including the bear, who could not know that Preminger who feared no man has a pathological fear of animals. The giant beast put his giant paw with the giant claws on Otto's lap. Otto went white and did not dare to move: 'Call the trainer, call the trainer!' he whispered almost inaudibly. It took a few tense minutes to detach the bear from the petrified Preminger.

The film completed, he showed it to United Artists who had a big stake in it. Preminger knew he was in for a rough ride. The script violated a few of Hollywood's sacred taboos. Executives looked shocked when they heard the dialogue which was spiked with the kind of remarks which were acceptable on the stage but had never before been made on the screen. 'Lots of girls don't mind being seduced . . .' – it was the first time the word 'seduce' had been used in a movie.

'Men are usually so bored with virgins!' was one of Maggie McNamara's lines. Not only was the sentiment immoral, the word 'virgin' almost burst a few blood vessels. Even worse: 'You are shallow, cynical, selfish and immoral,' she says, 'and I like you!' Immorality likeable? Shocking! But this was really what the play – and the movie – was all about.

The reaction in the screen-room was a flare up: 'You will never get this past the Breen Office!' – the self-censorship body of the Motion Picture Proprietors Association. 'Why not make a few cuts?' Otto would not hear of it. It was not a matter of a few cuts which would have left the comedy virtually intact. For him, it was a matter of principle. He had had enough of studio censorship, censorship by the Hollywood bosses, interference, interference, interference. Wasn't it to escape from this sort of thing that he had declared his unilateral independence? 'No more!' he decided.

The Breen Office promptly refused to pass the film unless the word 'virgin' was eliminated and the reference to seduction in another place. The Catholics condemned *The Moon is Blue* from the pulpits and instructed congregations to boycott it.

Preminger remained adamant. Was the much-vaunted Seal really necessary? 'The Supreme Court', he argued, 'has recently ruled that films are entitled to the same protection under the First and Fourteenth Amendments of the Constitution as the Press.' He fought the ban in the courts – in the event only three States, Maryland, Ohio and Kansas, persisted.

'I am not a crusader or anything like that,' Preminger explained. 'But it gives me great pleasure to fight for my rights. If you don't fight for your rights you lose them . . .' He invoked the memory of the totalitarian countries, and attacked the rules to which the Breen Office was working: 'The Motion Picture Code', he said, 'was written twenty-three years ago and I knew I didn't have a chance when I submitted *The Moon is Blue.*'

United Artists helped him to break the power of the Breen Office by agreeing to distribute the picture without the stamp, and Preminger turned on the Catholics: 'I don't mind the clergy telling their flock not to see it,' he said, 'but at the same time I see no reason why they should prevent people of other faiths from seeing it . . .' There was a profitable side product of the controversy. As David Niven was not slow to point out: 'The publicity ensuing from the Catholic ban helped enormously!' The lesson – Provocative Subject equals Protests equals Publicity equals Profits – was not lost on Preminger.

The Moon . . . without the Seal spread like wildfire through the United States. It was shown in eight thousand theatres. In Germany it was the star attraction of the Berlin Film Festival. The French liked it but, far from contemplating protests, thought it was a little naïve. It earned David Niven the Golden Globe Award from the Foreign Press Association for the best comedy performance of the year. And it made Otto Preminger a herald of the permissive society.

Preminger with the cast of *Exodus:* Paul Newman, Eva Marie
Saint, Jill Haworth, Sal Mineo

Exodus: Preminger watches Jill Haworth and Sal Mineo

Willi Frischauer with Preminger in Israel during the shooting
of *Exodus*

Advise and Consent: Don Murray, Preminger and Charles
Laughton on set

In a brief rearguard action, Censorship raised its head again in London where the film landed in the lap of the Board of British Film Censors. The Board's General Secretary Arthur Watkins arranged for a small team to view it, among them John Trevelyan (who eventually succeeded him), Sir Sidney Harris, the President, and a woman examiner who must remain nameless.

'What do you think of it?' Harris asked Trevelyan. 'Would you pass it?'

'Certainly! It is the most delightful comedy in years.'

The woman censor was asked next: 'I would entirely refuse a certificate,' she said. 'I loathe the film, I can't stand that girl . . .!' She had no rational objection, did not suggest any cuts but wanted to get rid of the film entirely: 'In the event', Trevelyan said, 'a few token cuts were made and the film was passed and greatly enjoyed by British audiences.'

Otto Preminger and John Trevelyan met and got on well with each other. The anti-censor movie maker and the censor became friends.

XIV

In the Black

'Mamoulian had been fired and a new director –
Preminger as it happens – was in charge.'

Mamoulian, TOM MILNE

While the huge financial rewards of a smash hit, the first on
his own account, were as yet only a gleam in his eye, Otto
Preminger lived in style, maintained establishments in Hollywood and New York, paid massive alimony, spent a great
deal in night-clubs and kept up appearances with assurance,
if with difficulty. Almost impossible to visualise but, to tell
the truth, he was extremely hard up, living from hand to
mouth and never knowing where the next jar of caviar was
coming from.

Only when the bad patch was over did he, like so many
wealthy Americans, begin to flirt with his lean years and tell
all and sundry what a hard time he used to have and how
much tax he used to owe. The crunch, according to him,
came with an alert from his business manager in Hollywood:
'The Revenue have attached your house!' was the grim
signal. The house in Bel Air, decorated and furnished with
love and taste, was Otto's pride. 'Sell it!' he commanded as
ruthless with himself as he could be with others.

The proceeds cleared his debt and he never had that kind
of trouble to boast about again. He could have raised the
money by less drastic means but the sale of the house was as
good a way as any of breaking his last personal link with
Hollywood.

Hugh Herbert accompanied him on a trip to Europe, first
stop London. A sentimental journey? In some ways it was,
at least for Herbert. Educated at a British public school

(though born in Vienna), he dragged Otto along to visit his old haunts. Preminger, too, renewed contact with the past. Among London's large colony of Austrian and German refugees were many of his old friends.

Expansive, good-humoured and beaming with benevolence, he invited them to his big apartment at the Dorchester Hotel in Park Lane – 'The best hotel in the world, always the same valet to greet me, always keeping the liquor bottles for my next visit!' The day's first wave of cronies arrived early but even latecomers were summoned to the bathroom where their host from overseas was soaking in the tub like a Roman emperor. His practice was to keep them talking throughout his ablutions and meticulous towelling until he moved on to the bedroom, still minus clothes, a faun-like and very, very manly figure.

Gossip flowed freely but not idly – for him it was a means of keeping himself informed – and continued at the breakfast table. The sessions were repeated on every one of his visits, and it was not much different when he turned up in Paris or Rome or wherever he went in Europe. Among the London regulars were Pem (Paul Markus), the former Berlin showbiz columnist who kept a close tab on stage and film personalities, and Alexander Paal, Hungarian-born ex-husband of Eva Bartok – Paal later went to work for him. On many such occasion I exchanged memories of Vienna with Preminger.

Presently he went to Vienna to see for himself but this visit was less convivial. He met actors, directors, managers he used to know but there was a distance, a barrier. The Nazi period, the war – he in the States, they under Hitler. What had they been doing in these years? Had they been Nazi sympathisers or worse? He was uneasy, suspicious. When Viennese claimed the 'celebrated Hollywood director' as one of their own, he was irritated or amused or both.

The central figure of a typical vignette he paints with glee is the concierge of the famous Hotel Sacher, also known as 'Hotel Habsburg' because of the young archdukes who used to frequent it. The hall porter, Otto recalls, went into a most enthusiastic and deferential reception routine: 'Willkommen, Herr Doktor, Willkommen!' A day or so later, the 'Herr Doktor' was about to take a young lady up to his apartment – in all innocence, of course – when the same porter who had greeted him so effusively stopped him sternly: 'No ladies permitted in the rooms!'

'Who says so?' asked Preminger.

'Police regulations!'

'Get me the police president on the telephone . . .!' The notorious Preminger gall was rising.

A typical Viennese, the porter was bending with the storm: 'But, Herr Doktor . . .' he tried to pacify the irate guest, 'how long would the lady be staying?'

'Oh, a few hours, I suppose,' Preminger barked.

'Ah so! If it's only a few hours, it will be quite all right!'

'That's Vienna for you!' Preminger says.

He was back in New York in no time, back in Hollywood in fact but only to discharge a debt. He did not owe money, to be sure, but he owed a picture, the last he was under contract to make for Twentieth Century Fox. The script he was given was based on *River of No Return*, a story by Louis Lantz. He liked it. The producer was Stanley Rubin, and Preminger's interest in the whole project was marginal: 'It was simply an assignment,' he told Peter Bogdanovich, the young film writer and director.

Arrangements were made for the picture to be shot in Alberta, Canada. The stars assigned by the studio – Robert Mitchum and Marilyn Monroe. Marilyn Monroe? Marilyn Monroe, the sex bomb, the living legend, the scourge of directors and producers, the stories about her!

Well, Otto, what was she like? At close quarters? To work with? As a person? Surely, he had a fund of anecdotes about their time together. Over the years I have tried to pump Preminger about Monroe. The well was dry: 'She was vulnerable,' he said, 'insecure. Poor girl . . .' Then he mumbled something about the people around her and her making enemies . . .

I did discover, though, that he had complained bitterly about her always being late: 'It is okay for a star to be late, one time, two times,' he was quoted as saying. 'But fifty-four to fifty-six times is too much. It is beneath the dignity of any director to have to endure this . . .!'

By contrast, Billy Wilder who had similar trouble with Marilyn Monroe, never knowing her lines, always arriving late, when asked why he suffered it, replied: 'Look here! My old aunt would always be punctual and always know her lines . . . Only no one would go to see her!'

Preminger was also credited with one wounding blow: 'Directing Marilyn Monroe is like directing Lassie – you need fourteen takes to get the bark right!' But he does not confess to the authorship.

He did talk about shooting *River of No Return* in cinemascope, though: 'It's more difficult to compose but you see more. It embraces more.' He obviously did not embrace Marilyn Monroe or take her to his heart. For some reason or other, he has drawn the veil over that beautiful body.

To help a mediocre picture on its way, a publicity campaign of outsize proportions was set in motion. Trainloads of free literature, mountains of Marilyn Monroe stills, even gramophone records were unloaded on exhibitors and the public. Audiences liked Monroe better than her director. Behold – the picture was a success.

By the time movie fans saw Marilyn, as presented by Preminger, a pink, fair-haired, sexy saloon singer caught up in the gold rush and battling against the river of no return, the director was thousands of miles away – in Europe. Even for a patriot it was a good time to be away from America as the shrill and discordant notes of the McCarthy affair pursued him across the Atlantic.

The witch-hunt organised by the junior Senator from Wisconsin did not make a pretty picture and Hollywood did not come out of it with much credit. Among the eminent and talented writers banned by the studio bosses because of their alleged liberal or left-wing views (or because they 'hid behind the Fifth Amendment' and refused to incriminate themselves) were several whom Preminger knew well.

He settled down in Paris for a while and, from an apartment in the Ile St Louis overlooking the Seine, followed the half-sinister, half-clownish Senate hearings which were moving to a climax. He made no comment – in this period of political aberrations anything he said could one day be held against him by one side or the other. But, like other Americans, he applauded the triumph of the little known, inconspicuous, mild-spoken army attorney, Joseph Welch, who demolished Joe McCarthy in open session and became a national hero as a result. The condemnation by fellow Senators put an end to McCarthy's shameful run and he died, it seems fittingly, as an alcoholic.

McCarthy was disgraced but the Hollywood scriptwriters with the stigma of the 'Fifth Amendment' upon them remained black listed. Preminger, on the other hand, when he returned to the United States was received with open arms and found a major new assignment waiting for him. Zanuck was all *bonhomie* – there's an almost untranslatable Austrian proverb which says, 'Pack schlägt sich, Pack verträgt sich', which means that people fight one day and make it up the next and so on. Ever since the success of *Laura* Preminger and Zanuck were friends.

What Zanuck asked him to do was to translate Oscar Hammerstein's smash-hit *Carmen Jones* to the screen. Harry Kleiner transported Georges Bizet's *Carmen* from nineteenth-century Spain to contemporary America. The violent, tragic triangle is set in an American all-black milieu with prize-fighter instead of the traditional toreador, a GI instead of a Spanish corporal and Carmen working in a parachute factory instead of a cigarette factory.

At first glance, Preminger was sceptical: 'There's no all-

black community like this in the United States,' he argued.
It would have to be approached as a fantasy . . . He was, of
course, familiar with *Carmen*, a favourite in the old Vienna
Opera's repertoire. The atmosphere of rampant sex and
conflict was dramatic. Preminger knew all about the human
emotions and about women – black women fascinated him.

Recruiting the cast was an exhilarating experience. For the
name part, he chose the delectable Dorothy Dandridge.
When he saw the youthful Diahann Carroll in a California
night-club, all sex and sophistication, he offered her one of
the supporting roles: 'I thought she was very talented,' he
told me (by which time Diahann was a celebrated international diseuse, star of the black-white television soap opera
Julia and the much publicised girl-friend of David Frost).

For other parts, he managed to get Pearl Bailey and Olga
James – the whole establishment of black talent was assembled under the Preminger umbrella. They liked him
because he abhorred colour prejudice. Indeed, before
Preminger all men and women were equal although his kind
of non-discrimination, of making no distinction whatever
between black and white, did not commend itself to one
particular Negro.

Shooting was already in progress when an editor of a small
Los Angeles Negro paper made derogatory comments and
threatened to print an unfavourable article about him.
Preminger was undaunted. Within the hearing of the entire
cast he sailed into the black journalist: 'I don't discriminate
in any way,' he shouted. 'If someone is a sonofabitch he is a
sonofabitch. And you just happen to be a double-crossing
Black sonofabitch!' The entire cast applauded.

An idea struck Preminger, and *Carmen Jones* enabled him
to test it. Did the public ever read credits and titles on the
screen? Could people be made to pay attention from the
word go and was it not possible to devise a symbol for a
specific film and imprint it on everybody's mind? He called
in a young designer, Saul Bass, and asked him to produce a

graphic idea to lift credits and titles out of the rut, something that would stand for *Carmen Jones*.

Saul Bass was a happy choice. His designs for *Carmen Jones* were a work of art and became a trade mark which everyone associated with Preminger. Preminger put them on posters, on his letter headings, inter-office memoranda and all material emanating from his office. While the film was being shot and shown, it was *Carmen Jones* and Preminger, Preminger and *Carmen Jones*. As time went on, Saul Bass designs for Preminger films became ever more effective and started a fashion. Some of his work for Preminger has since found a home in the New York Museum of Modern Art and he has been honoured all round for his movie work.

The *Carmen Jones* tag stuck to Preminger across five years – he even learned to sing the familiar Toreador chorus with Harry Kleiner's apt words: 'Stan' up and fight until you hear de bell, Stan' toe-to-toe, trade blow for blow' – when he became involved in another all-black production and, indirectly, in another joust with Rouben Mamoulian.

The ageing Mamoulian dug up his first big theatrical coup, the original non-musical stage play *Porgy* (based on DuBose Heyward's novel) which was a smash hit in the twenties. It told the story of a bully named Crown who kills a man in a street fight and his girl-friend Bess who finds shelter with Porgy, a cripple. In the end Porgy kills Crown while Bess is lured to New York by an interloper.

George Gershwin eventually set the piece to music (including the tune which Preminger wanted for *Laura*), and Mamoulian directed the musical with the same sure touch as the straight play thirty years earlier. The novel, the play, the musical: by the iron law of show business there had to be a movie as well. Sam Goldwyn hired Mamoulian to direct the film of *Porgy and Bess*.

Sam Goldwyn was never an easy man to get on with and Mamoulian was as difficult as ever. They quarrelled and their row flared up literally – a fire destroyed the elaborate

and costly set. With it, the Mamoulian-Goldwyn collaboration was in ashes. To rescue the movie from the ruins,
Goldwyn turned to the only man who had made a highly
commercial film with an all-black cast, Otto Preminger. For
a second time Otto stepped into Mamoulian's shoes but the
Goldwyn-Preminger alchemy was no less combustible than
the Goldwyn-Mamoulian mixture.

They fought a war of attrition as wearying as the Battle of
the Somme. A lot of mud was thrown up as the two stubborn
individualists of the movie industry waded into each other.
Goldwyn held the power and the purse strings, Preminger
commanded the skill on which the multi-million project
depended.

The talent that carried *Carmen Jones* to success was called
in once more. Dorothy Dandridge was Bess, Pearl Bailey
came in and Diahann Carroll was there again. The trio of
black beauties was joined by Sidney Poitier and Sammy
Davis Jr. Ira Gershwin collaborated on the songs which were
soon on everybody's lips: 'Bess, you is my woman now!', 'I
love you, Porgy' and 'Oh, I got plenty of nuttin . . .' shot to
the top of the charts. Preminger turned the whole thing into
a symphony of visual and melodious delight.

It was a hit, though the critical reception was not unani-
mous. *Time* Magazine which has few good words to say about
Preminger and his works remarked that 'as an attempt to
produce a great work of cinematic art [*Porgy and Bess*] is a
sometimes ponderous failure'. Some black chauvinists objected (as they often do when liberals try to give the black
man a leg-up) that the picture perpetuated Negro stereo-
types.

As to Sam Goldwyn – he ended up at the head of
Preminger's personal rogues gallery, a favourite target for
the kind of stories he loves to tell about his adversaries.
Though he always resented interference, Preminger's complaint is that Goldwyn did not come up with a single idea or
suggestion. Goldwyn, he says, refused to give credit to

anyone – except Goldwyn. Goldwyn did not even know that a film could be reduced from standard size to 35 millimetre. Goldwyn was supposed to have been worried when a cameraman admired his Picasso – what if the fellow expected it as a present.

Preminger was not alone in his view of Sam Goldwyn. Billy Wilder warned him: 'This is going to be Goldwyn's last picture. Be careful that it isn't your last picture, too!' And Rouben Mamoulian accused Goldwyn of 'deceit and culumny' and threatened to expose 'his publicity greed, his professional hypocrisy and selfishness'.

As with most conflicts in movieland, money was at the root of the fight between Goldwyn and Preminger. Dissatisfied with Goldwyn's offer of a ten per cent participation in the profit, Preminger agreed to leave him to decide the figure when the work was done but this was never put in writing. Once the picture was completed Goldwyn lived up to his best-known Goldwynism: 'A verbal contract isn't worth the paper it is written on!'

When Ingo Preminger, acting as his brother's agent, reminded Goldwyn of the arrangement, he received a dusty answer: 'Otto has left the profit participation to me? No participation!' Preminger did not get a penny and, to remain in the Goldwyn idiom, has repaid him with his own coinage of studied denigration.

It is difficult not to write a satire.

XV

Drugs - And A Virgin

'You know what you're letting yourself in for. It ain't
pretty 'n it could be dangerous.'
Frankie in *The Man with the Golden Arm*

Without resting on the laurels of his *Carmen Jones* hit (and
with another picture, *The Court Martial of Billy Mitchell*, in
the can after an aggravating, brawling production), Boss
Preminger – his own boss now at least in name – was groping
for a new subject. There was plenty of money in the kitty,
enough to afford the rights in a best-selling novel, the safest
vehicle to success.

Preminger, though, was in the frame of mind when any
odd best-seller would not do. The ingredient he was looking
for was – controversy! A topical, acute problem. In movies
seduction, attempted seduction of a virgin was now old hat,
thanks to him. He had given Negro performers their chance.
What next?

While searching for new ideas, one subject kept rising to
the surface. He had been reading Nelson Algrin's *The Man
with the Golden Arm*, and his thoughts returned to it again and
again. There was no rush for the film rights, no risk of
competition. Who would dream of putting the drug scene
on the screen? Drugs were a growing social problem but . . .
well, just 'but'! For Preminger, the 'but' became an incentive.
Come the censors in arms and he would shock them!

What did he care whether his film would get the Motion
Picture Proprietors Association's Seal? Another good old-
fashioned row could only help. *The Man with the Golden Arm*
it was! But a controversial film such as he had in mind
would have to have a high standard and definite artistic
merits. The cast would have to be worthy of the battle ahead

– that there would be a battle, of this he had no doubt.

For the star part of Frankie, the junkie poker dealer, Preminger thought of either Marlon Brando or Frank Sinatra. He had thirty-odd pages of the script ready and sent copies to their agents. Next day Sinatra's called and told Preminger:

'Frank likes the script very much.'

'I'll send him the rest as soon as it's ready,' Preminger replied.

'No, no,' the agent came back, 'he wants to do it without reading the whole script!'

When Preminger told Brando's agent that he had already engaged an actor for the part he encountered utter disbelief: 'He thought I was bluffing,' Preminger recalls.

The news of the Sinatra–Preminger deal soon made the rounds, and aficionados of the studio fight licked their chops – what a battle royal it would produce! The terrifying, autocratic director and the temperamental star who could be a little dictatorial himself. Their encounter might well turn out more gripping than the picture they were making . . .

Casting the part of the junkie's girl-friend was the next job. Preminger's choice fell on a girl called Marilyn – Marilyn Novak – who had to change her first name because of the other Marilyn and became known as Kim Novak. She started her career as 'Miss Deepfreeze', peddling kitchen appliances and was built up as a star (to replace Rita Hayworth) by Columbia chief Harry Cohn who only addressed her either as 'Novak' or 'Polak'. She was diffident and difficult.

Her tantrums were no secret in the trade but an emotional star did not worry Preminger. Kim Novak was under contract to Cohn at 750 dollars a week, although her film *Picnic*, directed by Joshua Logan, was a smash hit and she was acknowledged as a top star. If Harry Cohn needed proof that his Svengali act on Kim was paying off, Preminger promptly provided it for him. When Otto asked if he could borrow her to play opposite Frank Sinatra, Cohn demanded an astronomical figure. There was much hard bargaining but Cohn would not accept a penny less than 100,000 dollars. Preminger paid.

The original plan was to shoot the film in Chicago, the book's original setting, but the mathematics of the scheme did not work out. It had to be Hollywood. When the principals got together, there was enough explosive in the studio to blow up into a major conflagration. In the event, there was no explosion.

'Herr Doktor!' Sinatra greeted Preminger, good-humouredly aping the director's heavy accent. Throughout their work together, he called him either 'Herr Doktor' or 'Ludwig', the middle name Otto had long dropped. Preminger retaliated with a nickname of his own for Frank, 'Anatole', a character in a play by Arthur Schnitzler.

So determined were the two warriors not to provoke each other that they behaved with perfect courtesy. There was just a hint of an incident when, after seeing the first day's rushes, Frank took 'Ludwig' aside and told him that he ought to fire the camera operator: 'He's no good!' Frank said. Preminger's reaction was almost gentle: 'Anatole,' he answered quietly, 'on your pictures, when you are a producer, you can do the hiring and firing. On my pictures, I will do it!' It is a regular Preminger gambit. The operator stayed, and Frank did not bring up the issue again.

Sinatra, who was said to have driven directors to despair by never turning up for work before noon, was on the set bright and early every day: 'I never believed these stories about Frank not wanting to work in the morning . . .' Preminger said bravely. Sinatra returned the compliment declaring he would rather work with Preminger than with any other director – no wonder! Even before the picture was completed, it was evident that, under Preminger's direction, he had surpassed his famous performance in *From Here to Eternity*.

There was no problem with Kim Novak either. Preminger paid her one of the stereotype showbiz tributes: 'She is full of basic honesty and warmth.' A little less conventual, Joshua Logan's verdict was: 'Trying to hide what she's got is like trying to hide an elephant in a phone booth.'

The Man with the Golden Arm showed 'what Novak's got' to full advantage. Everybody was impressed, including the censors. But they, predictably, refused the new Preminger picture the Seal. No use Preminger arguing that it was a valuable social document which would deter people from resorting to drugs – under a twenty-five-year-old embargo, any film about illicit drug taking and peddling was automatically taboo, whether it was a valuable social document or not.

United Artists, the distributors, refused to bow to the adverse decision of the Hays Office (Hays succeeded Breen) and walked out of the Motion Picture Proprietors Association: 'We shall submit the picture to local State censors,' they announced. Over a thousand theatre owners promptly elected to show the picture, Seal or no Seal. State by State, the barriers fell and *The Man with the Golden Arm* was booked from one end of the country to the other.

Quite unfairly in this instance, the controversy went down in movie annals as another 'scandal'. Since *Carmen Jones* had involved Preminger in a brief copyright dispute with the heirs of Bizet (which was settled with a small payment), the tag gained world-wide currency: 'Otto Preminger – Accustomed to Scandals' was the headline of a German newspaper when he visited Munich.

As the premiére of *The Man with the Golden Arm* approached he went through a crowded, frantic promotion schedule worked out by Nat Rudich of United Artists' publicity department – TV appearances, radio shows, newspaper interviews. He talked his head off about drugs, prouncing on the various causes of addiction with the authority of a movie man who had 'studied' his subject for a few weeks.

What he said sounds a bit obvious now but it was interesting enough at the time.

Going through the list of his personal guests for the opening night, he found that, by some mix-up, his favourite uncle, a seventy-years-old gentleman, had been assigned the worst possible seat – in the first row: 'He blew his top!' Nat Rudich recalls in a tone which echoes Sherlock Holmes' 'Elementary, my dear Watson!'

The poor chap responsible for the seating arrangements felt the lash of Preminger's wrath: 'I will have nothing to do with him!' Turning to Nat Rudich, he demanded: 'You must handle the whole thing!' He insisted on seeing the new seating plan, and Rudich took the tickets to Preminger's office: 'It was my first lesson of Otto's method,' he said. 'He took over, arranged the whole thing himself – he insists on being involved in everything, on being told every little thing. He takes responsibility. He and nobody else.' Rudich carried out Preminger's instructions to the letter, and Preminger made a mental note that here was a man who would do exactly as he was told.

'I also lived a private life,' Preminger told an interviewer who catalogued his multifarious activities. It did not seem possible but, living in the glass house of public prominence, he yet managed to keep his private life private. That his second marriage was breaking up was nobody's business but his own. Like many peripatetic and prosperous showmen, he preferred a hotel suite in Manhattan to an apartment. Places which cater for the leisure of the rich counted him among their regulars – Billingsay's Stork Club, Twenty-One or El Morocco, where movie tycoons rubbed shoulders with millionaire Greek shipowners, and whichever Manhattan restaurants were in vogue.

Attractive women with showbiz ambitions clamoured to be taken out by him and he liked the company of attractive women with or without ambitions. When he was not casting a picture, he was casting around for pleasant female companions and found plenty to choose from. It was glamorous and great fun but the popular conception that he was spending every night in the arms of some gorgeous paramour was a little far-fetched.

Many a long evening was spent with interesting but not exactly glamorous male friends playing gin rummy, often at the house of fellow producer Sam Spiegel. Though the amounts at stake were well within their reach, the game was fierce, tempers clashed and often erupted in arguments.

Adept at finding other people's weak spots, Preminger pummelled away with the single-mindedness of a boxer who has his opponent on the ropes. At the receiving end of Otto's taunts, Sam, on one occasion, was so exasperated that he forgot he was in his own drawing-room, jumped up and shouted: 'I'm going – I shall never set foot in this house again!'

Who would have thought that, at this moment in time, Otto Preminger was largely preoccupied with finding a simple, unglamorous, virginal girl? But this is what kept him busy. The idea probably originated with a wish to get away for a while but when he told friends that he was planning to spend some time in Europe they thought he wanted to put distance between himself and his wife before the trouble started. He neither confirmed nor denied their suspicion.

He was, in fact, deeply immersed in a major new project and his eyes were on England – for several reasons. For an American producer there were many advantages in making pictures abroad. Quotas dictated the number of American movies which could be shown in some European countries, and Preminger, often a few steps ahead of others, was one of the first to plan evasive action to get round the difficulty. Secondly, he was thinking of a very European subject which ought to be handled in a European setting.

The play he planned to translate to the screen was George Bernard Shaw's *Saint Joan*. Shaw's Joan of Arc was a young girl who hardly understood the religious conflict of which she was the victim and never really knew why she was condemned to die at the stake. She was a country girl pure and simple, certainly pure, natural, unsophisticated.

At some later stage it was said that Preminger first approached Audrey Hepburn who declined the part. It was no more than a passing thought. How much more effective to fill the role with a new girl who was truly in the mould of Shaw's character! But how to find her? Preminger's plans were ready. With much beating of the propaganda drums he announced that he wanted an unknown for the star part in his next movie, even a newcomer to the screen, and that he would tour the country – tour America and Europe – to find the right girl.

When he organised a big search, asked girls to submit their photographs and set out on his tour of inspection and screen testing, the industry was convinced that it was a gimmick. Surely, Preminger, having extracted maximum publicity from his public viewing of several thousand applicants and the whole paraphernalia of his trips, would fall back on an established star who was probably already under contract to him.

Preminger was not that transparent! His gimmick was that the search was not a gimmick. There is an old Jewish story which tells of two rival salesmen travelling in the same compartment: 'Where are you going?' one asks and the other replies: 'To Cracow.' When he gets out at Cracow, the other man flares up: 'You said you were going to Cracow and now you are really going to Cracow! Why were you lying?'

Some twenty thousand miles, half a dozen countries and some eighteen thousand applications and photographs later, the huge flock of hopeful Saint Joans was whittled down to three thousand, most of whom Preminger interviewed personally. One hundred and fifty of them were summoned to Chicago to give a rendering of a passage from Shaw's play on stage while Preminger watched, and studied their photographs and applications.

One applicant who struck a chord as soon as he saw her was a seventeen-years-old American small-town girl by the name of Jean Seberg. She seemed to have all the qualities he was looking for, radiated the innocence of a virginal girl, unspoilt and genuine, but with strength and character lurking behind that fresh, freckled complexion and the steel-grey eyes. Her application listed a few plays she had done with the local stock company, the sum total of her theatrical experience.

Preminger halted the proceedings: 'How old are you?' he demanded.

'Seventeen,' replied Jean.

'I don't believe it,' said Preminger.

After a second reading, later in the day, Preminger told her: 'You're a very talented girl. I want you to come to New York for further tests.'

When Jean presented herself in New York, there were two other girls. Preminger coached each of them in turn. Once more Jean recited Joan of Arc's speech repudiating her confession and asking to burn at the stake rather than languish in prison for the rest of her life. As soon as she had finished, Preminger tore into her roughly with a barrage of criticism: 'You're a ham and a phoney,' he said. 'You can't act and you will never be able to.'

He went on in the same vein until Jean Seberg looked desperate: 'I'll rehearse this till I drop dead,' she said. Preminger walked over and embraced her. He went with her to her dressing-room: 'Who bought you these violets?' he asked, pointing to a bunch on the table.

'I bought them myself,' Jean replied. 'I like violets.'

'Well, I'll buy you a whole roomful the day we begin shooting in London,' said Preminger and hugged her again. That was how she learned she had been chosen.

To see Jean in her natural environment, Preminger

travelled to Marshalltown, Iowa (Pop: 6000), where she worked in her father's drugstore − largely, she confessed, so that she could read all the movie magazines. She taught in Sunday School at the local Lutheran Church, dreamed of a career in Hollywood and prayed to God to make her a star. Until Preminger took a hand there seemed precious little hope of her prayers being answered.

Her parents were delighted and quickly agreed to Preminger's fantastic proposition. He was going to make Jean a star. She would get a big salary, astronomical by the standards of Marshalltown drugstore economics. She − or rather they since she was a minor − would have to sign a long-term contract: 'Seven years is the accepted period!' Her pay check would grow from year to year.

He, Otto Preminger, would have the sole rights in her services, unless he assigned them to another producer. He would take her to Europe, to France where Joan of Arc lived and to England where the film would be shot, would give her an ample expense allowance and a complete wardrobe. He would promote her, instruct her, direct her and guard her in *loco parentis*.

Once Otto's decision was made things began to happen. Arrangements were made to introduce Jean via press, radio and television to the movie fans. United Artists who sponsored the production were involved in the promotion from the outset and, again, Nat Rudich was assigned to the job. The campaign was launched with an announcement on the Ed Sullivan show with Jean repeating her screen test performance. A big press party followed. For the next day, Rudich arranged for Preminger to appear on the Today Show to be interviewed by Dave Garroway. There had not been such a spate of advance publicity for a new actress in many a moon.

Presently, the Preminger circus moved to Europe. He took Jean Seberg on a pilgrimage of the Jeanne d'Arc country, to Domremy where the Maid was born, to Orleans where she defeated her enemies, to Compiegne where she was captured and to the Cathedral of Rheims where she had crowned a French king. The highlight of the tour was Paris where Jean was given the full star treatment, was photographed in the Bois de Boulogne and other typical backgrounds and was introduced to Marcel Pagnol and Charles Chaplin. For the little girl from Marshalltown, whose most expensive dress cost fifteen dollars, Preminger ordered seven *haute couture* outfits from Givenchy.

Production was due to start in London in January 1957, and Otto Preminger installed himself in the Dorchester Hotel in a suite overlooking Hyde Park. He set up an English company, Wheel Productions, with his friend Jack Dumphy on the board, and offices at the expensive London address, 146 Piccadilly. The more prosaic production chores were in the hands of George Thomas, his PRO-factotum, who dealt with labour and tax problems. (The employment quota was eighty per cent British, the rest foreign.) While George Thomas worked with his new boss in London, Nat Rudich attended to the American end.

To deal with the British press, Preminger engaged a man by the name of Leslie Frewin whose first release was to publicise his own appointment. Preminger decided he might be better off with another P.R.O. The man most highly recommended was Bill Batchelor, a veteran of the British film industry whose clients, at one time or another, included the late Alexander Korda and Marilyn Monroe.

'Bill Batchelor!' Preminger greeted him when he presented himself at No 146. 'I want you to work for me. You have a good reputation.'

'I would like to work for you,' was the reply. Preminger asked Batchelor to bring along as many press people as possible: 'What I want you to do, Bill,' he told him, 'is just to introduce me. Whatever they write about me, you will not be to blame.' Batchelor liked Preminger's style: 'His door was always open,' he said. Whenever he showed his face,

Preminger called out: 'Come in, Bill! I like you – we get on well.'

One of the people anxious to work with him was Martin Schute, a promising young Columbia executive in London who applied for the job of production manager: 'How old are you?' Preminger asked without much ado.

'Thirty-one.'

'Too young!' So that was that.

Jean Seberg occupied an apartment at the Dorchester one floor above Preminger's. He kept her on a tight rein. He told her what to wear, what to say, when to go to bed, when to rise, how to spend her day. She belonged to him, body and soul. No, not body. Jean snuggled up to him when they were together, he embraced her a lot and ruffled her short-cropped hair affectionately but appearances were deceptive.

The inevitable rumours of a personal involvement, of Jean having a crush on Otto or Otto's paternal affection changing into romantic attachment were fed by a scurrilous piece in the American scandal magazine *Confidential*. They were so much nonsense but a bit of gossip and implied scandal could do no harm to the publicity.

Jean fitted Preminger's concept of Joan of Arc but, with her shortish legs and unsophisticated manner, was not really the type of girl who attracted him. Besides, he was determined to protect her greatest asset, her innocence, her virginity against all comers. Schoolmaster, instructor, trainer, slave-driver – yes! Lover – never!

It was at this stage that I first met her. When she joined us in Preminger's sitting-room, he greeted her warmly: 'Would you like a drink, Baby?' he asked. 'Some juice?' Jean's eyes wandered towards a bottle of champagne: 'OK, Baby,' he said indulgently. Half an hour later he was the stern father-figure once more: 'Time to go to bed!' he ordered her. She submitted herself to the discipline with almost masochistic pleasure, obviously convinced that she would emerge from ordeal by Preminger as a great actress.

She looked as cool as the December day outside and was evidently everything the publicity boys cracked her up to be – virginal, fresh, almost rural, just like Saint Joan. If Joan of Arc did not know the fate that awaited her, Jean Seberg was under no illusion. Somewhere along the line she sent Preminger a picture postcard showing a green monster cracking a whip. The caption read: 'My, but we do have fun, don't we?'

XVI

Otto Under Fire

'I made the mistake of taking a young, inexperienced
girl . . . and wanted her to *be* Saint Joan – which of course
she wasn't. I didn't help her to understand and act the
part, indeed I deliberately prevented her, because I was
determined she should be completely unspoilt. I think the
instinct – to cast a very young, inexperienced girl – was
right, but now I would work with her for perhaps two
years until she understood the part right through. Well,
that was a big mistake and I have nobody to blame but
myself.'

Otto Preminger, in an interview in *The Times*
22 November 1962

The scene was set for the public execution. Rouen town
square was jam-packed with the populace pressing towards
the tiny figure of the girl chained to the stake. Her face
mirrored suffering, resignation and deep faith. Though
childlike, almost boyish with her cropped hair, she looked
strangely beautiful. The executioner approached to put the
light to the tightly packed bundles of sticks below the
bigger logs. Tension was mounting as the dramatic climax
approached.

The realism of the set at Shepperton Studios was astonishing. Only the big mobile camera gave the game away. This
was the critical moment, difficult both technically and artisti-
cally, for Joan of Arc to be devoured by the flames. Newspaper reporters and photographers called in to witness the
great occasion stood by at a respectable distance.

Pyro-technicians had prepared the stake from which flames
were expected to shoot up impressively and lick the garments
of the chained Jean Seberg without touching her body. The
script provided for the executioner to move into shot and

ignite a controlled supply of inflammable gas in the carefully constructed system of tubes below the wood.

The cameras were turning and there was a gasp from the crowd, the crew and the press as the flames engulfed Jean Seberg. The scene was certainly not lacking in realism. Smoke welled up and she gave out a scream, drew her hands instinctively to her face and – quite contrary to the script – tried wildly to free herself from the chains which tied her, neck and body, to the stake.

The 'executioner' was the first to realise that fact was taking over from fiction and that the fire was getting out of hand. He rushed to Jean's rescue, untangled the chain round her neck while technicians freed her from the other chain and dragged her away. All the while, the camera turned and cameraman and director high up on the platform could do nothing but watch.

Hair singed and fingers blistered, Jean was put on a stretcher and covered with a blanket. Apart from slight shock she was quite all right: 'I smell like a burnt chicken,' she managed to joke. She would need a new haircut . . . With so many reporters and photographers present the incident was bound to make headlines and front-page pictures but sceptical voices were heard asking whether it was not all a publicity stunt: 'What do they think,' Preminger muttered. 'Would I risk burning the star of my picture?'

What apparently happened was that a bubble of air somewhere in the system had bolstered the flames. You could call it a technical hitch or a mistake. It was not the only mistake – the question was whether the whole production was not a mistake.

In his *Times* interview, Preminger said that he dropped into a New York cinema to see Saint Joan five years after he made the picture. Looking at it in a completely detached way, he realised how many things he had done wrong: 'Basically,' he conceded, 'I tried to be too faithful to the play . . . didn't see that, as it was a play which works on the intelligence, it has to be understood before it can be played.'

The language matched the extraordinary thought process – a play which 'works on the intelligence' must be understood before it can be played! But producers, accustomed to play God – dictatorial power over their discoveries, huge budgets to back them up, publicity machines to dazzle the fans, criticism dismissed as hostility – can simply shrug off mistakes and move on. Though he admires Alfred Hitchcock, Preminger is fond of pointing out how many poor pictures the master has made for every one that became a smash hit.

Apart from rushing little Jean Seberg into this complicated role utterly, deliberately unprepared, Preminger conceived the crackpot idea (euphemistically described as 'off-beat casting') of giving the part of the Dauphin, the future King Charles VII of France, to Richard Widmark whose fame rested on his portrayal of pathological gangsters with a hysterical sneering laugh.

Crackpot? Not altogether! It was intended as an inducement for American fans who would want to see at least one of their own favourites in the alien cast. The rest were English actors of high standing, Sir John Gielgud, Richard Todd, Anton Walbrook, Felix Aylmer, Bernard Miles. The choice of Graham Greene as scriptwriter added another big name to the credits.

If the producer-director was uncharacteristically subdued, it was probably because his misjudgment already weighed on his subconscious – there was no question of allowing the slightest hint of doubt to rise to the surface. The shooting was completed in ten weeks. Editing and cutting went with the usual precision.

Newspapers and magazines were taken in tow and boosted the picture to high heaven long before the critics had a look at it. The advance ballyhoo, master-minded by the French publicity expert Georges Cravenne, was fortified with a twenty-minutes documentary on the picture's genesis which, as so many trailers, turned out to be better than the product it publicised. The setting of the ceremonial premiére was unique – for the first time in its history, the Paris Opéra consented to usher in a motion picture.

The glorious, euphoric setting did nothing to mollify the critics. Their reaction was devastating. Wherever the picture was shown the reviews were poor. Little Jean Seberg's performance came in for some harsh comments. Preminger ran her a close second. Graham Green was reproached for taking liberties with Shaw's text: 'Perhaps the law that protects public monuments', one critic suggested, 'should be extended to include literary treasures.' *Time* Magazine wrote: 'Shaw's Joan is a chunk of hard brown bread dipped in the red wine of battle and devoured by ravenous angels. Actress Seberg by physique and disposition is the sort of honey bun that drugstore desperadoes like to nibble with their milkshakes.'

The film was said to be 'The Greatest Box Office Flop of All Time'. As if it mattered! Even before her disastrous début ('Jean's biography is all in the future,' warbled the publicity), Preminger announced that she would play the lead in his next picture. It would be a film version of *Bonjour Tristesse*, a first novel by the eighteen-year-old Françoise Sagan, which sold over 60,000 copies in France and 1,625,000 in the United States.

Hailed as 'mature' by some, dismissed as 'degenerate' by others, the novel depicts a French teenage girl on the verge of incest, consorting with her father's mistress and, more intimately, with the boy next door. The romp follows the smart set from beach to bed on the Riviera and from the Bois de Boulogne to the boudoir in Paris.

For Jean Seberg there was nothing but to throw herself into her new assignment. She studied the novel and learned French: 'So I shall be able to talk to Françoise Sagan.' In London or Paris, wherever I saw her, she was buried in her dictionary, mouthed French words and listened to her own accent, polishing, practising, as if her whole future depended on it. In the event, it did.

Preminger's bland countenance disguised his own reaction. His friends thought that he was hurt and uncomprehending like a little boy wondering what he had done wrong and more intense and erratic than usual even in his private diversions. But the pattern was still the Hollywood producer's stereotype. Hotels – the Dorchester in London, the Plaza Athénée in Paris, Ambassadors in New York – were his habitat.

On his obligatory rounds of the fashionable restaurants and night-clubs, he was rarely without a beautiful girl, a choice quarry of informers who kept him under observation to pick up titbits for *Confidential*. They registered one particular French girl who turned up in his company rather more frequently than others. Though he was as yet unaware of the snoopers' attention, magazine reporters were not the only ones sniffing at his heels.

Unhappily married movie producers face all manner of hazards. In this period, one voluptuous international actress who was much in the news eagerly sought his company – impossible to say whether her interest was in Preminger, the man, or Preminger, the producer. Not too sure himself, he asked her out to dinner but decided to take another couple along lest an evening *à deux* should become embarrassing.

Even in the car *en route* to a night-club, his celebrated companion pointedly mentioned a piece of jewellery, price 10,000 dollars, she had recently seen in Rome. How she would love to have it! 'Let's fly to Rome for the weekend!' she suggested to Otto – the implication was only too evident.

Whether it was the blatancy or the price, Preminger did not take the hint. His interest in the lady vanished abruptly. For the rest of the evening, it was as if she did not exist. He never addressed another word to her until he made his farewell, leaving his car to take her back to her hotel.

Similar situations arose frequently. If he was perhaps not always so uncooperative, he certainly did nothing which the snoopers could interpret as newsworthy or, not to put too fine a point on their purpose, as adulterous. Visits to the movies, the theatre, cocktail and dinner parties – the usual thing. His pursuers did not give up.

He was in his Dorchester suite one morning in September 1957 when the telephone rang. A friend was on the line: 'Otto, have you seen the story about you in the latest issue of *Confidential*?'

'The cover story, I hope!' Otto joked. The flippant remark hid a growing apprehension. He sent for a copy of the magazine which carried the kind of revelation of which prominent showbiz personalities are regular victims.

'Preminger was relaxing in his suite at the Dorchester after an all-day session looking at hopeful stars,' he read, 'when he heard a knock at the door. He had a visitor, a saucy young English miss who had been recommended by a friend of his . . .'

He was not looking for hopeful stars, no actress had been recommended to him recently but, according to the two-page article, he gave the doll a quick once-over and his first question was: 'Are you any good at love scenes?'

'Yes, very good!' the cutie was supposed to have answered.

With his vivid imagination, the writer described how Preminger had offered the girl a bath in the tub which he laced with a bottle of perfumed bath oil, how he had told the unexpected visitor that he expected another girl soon:

'She figured this must be a hint to clean the tub when she was finished,' the story continued, 'because she assumed another audition meant another bather. She took an extra ten minutes to carefully swab out the tub and then slipped into something while the producer waited impatiently, wondering whether his guest had gone down the drain. She finally came out, pink, powdered and ready for the audition.'

On it went in this vein, Arabian Nights or American Nights, as a *Confidential* contributor imagined them to be. The piece had sinister overtones if for no other reason than that, three thousand miles away on the other side of the

Atlantic, Mary Gardiner-Preminger was at this very time filing divorce papers. A copy of the article joined accounts by other Preminger-watchers, paid or unpaid, frustrated film stars and rebuffed blackmailers, in the dossier which was slowly building up. Taken at face value, it would show Otto Preminger as a philanderer using his position as a movie producer to lure young would-be actresses into his parlour.

Though it was soon actively pursued, the accusation was wide off the mark. There was indeed another woman who really interested him – or, to be accurate, began to interest him. She was not a good-time girl or budding actress in London nor was she currently in New York. The trail which the posse of investigators did not pick up for some time led to Paris.

In the French capital, moviemen, the higher echelons of the Hollywood fraternity, were thick on the ground, coming together at cocktail parties, dinners and functions. For Americans on this wavelength, it was impossible not to run into each other. One significant encounter was recently described to me: 'Otto and I met at a dinner party of mutual friends in Paris,' said the tall brunette who manages to look lady-like and sexy which is exciting but extremely rare. An American girl then known as Hope Bryce, her impeccable elegance suggested a top model and fashion designer which she was.

When she and Preminger found themselves in conversation, they realised that they had met before in the United States – was it in 1951? And where? 'At the Westchester County Club . . .' Yes, of course, but wasn't she a friend of Mary's – his wife Mary? Didn't she and Mary once share an apartment? It all fell into place.

Hope told Otto that she was married not long after their first encounter – her married name was Mrs Dirk Leys – but was separated from her husband. What was she doing in Paris? Well, she had been working with Givenchy at his workshop in New York's Seventh Avenue and designing clothes for a number of American movies. She was in Europe to do a little work, have a little fun.

What a fortuitous constellation! A beautiful woman, a fashion designer, association with the movie industry and with Givenchy who happened to be Otto's favourite couturier and was designing the costumes for *Bonjour Tristesse* . . . There was a great deal to talk about. There was even, come to think of it, an excellent opportunity to work together. Hope's advice and cooperation could be invaluable for him. They agreed to keep in touch – in close touch.

Preminger himself was bound for New York with a copy of *Saint Joan* to show United Artists and discuss the picture's American distribution. Almost *en passant* he asked Nat Rudich whether he would like to join him full time: 'Let's have lunch and talk about it,' he suggested. As they strolled towards the elevator he asked Rudich: 'How much do you get from United Artists?' Rudich told him the figure, adding that he would want more: 'All right!' Preminger answered. And the deal was done. His new employee's first job was to set up a New York office – 'I started at 1600 Broadway,' Rudich said, 'and there was just me and a girl' – and to arrange the *Saint Joan* previews.

From United Artists to Columbia – *Bonjour Tristesse* was under their auspices. To put the final touch on the financial aspects of the production, Otto saw Columbia President Abe Schneider, Harry Cohn's successor. The budget was fixed at 1.7 million dollars with Columbia reserving the right to check expenditure. For Preminger setting up the deal was almost as exhilarating as directing the picture. Drawing on his tremendous energy he set a terrific pace with which his associates could hardly keep up. He was anxious to start shooting but there were problems.

The script was the first hurdle. Françoise Sagan was disgruntled because, in the inexorable way of these transactions, an early bird had acquired the film rights when *Bonjour Tristesse* was as yet an unpublished manuscript by an unknown author. He paid the risible sum of 10,000 dollars which was all she received. The price Preminger paid by the time it was a world-wide best-seller was many times that amount but the difference went into other people's pockets. Little help could be expected from her, and in this period relations between her and Preminger were cool.

First choice of script writer was the practised and well-established Sam Behrman. He and Preminger arranged to meet in the milieu of the Sagan book to co-operate on the script – Preminger says he can only direct a film if the script is filtered through his mind scene by scene. As their headquarters he chose the Riviera's exquisite Hôtel du Cap in Cap d'Antibes where they hammered away in harness. It was a rough ride.

To unwind from the daily chore, Preminger sought the excitement of the baccarat tables at the Casino. One night after a losing streak he was about to leave a few thousand dollars the poorer when Jack ('Warner Brothers') Warner walked in. 'You can't desert me!' Jack called over and persuaded Otto to resume the game and join him at the big table in the Cercle Privée.

The stakes mounted and Otto, normally a modest drinker, gulped Scotch whisky and gritted his teeth. The game broke up at 3 a.m., Otto heaved himself out of the chair and cashed his chips. He had not only made good his losses but emerged a couple of thousand to the good. Jack Warner was the principal loser – for him it was a small game.

The script did not turn out as well. The Behrman effort was abandoned and Otto called in Arthur Laurent and started all over again. The Preminger-inspired final version drew a moral from the highly immoral tale. The end of the script showed the principal characters disillusioned with their empty lives and with nothing to look forward to except saying Bonjour to every sad day.

Preminger toured the Côte d'Azur for locations and finally picked the handsome villa of Pierre Lazareff at Le Lavendou as the central setting. He would be staying at the Hôtel de Paris in Saint Tropez, a few miles pleasant drive down the coast.

In the meantime, it was back to Paris and his suite at the Plaza Athénée. One or two engagements had to be finalised to complete the cast, headed by his old friend David Niven (as Jean Seberg's 'father'), Deborah Kerr, the English star, and Mylene Demongeot, an up and coming French actress.

Preminger was in close touch with Mike Frankovich, head of Columbia's London office. Frankovich advised him that he was sending a Columbia man to join him, name of Martin Schute: 'I know him,' Preminger said, 'I like him!'

'I went to Paris to discuss the budget with Mr Preminger,' Schute told me.

The producer-director received him with open arms but there was an abrupt change of mood when Schute demanded to see the figures: 'The only person with whom I will discuss the budget is Abe Schneider,' Preminger told him acidly.

When Schute tried to insist, the Preminger fury hit him with full force: 'We had a blazing row!' he says. It was like a row between a sapling and the lightning that strikes it.

Schute went to his hotel and called Frankovich: 'I can't talk to Preminger. He won't talk to me!' Shades of the old days in Hollywood when Preminger was at the receiving end of such treatment.

Frankovich pacified his young emissary: 'Don't worry!' he told Schute. 'Otto is a highly professional man. He won't cheat us. Just keep your eyes and ears open and let me know what goes on.'

'It was the only row I had with Preminger,' Schute says. He quickly understood that he was not expected to offer his views, that Otto Preminger would not permit him or anyone else to say how he should go about his business. He was less ferocious than his bark. All cheques were readily passed to Schute to be countersigned on behalf of Columbia: 'I got to know him,' Schute added. 'Eventually he asked me to stay

Advise and Consent: Preminger with Frank Sinatra and
Peter Lawford

Preminger directing Dyan Cannon in *Such Good Friends*

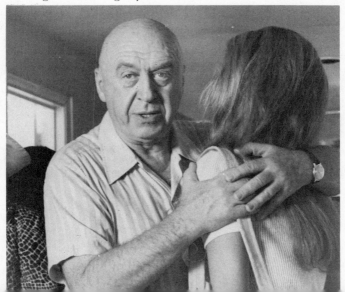

Preminger with his twins, Mark and Victoria, 1963

and work for him.' It was the beginning of an association
that lasted many years.

From the Lazareff villa at Le Lavendou, the private beach
sloped gently towards the sea. On the edge of the water little
Jean Seberg in her Givenchy swimsuit looked up at Otto
Preminger like a pathetic puppy who had misbehaved on
the carpet. Preminger glared back at her, his chin thrust out
and his lips moving without making a sound.

The camera was focused on Jean and the assorted crowd
of technicians and aides – assistant director, assistant producer, assistants to the assistants, clapper boy, script girl,
cameraman, electricians, property men, make-up girls, hair-
dressers – formed a circle around star and director who faced
each other with evident distaste: 'Again!' Preminger bellowed
at last.

An assistant approached with a bucket of water and
emptied it forcefully over Jean. A shiver shook her slim body.
She looked unwell. Preminger checked the position of the
camera, let his eye roam into the distance where boats with
neck-craning holiday-makers intruded. Declining the prof-
fered loud-hailer, he shouted: 'Out! Get these people out of
shot!' His shout was echoed down the line. There was much
waving and gesticulating. The boats would not move and
the aides shrugged their shoulders resigned to impotence.
How could you control the whole coastline?

Turning to Jean Seberg, Preminger said quietly: 'Now do
it again!' Two seconds later he shook his head disapprov-
ingly: 'You must smile!' he insisted. Cecile, Sagan's principal
character whom Jean portrayed, was supposed to be coming
out of the sea with a happy smile to greet her father (David
Niven) but, instead of getting in and out, she was doused
from a bucket.

'Again!' Preminger ordered. The torture by water was
repeated. 'Smile!' he persisted. It sounded as if he asked her
to cut her throat. Once more the bucket was forcefully

emptied over her. She was splashed a fourth, fifth, sixth time.

For a seventh time the water hit Jean. She pursed her lips, took a deep breath, ran the few strides the scene demanded, and – by God! – smiled. It was not much of a smile, not much of a scene but the director seemed to think that it was as good as he was likely to get. The camera rolled, the smile stayed mercifully intact until, like a reprieve at the foot of the gallows, he brought the ordeal to an end: 'Cut!'

Preminger turned on his heels. His stern features relaxed as he greeted me: 'You have arrived!' He shook hands with the American film writer Hyams with whom I had flown in from London that morning.

Tears in her eyes, exhausted and shivering in spite of the sun, Jean Seberg was towelled down by solicitous hands and led away. She was feeling rotten. Almost every one of her scenes involved a test of nerves. Witnesses assumed that Preminger no longer believed in the wisdom of his choice, and that Jean Seberg was made to suffer for his mistake and her own inadequacy.

It was a fanciful suggestion. Indeed, almost invariably, the stern master abruptly became the fatherly friend, all solicitude and concern, putting his arm protectively around the girl's shoulders, drying her tears, talking sweetly and reassuring her as if the whole business hurt him more than he hurt her.

The clashes made better copy than the reconciliations. Stories of Preminger's treatment of Jean Seberg were bandied about in film centres all over the world. Tied in with his 'Nazi' reputation, vintage *Stalag 17*, they merged into a composite picture of a heartless bully who tramples on the feelings of defenceless performers. It was not pretty to watch but it was not as bad as all that.

Actually, the general atmosphere of the unit was rather convivial. To keep his stars and his crew happy, Preminger encouraged them to bring their families along and paid their expenses, a practice which other producers soon copied.

David Niven had his handsome Swedish wife Hjordis with him, Deborah Kerr, her day's work done, dined with her little girl and a nanny, Mylene Demongeot's future husband was in the party.

Accompanied by some of her swinging friends, Françoise Sagan drove over from Saint Tropez for a brief visit. We watched one morning's shooting together but she was sparse with her comments. Come evening, Preminger shook the dust of a ten-hour working day from his feet and delved into an active night life. Parties sprouted all along the Riviera with wealthy French industrialists competing for the company of the director and his stars at cocktail and dinner parties in their villas and yachts.

The Côte d'Azur sequences completed, Martin Schute made good the damage in the Lazareff villa before rejoining the *Bonjour Tristesse* unit which moved on to Paris. An early scene was set in the Bois de Boulogne. That morning David Niven telephoned a production assistant to ask at what time he would be required: 'Not at all, today!' was the answer. A day off – David decided to drive to Le Touquet for lunch and, perhaps, a brief session at the Casino. He was totally unaware of the storm clouds gathering in Paris on this perfect summer's day.

'Where is Mr Niven?' Preminger demanded when he arrived in the Bois to direct a scene which may or may not have originally been scheduled for a later date. 'Where is Mr Niven?!' The voice assumed the familiar menace. There was a lot of scurrying around, telephoning and messengers being despatched in all directions.

The sun was setting when the debonair star with the perfect manners on and off screen was at last recovered from Le Touquet and rushed to the Bois de Boulogne: 'Where have you been?' Preminger asked, less than politely. A wasted day had not improved his temper.

The two contestants faced each other like duellists at a distance of twenty feet. Niven tried to explain, Preminger did not want to listen. Their exchanges became more and more heated and developed into a shouting match, Niven giving as good as he got. In an aside to Martin Schute, who was watching the contest, Preminger whispered: 'Get me the Niven contract . . . We may have to cancel it!'

Combat continued until the duellists, having inflicted maximum verbal injury on each other, separated without reconciliation. As Preminger, still red in the face, turned away, a smile appeared: 'It will make good publicity,' he said to Schute. He guessed right. Next morning's newspapers in France, Britain, even in the United States, published blow by blow accounts of the battle of the Bois de Boulogne.

By this time Preminger and Niven had already made it up. Niven restored a sense of proportion to the incident: 'Otto's voice is like my moustache,' he said. 'It's part of him. But sometimes it grows too big and it frightens the pigeons!'

It continued to frighten Jean Seberg, although, having graduated from vierge (Saint Joan) to demi-vierge (Françoise Sagan's Cecile), her private life was no longer Preminger's concern and there was no longer any need for him to keep the suitors at bay. Still smarting under her *Saint Joan* disaster and her nerves worn thin after a year of the Preminger régime, she was sorely in need of affection and psychological rehabilitation.

She fell in love with the first young man allowed close enough to attract her attention – François Moreuil, a twenty-four-year-old French lawyer so full of fun and nonsense that his friends called him 'the charming idiot'. They were married in Marshalltown which gave the local girl a grand reception, spent their wedding night on a plane to New York and returned to Paris the following day.

The reception *Bonjour Tristesse* received from the critics was less cordial, if anything it was worse than the *Saint Joan* flop. Again, Jean Seberg was soundly whipped by the critics: 'I think the critics were punishing me for allowing Otto Preminger to force me down their throats,' she said when the pain subsided. 'As a person I was utterly crushed and humbled.'

Preminger sold her contract to Columbia without much profit to himself – she did not rate much more than he had invested in her costly publicity build-up – and Columbia put her into a few minor movies, type-casting her as 'an American girl in Paris'. She hated every minute of it but battled on bravely. In 1961 she was given a big part in a low-budget film, *Breathless* ('because nothing else was offered and Columbia saw a faint hope of making a tiny profit out of me at last'). It was an instantaneous smash hit.

Jean Cocteau saw her and expressed his 'unreserved admiration'; Jean-Paul Sartre spoke of her 'exceptional triumph'. The critics applauded her. Better films and better notices followed. She was, in her own words, 'accepted as an actress'. The 'new wave' moviemakers adopted her as their own star but some of the parts she played shocked the good folk back home in Marshalltown, Iowa.

She parted from her 'charming idiot' and married a leading French intellectual, Romain Gary, winner of the Prix Goncourt, the French literary accolade, who transported her into a new world. She read a great deal, learned a lot, mixed with eminent people and was wholly accepted in the circles who lionised her husband. They lunched with General and Madame de Gaulle, a rare distinction, were invited to the White House – the American girl in Paris became something more than a mere movie star.

Though better known in Europe than in her native country, she yet remained as American as blueberry pie: 'Preminger warned me from the beginning not to lose my roots,' she said. Their paths did not cross again but, however painful her initiation, it is not fair to suggest that she made the grade not through Preminger but in spite of him. It is not unusual for a star to be launched on a sea of her own tears, and a star is what Jean Seberg wanted to be more than anything.

XVII

Matrimonial and Malaysian Jungles

Throughout the shooting of *Bonjour Tristesse* in the south of France, an ethereal young woman, her slim limbs covered to protect her from the sun and with a black balaclava hiding all but a tiny circle of her pretty face, was never far from Preminger's side. She looked after him as diligently as after the cast's Givenchy outfits: 'This is Hope . . . Hope Bryce,' Otto introduced her.

After their meeting in Paris earlier in the year, he had put her on the payroll. The elegant and serene 'wardrobe mistress' seemed a perfect foil for her combustible companion. They were inseparable on the Riviera, in Paris, in London – and in New York when Otto returned to the United States.

'I resumed my career,' Hope told me. As a top model she was much sought after but also worked for WINS radio and later, while Otto was shooting *Porgy and Bess*, went to work for RTLA Television in California.

Preminger was fighting on several fronts. Even before his running battle with Sam Goldwyn developed, his matrimonial skirmishes became fierce and troublesome. Suing him for divorce in Los Angeles, Mary Gardner-Preminger accused him of infidelity with two London girls who were named (*Confidential* was the basis of the accusation), though at least one of the names turned out to be fictitious. The divorce petition also claimed that he had been 'keeping company' with a Frenchwoman for three years and threw in a few instances of 'cruelty' for good measure.

Presently, his lawyers went over to the attack. In a counter-petition to the Supreme Court of Los Angeles, they accused Mary of leaving her husband in 1956, and of committing adultery 'on numerous occasions'. Michael Rennie, the British actor, was named as co-respondent.

As in most of these cases, the parties' main concern was with the financial settlement. Mary claimed that Otto's income was 200,000 dollars a year and asked for alimony of 3000 dollars a month. He offered a fifth of that amount as appropriate. In the final analysis it was the alimony not the inevitable end of the marriage which was at stake.

Preminger did not allow the unpleasant proceedings to distract him from his work. In strictest secrecy, he followed up an important tip. Pierre Boule, whose book *Bridge on the River Kwai* became a money-spinning movie without compare in recent years – it earned producer Sam Spiegal a huge fortune – had completed a new novel, *The Other Side of the Coin* which, like *River Kwai*, was set in the Far East Jungle but this time against the background of guerrilla warfare in Malaysia.

The manuscript was still with the French publisher when Otto flew to Paris to read it. Before Sam Spiegel, anxious to repeat his *River Kwai* smash, could get his hands on it, Preminger snapped up the film rights – typically both producers were backed by Columbia funds. Sam Spiegel did not relish being pipped at the post, and his friendship with Preminger came to an end. He would not talk to his old friend, who took the rebuff badly.

To investigate the terrain of his new project, Preminger prepared to go to the Far East. He persuaded A. E. Hotchner, Ernest Hemingway's friend and author of *Papa Hemingway*, to write the script and go with him on his trip. Next he looked for an assistant to come along – who better than young Martin Schute with whom he had worked so well.

Schute was in Spain supervising a Columbia picture when Mike Frankovich recalled him to London: 'Otto Preminger has asked Abe Schneider to let you go with him to the Far East,' Frankovich told him. 'Ever been there?' Schute shook his head. 'Never mind,' Frankovich said, 'you'll be going

167

there next Saturday!' All Schute could say was a weak 'Oh!' Within forty-eight hours he was on his way to New York to join the Preminger expedition, final destination Singapore, Kuala Lumpur and the jungle.

Departure for the Far East was fixed for 10 May 1958: 'Otto was in a happy frame of mind,' Nat Rudich recalls. He and his wife joined Preminger at his hotel for a farewell breakfast of caviar and champagne. Hope Bryce was with them. Otto gave Rudich a pair of cufflinks, Rudich reciprocated with a cap with mosquito netting. Then the party drove to Kennedy Airport. Another escort followed, uninvited, unobtrusive and unnoticed.

As other prominent travellers, Preminger was conducted to a private lounge where the final farewells were made. As he, Hotchner and Schute boarded the aircraft well ahead of the other passengers, the Rudichs and Hope Bryce slipped out of a side entrance and returned to Manhattan where the Rudichs deposited Hope at her apartment.

Otto Preminger was already on the other side of the globe when the *New York Daily Mirror* hit the streets carrying a sensational story. It told of a new deposition by Mary Gardner-Preminger amplifying her divorce petition. Based on the testimony of an inquiry agent who had kept Preminger under observation, her new accusation was that her husband had gone off on a round trip of the world – with Hope Bryce. 'I did not see the paper and knew nothing about it,' Hope told me. A girl-friend whom she telephoned answered her with surprise: 'What, you are here? I thought you were in Malaya!'

The canard did not help Mary Preminger's case but the lawyers eventually worked out a divorce settlement. Preminger will not give the figure but it is no secret that it provided for a single payment of 200,000 dollars to his wife. Having bought his way of the matrimonial jungle, he was heading for the Malaysian swamps.

Well, not quite. His first stop was Kuala Lumpur and his

first objective to deal with financial aspects. As the Malaysian law stood, an American movie star, obliged to pay some eighty per cent of his income in United States tax, would still be liable to thirty per cent Malaysian tax, which added up to more than he could earn. Preminger explained the position to members of the Malaysian government who accepted his arguments and agreed to change the law.

This hurdle cleared, he and his party drove to the Dunlop Plantation outside Kuala Lumpur to meet leading planters. It was a convivial get-together until the head planter launched out on some fascinating stories about snakes. There was this young boa constrictor one of his friends had brought from the jungle and kept in his bathroom until, one day, the slippery reptile wriggled down the pipe. He just caught the tail but the more he pulled the more the snake pulled in the other direction. The planter had to dig up ten yards of sewer to get it out.

As the story unfolded Preminger's face grew paler and paler. Finally he confessed: 'I've had one phobia since childhood – snakes!' He did not particularly like any animals. The planters tried to reassure him but his enthusiasm for the project seemed to wane.

Back in the United States, the script did not turn out to his liking, and he thought that, before another screenplay could be completed, the troubles in Malaya might be over and the subject outdated. He kept talking about all those snakes hiding in the homes of the planters and of the snakes infesting the jungle where the film would have to be shot. It came as no surprise when he called the whole thing off because of 'technical difficulties'.

Snakes or technical difficulties – Preminger will not produce and direct a movie if he is not totally enthusiastic about it. Neither did he abandon Pierre Boule's *The Other Side of the Coin* without having the film rights in another best-selling novel in his locker. It was a story after his own (director's) heart – a courtroom drama of murder and rape breaking enough taboos to make an American censor's hair stand on end. The author, writing under the pseudonym of Robert Traver, was a Justice of the Supreme Court of Michigan, name of John Voelker, who drew heavily on his experiences as a young lawyer. The novel's title, *Anatomy of a Murder*, hinted at his clinical approach.

The more Preminger immersed himself in the subject, the more it gripped him, a mood he hoped to communicate to his audiences. The plot revolves around a young couple, Second Lieutenant Frederick Manion and his attractive, sexy wife Laura who are living in a caravan in Michigan. Laura Manion is raped and her husband stands accused of murdering the rapist. A central figure is an intensely sincere and persuasive young lawyer, and there is the judge, earthy, courageous, with quiet authority. The treatment cried out for the novel's original setting and a Michigan courtroom in which the drama unfolds.

Commuting between New York (a new, elegant penthouse office in Fifty-fifth Street) and Hollywood (Columbia offices), Preminger searched for stars suitable for the key parts. James Stewart, who immediately came to mind as the young lawyer, happened to be available, liked the script and agreed to take the part. Among actresses he considered as 'the woman in the case' was a girl he remembered seeing in an Elia Kazan film, *A Face in the Crowd*. To others, Lee Remick may still have been a face in the crowd but she seemed to have what he wanted: 'Find Lee Remick for me!' Preminger asked.

When the young lady presented herself at his office, personal contact confirmed his impression. She was attractive with an expressive unconventional face. She was also, alas, very obviously pregnant – in her eighth month, in fact. By the time shooting started Lee Remick would have had her baby but it was a risky thing . . . Still, he gave her the script to take home with her. She had not finished reading it, when Preminger was on the phone to her: 'I'm sorry,' he said,

'I've signed Lana Turner for the part. But there is the second lead – would you like to play it?'

'I did a very brave thing,' Lee Remick said to me when we discussed the incident, 'or, perhaps, a very foolish thing.' She told Preminger: 'No, thank you, I really would not!'

Lana Turner was learning her lines and studying the role. Preminger chose Ben Gazarra to play the outraged husband and murderer. Eva Arden and Kathryn Grant were engaged. Otto sent a cable to Hope Bryce asking her to become the film's 'costume coordinator'.

The judge was a problem. Burl Ives was one possibility – he had the physical attributes and a high standing. Preminger and his aides discussed him at length but the idea was abandoned: 'Why not have someone real – a real judge?' Nat Rudich said.

The suggestion opened up an interesting new line of thought. A real person – wasn't this exactly what Preminger had in mind? But who . . .? The name of one worthy legal figure cropped up – the brave man who stood up to Joe McCarthy in those dramatic Senate hearings, the army lawyer who finally demolished the evil Senator with a few telling blows, Joseph N. Welsh.

'He would never do it!' Preminger said but his tone indicated that he was already determined to get Welsh come hell or high water. He telephoned the ageing lawyer's home in Boston. Mrs Welsh answered and listened to the proposition. Her reaction was not unfavourable. Yes, she and her husband would be glad to talk it over with Mr Preminger.

Preminger's dedication to authenticity made a strong impression. His knowledge of the law and legal procedure was profound. That the author of the book was an eminent legal personality was another incentive. Joseph Welsh promised to think it over but his friend Ed Murrow and others advised against – it might well dilute the public conception of him as a distinguished national personality.

Welsh was not bothered: 'What are the hours I would

have to work?' he asked Preminger. 'Nine to five,' was the answer. 'What would my wife be doing all this time?' 'I have an idea,' Preminger said. 'She can join the cast and play a member of the jury.' That decided it.

Later, Preminger praised Rudich publicly: 'A young man in my office, Nat Rudich, made the suggestion to offer the part to Mr Welsh,' he told a press conference. 'I am most grateful!' Said Rudich, highly gratified: 'The first time a Hollywood producer ever gave credit to an underdog!'

Loyal to the original story, Preminger chose Marquette in the Michigan peninsula as the location and arranged for the use of the courtroom. He decided to cast local people in the crowd scenes rather than the same old hackneyed Hollywood extras who turn up in every other movie. He asked the author to act as legal adviser: 'I am willing,' Justice Voelker said, 'if you undertake to keep strictly to the legal procedure.' Preminger promised to do just that.

Shooting was scheduled to start on 23 March 1959. Speed was vital. Preminger wanted to cash in on the interest in the novel which was heading the best-seller list – it stayed at the top for over forty weeks. The paperback edition was just coming on the market, eventually to sell close on three million copies. The picture could ride high on this wave of popular acclamation.

He allocated eight weeks to the shooting: 'There were many bets that I would not finish in time,' Preminger chuckled. He was so confident that he arranged for a preview in San Francisco for 17 June and booked the picture into the three main theatres in New York, Chicago and Los Angeles.

Preparations went ahead almost too smoothly for comfort. As always, he checked every single detail. The big hitch came over the question of Lana Turner's outfit. Hope Bryce tried to get away from the Hollywood style: 'Everybody was using a Hollywood designer, the same designer,' she told me. 'I thought in terms of New York rather than Hollywood. I went to a riding shop and chose a pair of Weskin cowboy pants for Lana Turner.'

Lana Turner would not have them: 'I want my clothes designed by Jean Louis!' she insisted – Jean Louis, Holly-wood's leading movie designer.

'Certainly not!' Preminger told her. 'I want clothes that look real!' He was not backing his costume coordinator for personal reasons. Lana Turner was playing a junior officer's wive living in a trailer: 'She could not afford Jean Louis,' Preminger said. It was ridiculous to dress her up as a glamour puss.

Accustomed to having her own way, Lana Turner would not budge. Preminger certainly did not. He told her agent: 'If she doesn't like it, she can turn the picture down!'

The agent thought he was bluffing. Lana Turner sent back word that she would not wear the cowboy trousers. But Preminger was not bluffing and that, as far as *Anatomy of a Murder* was concerned, was the end of Lana Turner.

Lee Remick was still pondering the wisdom of her own refusal. She was barely twenty-one and at a very early stage in her career. Even a second lead in a Preminger movie would have been a step forward. She was not left long to ponder. Preminger called her from California: 'Have you had your baby?'

Baby Kate was four weeks old: 'Almost straight from the clinic.' Lee told me, 'I flew to California.' As she stepped into Preminger's office he said: 'The part is yours.'

She was exhilarated. The three films she had made were nothing compared with this. The script was exciting, the part marvellous. She went away in a daze but when she told friends of her good fortune there were raised eyebrows: 'Preminger?!' they said as if she was entrusting herself to the tender mercy of the Gestapo. 'He will insult you! He will scream at you!' She was frightened, really frightened, she says.

When she met Preminger again, Hope Bryce was with him.

They could not have been more charming. There was no problem about style or fashion: 'The outfit Hope Bryce suggested was perfectly suitable for a girl who lived in a trailer,' Lee said. She gathered that there had been some trouble with Lana Turner over the clothes. 'I had no cause at all to question the design.'

Things moved with a speed she came to accept as Preminger's usual tempo. The following day she and Joseph Welsh were introduced at a major publicity lunch at Romanoff's. The press, the photographers, all the media were there.

Almost at once they moved on to Michigan. They were accommodated in the leading hotel. Only Joe Welsh had a complaint – he grumbled about inadequate heating. Lee Remick had nothing to grumble about: 'Otto was extremely nice to me,' she recalls. 'I had this going for me that I had produced this little baby girl who was only five weeks old when we started shooting . . . Preminger was absolutely charming. Every evening he complimented me on my work.'

Word went round that he was unusually benign in Joe Welsh's moderating presence: 'Would you mind if we moved your chair a little sideways?' he asked Welsh with uncharacteristic humility. He let the old lawyer decide the position of the teleprompters. Says Lee Remick: 'There was no incident throughout the production, none that I noticed . . . But there was his little assistant – I can't remember the name – whom Preminger was giving a hard time.'

The authentic setting of the Marquette courtroom forced Preminger to focus his camera at more realistic angles than in a studio, which was exactly what he intended. It enhanced verisimilitude: 'You can't move walls,' he said. The real-life atmosphere inspired the performers: 'It's almost immoral,' Joe Welsh told a *Newsweek* reporter, 'for Jimmy Stewart to become such a good lawyer without having to work at it as I did.'

Welsh himself felt very much at ease. No real judge at a

real trial could have handled the situation more authentically than he when the key question of Laura Manion's 'undergarments' came up in the big scene. He seemed to be addressing a wider audience when he spoke his lines from the bench:

> For the benefit of the jury, but more especially for the spectators, the undergarment referred to in the testimony was, to be exact, Mrs Manion's panties . . .' [Pause while he waited for a snicker in the courtroom to subside] I wanted to get your snickering over and done with. This pair of panties will be mentioned again in the course of this trial and when that happens there will not be one laugh, one snicker, one giggle or even one smirk in my courtroom There isn't anything comic about a pair of panties which figure in the violent death of one man and in the possible incarceration of another.

However smoothly things went, Preminger could not escape his reputation. Friends and acquaintances whom Lee Remick met in the evenings looked at her quizzically: 'Was he awful?' they asked. 'Was he terrible?' She had to disappoint them. Preminger behaved impeccably and she thinks back with pleasure on this movie: 'It was a big step forward in my career. It established me,' she says. Does she feel she owes it all to Preminger? 'Not entirely. It was a very well-written script, an eminently playable role and a very good director. Everything fell into place.'

She never looked back. *Anatomy of a Murder* made her a big star. Her contract included an option for another two films but Preminger sold her to Columbia. Her next film was *Wild River*, directed by Elia Kazan. She never made another picture for Preminger.

Shooting was completed on 16 May exactly on schedule, and the first city to see *Anatomy* was Detroit. Preminger was backstage during the opening – the Chicago premiére was the following day – when an assistant rushed up to him: 'We can't open in Chicago tomorrow,' he said. 'The Censorship

Board wants to make cuts in five scenes!' Most of the 'offending passages' were in the testimony of the medical experts giving details of rape which had not been mentioned in any movie before.

Preminger gave instructions to postpone the opening and flew to Chicago. He went to see the Police Commissioner who also acted as Censor ('A very nice looking man with white hair').

'I hear you are very tough, Mr Preminger,' was the first thing the police chief said. 'My Board suggested five cuts, so I'll give them one but you must make the cut yourself!'

'What do you want me to cut?'

'Well, the word "contraceptive".'

Preminger shook his head in disbelief. The picture dealt with rape and all kinds of sexual implications: 'Why contraceptive?' he asked.

'I wouldn't like my daughter to go to the movie and hear that word,' said the police chief.

'How old is your daughter?'

'Eighteen . . .'

'Eighteen?' Preminger countered. 'I think she should be grateful . . . You ought to teach her . . .'

There was no meeting of minds. The Censorship Board, Preminger found, was composed of policemen's wives and – he has been dining out on this for years – one sergeant who used to be the police chief's driver. He decided to challenge the censorship in the only way possible which was to take the City of Chicago to court and sue for the issue of a licence:

'I did not feel that the picture, or any other picture for that matter, would necessarily be seriously hurt or destroyed if one line were cut,' he explained later. As an American citizen, however, he was determined to fight for his right of free expression: 'We are in duty bound to claim and defend this right,' he said, 'otherwise it would deteriorate and disappear.'

The Federal judge trying the case asked to see the picture.

A screening was arranged for the following day: 'You don't mind if I bring the family,' he asked Preminger. He came with his wife and two sons, aged eleven and twelve. 'I knew then he would find for me,' Preminger said. Indeed, the judge instructed the City of Chicago to issue a licence for the film without any eliminations or cuts. It was a famous victory.

The film which showed Preminger at his best – economy of style, a complex subject clearly presented, tension well sustained – was an outstanding artistic and commercial success. *Anatomy of a Murder* grossed four million dollars in the United States, another million abroad. Preminger, who had a share of the profits, made over half a million dollars.

It also enabled him to strike a blow for the basic principle of democratic justice – in Soviet Russia. Invited to visit Moscow and talk about his pictures, he took a copy of *Anatomy of a Murder* with him. Russian movie makers to whom he showed it did not query the sexual passages but felt that the officer accused of murder ought not to have been acquitted because he was a bad man. 'The evidence was not conclusive,' Preminger tried to explain, 'and in our country a man is presumed to be innocent until he is proved guilty beyond a shadow of doubt!'

Once more, in the mid-sixties, *Anatomy of a Murder* involved Preminger in a legal tussle when it was shown on television as part of a deal in which Columbia sold sixty pictures to television stations for ten million dollars. In New York, Channel Seven, the hundred and sixty minute run was interrupted thirteen times with a total of thirty-six commercials.

'The commercial interruptions destroy the value of the picture!' Preminger stormed. 'It is grotesque, it is uncivilised!' He claimed his contractual right to determine the final form and content of his picture. How dare Columbia – and 'Screen Gems', a subsidiary which transacted the television deal – allow the film to be mutilated in this manner? A big principle was at stake – the right of a director to protect the artistic integrity of his work.

Preminger took Columbia and 'Screen Gems' to court. The case was heard by Justice Arthur E. Klein in the New York County Court. Witnesses from every department of the industry gave evidence and one of the eminent directors who appeared in support of Preminger was Elia Kazan. The defendants were represented by four lawyers, Preminger made do with two: 'I don't need so many lawyers,' he said. 'I have a strong case.'

Although the judge seemed sympathetic, Preminger lost his case amid a hurricane of publicity which was not entirely unwelcome. 'I think the judge is wrong,' he said. 'The judge acted like a movie fan but he decided against me.'

Under the title 'Anatomy of a Commercial Interruption', the *New Yorker* spread an account of the proceedings and Preminger's behaviour throughout across eighty-seven pages. Presented in the manner of a film script, it culminates in a final scene with 'a full symphony orchestra . . . starting pianissimo and building up with mingled references to "There's No Business Like Show Business", "The Blue Danube" and "The Stars and Stripes Forever", to a deafening fortissimo.'

Otto Preminger's signature tune.

XVIII

Otto Invades Israel

In Hollywood the champions of Israel were thick on the ground. What an epic! What a human drama! What a triumph of the spirit! Jews, like Phoenix, rising from the ashes of Auschwitz, Buchenwald and Dachau to build their own state! The thought fired the imagination of Dore Schary, ex-scriptwriter and head of Metro-Goldwyn-Mayer, known to many as 'a professional Jew'.

Telling the story of this moving historic event, a first-class writer could set a literary monument to Israel. Dore Schary had the power and the means to lay the foundation stone. He called in Leon Uris, author of *Battle Cry* which was equally successful as a novel and a movie: 'You must write a dramatic novel about the birth of Israel!' Schary told Uris. He was prepared to underwrite the research and take an option on the book's film rights . . . One of the people with whom Uris discussed the proposition was Ingo Preminger, who had acted as his agent in an earlier film transaction.

After some heart searching, Uris agreed to go to Israel. His mission was to take two years. Hundreds of interviews and miles of tape recording later, he wrote a powerful novel entitled *Exodus* after the Book of the Old Testament ('Let my people go!' as it says in Exodus, Chapter 9, Verse 13). The Jews were the heroes, obviously; the British who operated the Mandate in Palestine the villains of the piece. Dore Schary took up his option and bought the film rights for Metro.

The transaction was hardly completed when it transpired that Metro had second thoughts. A movie based on the Uris manuscript was bound to be offensive to the British . . . Even before the novel was published, there was a risk that the film project would be shelved. When Ingo Preminger heard of the difficulties, he had an idea . . .

Ingo and Otto Preminger were as close as ever. Advancing age and long separation had not diminished their affection for each other. Though Ingo lived and worked in New York between 1938 and 1947 when Otto was mostly in Hollywood, and moved to Hollywood just when Otto made New York his main base, they frequently worked together, agent and producer, producer and agent, the obvious allies. Naturally, Ingo told Otto about the complications with the new Uris manuscript: 'Metro would not be averse to selling the film rights,' he said.

A Jewish subject, a best-selling author, the likelihood, nay certainty, of controversy – spelt p-u-b-l-i-c-i-t-y in his dictionary – was a concoction much to Otto Preminger's taste: 'Buy the rights for me!' Otto told his brother. Metro were happy to sell and Otto Preminger was launched on his most exciting project to date.

From his compact address book which lists friends and contacts all over the globe, he extracted the name of Meyer Weisgal who, a quarter of a century earlier, had been Max Reinhardt's 'angel' in the United States. One of Israel's founder fathers and unsurpassed fund raiser for Jewish causes, the venerable Meyer Weisgal was the head of the Weizmann Institute of Science in Israel. His uncanny resemblance to Israel's premier earned him the nickname 'The poor man's Ben Gurion'.

In the summer of 1959 Meyer Weisgal was at his home in Rehovot when, he says, like a bolt from the blue, a call from Hollywood was announced. It was the booming voice of Otto Preminger who informed him that he had acquired the film rights of *Exodus*: 'Will you help me make the picture in Israel?' Preminger asked. With an elder statesman like Weisgal supporting him, all doors would be open to him in Israel.

Weisgal asked to see the manuscript which soon arrived by

air in four telephone-book-size parcels – 'The postage stamps represented a king's ransom,' he thought. He started to read, then gave the manuscript to his son Mendy who took it with him to Jerusalem. A few days later Mendy called: 'Daddy,' he said, 'it's unadulterated . . . but I can't stop crying!'

'Preminger wanted to know my opinion,' Weisgal writes in his autobiography, 'not that he gave a damn for anybody's opinion. I told him that I thought it would make a good picture, providing he put his directorial genius into it . . .'

It would make a very good picture, provided he, Weisgal, supported the project and agreed to help, Preminger replied. 'We will give your Institute the Israel royalties and the income from all world premiéres,' he promised – 'we' being Preminger and United Artists. It would mean around one million dollars for scientific, cultural and artistic causes in Israel. Weisgal thought Preminger was joking when he added one condition – he, Weisgal, would have to make a brief appearance as Ben Gurion in the picture. Weisgal undertook to act as liaison between Preminger and the government of Israel.

The next step was to choose a scriptwriter. Leon Uris tried to write the script himself but it did not work out, at least not to Preminger's satisfaction: 'He is a passionate story-teller,' Preminger said, 'but he can't write dialogue.' Uris did not take kindly to it when his script was discarded.

But there was one splendid writer who could do justice to the subject – the gifted Dalton Trumbo, one of the Hollywood scriptwriters who were dragged before Joe McCarthy's Senate Committee and refused to say whether or not they were card-carrying Communists. Trumbo went to prison.

It was a long time ago, yet he was still tarred with the McCarthy brush, although Hollywood, hypocritical as ever, did not dispense with his talent. Trumbo did a lot of film work but his name never appeared on his credits. When his agent – yes, Ingo Preminger – suggested him to his brother, Otto made a quick decision: 'I shall have Trumbo,' he said, 'in his own right and his own name!' The McCarthy curse was broken.

The *Exodus* project stimulated Preminger more than any of his previous enterprises. It would be taking him away from the United States for a long time. Of course, Hope Bryce would go with him to Israel and work on his picture but it was no longer a matter of a loose association however personal. Neither he nor she had any doubts about their future together. They were earnestly talking about marriage. Otto's divorce was still in the pipeline but as soon as it was official they would be married. And if that moment arrived when they were in Israel, they would not want to lose a single day.

Otto established an advance base in London where he and Hope moved into the Dorchester Hotel. His apartment was like a railway station as he began to get his cast and his crew together. An unending procession of friends, agents, actors, technicians came to pay their respects or apply for jobs. Hardy Kruger, German star of *The Moon is Blue*, dropped in to recommend a German actor. Preminger's old pal, Alexander Paal, asked to join him as a still photographer and was engaged – some years later Preminger obliged Paal by making a brief appearance as an English butler in a film Paal produced for Hungary.

Martin Schute brought the news that he was leaving Columbia. Preminger thought for a moment, then asked: 'Will you spend a year with me making the biggest picture I've ever made?' Schute agreed on the spot and was appointed general manager of the Exodus production company.

Preminger moved around so fast that their talk was continued in Paris: 'Otto invited me and my wife to Paris,' Schute said. 'We had a marvellous lunch with him and Hope, and after lunch Otto and I walked through the streets for two hours, Otto talking about the script, how it ought to be written and the picture, how it ought to be made.'

He wanted a European crew and Schute suggested a girl as location manager: Eva Monley. Otto was doubtful but agreed to see her: 'What makes you think you can work for me?' he asked her a little aggressively. 'I coped with Darryl Zanuck,' Eva replied – she had only recently returned from Central Africa where Zanuck and John Huston made *The Roots of Heaven*. Otto did not need to hear more: 'We'll be going to Israel in a few days,' he told her. Eva Monley joined his team; he never had a more loyal assistant.

The unit he assembled was truly international. Art director Richard Day, winner of several Academy Awards, and Sam Leavitt, chief cameraman, were Americans, Martin Schute and Eva Monley headed a large British contingent, the electricians were Italian and eventually a large number of Israelis were recruited.

Work on the complicated budget started at once. As always, Preminger was cagey about the exact figure but calculations were based on two and half million dollars. The enterprise was so vast that every penny of that would be needed, if not more. His own emoluments as producer and director were in the region of a quarter of a million dollars, not counting his share of the profit which was expected to be big. Transport, accommodation, hundreds of extras, technical equipment, ships, a big building programme, the crew and a large expensive cast would absorb a small fortune.

Putting the cast together required ingenuity. Only a sensitive, intelligent actress could be credible as Kitty, the non-Jewish American girl who becomes attracted to the Jewish cause. Did Eva Marie Saint have sufficient depth? Preminger thought so and offered her a contract. A non-Jewish actor, the handsome blue-eyed Paul Newman was his choice for the star part of Ari, the forceful young Haganah underground fighter.

In the fine English performer Ralph Richardson he found the ideal General Sutherland, compassionate British commander in Cyprus where the death-defying Jewish refugees in SS *Exodus* break the British blockade to sail on their traumatic voyage to Israel.

There was an ulterior thought behind many engagements. the much-publicised Peter Lawford, member of the Kennedy clan by marriage and the Hollywood 'Rat Pack' by inclination, was cast as the British commander's unsympathetic and antisemitic aide. Gregory Ratoff was in it, of course – as a Jewish character who could almost have been himself. An important niche was reserved for a very special actor, Meyer Weisgal's son, who joined the cast under his stage name, Michael Wager. Two Americans, young Sal Mineo and Lee J. Cobb, were given contrasting roles, one as a young immigrant-turned-terrorist (or, if you will, freedom fighter), the other a moderate Jewish leader.

I happened to be with Otto at the Dorchester when a waif-like fourteen-year-old girl arrived with her mother. He interviewed and auditioned Jill Haworth who was virtually unknown and gave her a big part – shades of Jean Seberg. She was cast as the little Jewish girl Karen who is tempted to go to the United States but falls in love with the character played by Sal Mineo, gets caught up in the fighting and is killed. Jill Haworth signed a long-term contract – the birth of another Preminger star.

While Dalton Trumbo who, incidentally, had never set eyes on Israel, started work on the script in Hollywood, Otto Preminger and Hope Bryce flew to Israel, first of several round trips between Europe, America and the Middle East. Richard Day, Sam Leavitt, Martin Schute and Eva Monley went with them. Meyer Weisgal was at the airport to meet them: 'Preminger arrived on the scene,' he records, 'and Israel has not been the same since!'

While Otto's entourage surveyed Israel with a view to turning it into one vast film set, Weisgal took him in tow, showed him the country, explained conditions and introduced him to all and sundry. At Rehovot, the heart of his own empire, he gave a dinner party for his protégé to which he asked forty prominent Israeli politicians, bureaucrats, army and police officers, artists, actors, trade unionists.

One of the guests, Hope recalls, came up to her and introduced himself. He had a patch over one eye. 'How do you do,' he said. 'My name is Moshe Dayan – I am the father of Israel's Françoise Sagan.' The General reminded Hope that his daughter Yael, like Sagan, was only eighteen when she wrote her first novel.

Preminger made good use of the opportunity to explain what his production would involve. He planned to spend a couple of million dollars or more in Israel but it was evident that he expected value for money. He needed official co-operation from the authorities, the police, the unions, the youth organisations. It was going to be a major epic occupying almost four hours screen time. He was going to build a village, Ben Gafna, somewhere facing a real Arab village. As happened in 1947, he would blow up Acre Prison to re-create the dramatic liberation of two hundred and fifty Jewish and Arab prisoners, one of the biggest jail breaks in history.

Roads, squares, groves would have to be cordoned off. What he wanted was a free hand over parts of the country – Preminger remaking Israel to his own design. Once a film producer gets his teeth into a subject, he claims the right to change the landscape and control the people. Consultations with the Israelis started at once but, as Weisgal notes, government machinery was not ideally suited to help a film producer. Preminger and the government didn't exactly speak the same language – and he was not referring to Hebrew.

'Weisgal was a little dynamo,' Eva Monley recalls. Having established the contacts, he had his work cut out to keep the peace: 'Preminger is very demanding,' he explains, 'and usually in the right; but his manner of asking sends a shudder down the spine of government officials and bureaucrats!'

The shouting went on for months as Preminger returned to Israel again and again.

Attended by his two 'goyim' (Martin Schute and Eva Monley), he held court at the Dan Hotel, Tel Aviv: 'His door was never closed,' Eva Monley says, 'everybody could walk right in.' She thinks Preminger is superb: 'He makes a tremendous lot of noise and you have to live through his gusts of temper. When he explodes, you have to stand still.'

It did not always work out this way. Eva chose an olive grove at Canaa for an important scene and when Preminger arrived to inspect it he peered far into the distance: 'I want all this land . . .' he said with a sweeping gesture. He needed a long view. 'Have we got all this?' he asked. 'I was not instructed to get all that,' Eva protested. He was speechless with rage. That evening, she says, he complained about her answering him back: 'She argues with me! She is impossible! Get rid of her!' He promptly forgot all about it and Eva Monley carried on.

Two days later he challenged her arrangements for another scene with undiminished fury. Having learned her lesson, she let him storm and did not defend herself, just kept completely silent. He taunted her but she did not reply. Preminger stalked away angrily. Once more he complained bitterly: 'She won't talk to me! She is impossible!'

'It's his instant rage!' she says good-humouredly.

She and the others panted as they tried to keep pace with him: 'I am twenty years younger than he,' Martin Schute remarks, 'but I do not have his stamina.'

Authenticity was his God. He signed up Major-General Francis Rome, the British officer who directed operations against Jewish raiders in the forties, to advise him on military matters. The Israeli government loaned him the services of Colonel Gershon Rivlin, formerly of the Haganah underground army, to explain the methods of the terrorists. Rome and Rivlin became good friends.

It took six months to get Israel into shape. A vast amount

of technical equipment, lorries and motor cars was assembled. Shooting was scheduled to start on 27 March 1960, and to be completed in fourteen weeks. Nobody dared to question his timetable or say that it was impossible. Nobody believed it could be done.

Watching the technical preparations with one eye, he attended to the artistic side. He coached little Jill Haworth with great patience which did not leave him enough for others. The stars arrived at Haifa where the Hotel Zion was taken over as Preminger's headquarters. Many brought their wives and children. Paul Newman was with his wife Joanne Woodward. The day after his arrival he asked Preminger: 'Can we have a talk, Otto?'

'Certainly!'

'I have studied the script,' Newman said, and produced half a dozen sheets with comments and suggestions, and read them out. Preminger listened until he had finished. Every one of his aides could have predicted his response. 'Very interesting suggestions,' he said cuttingly. 'If you were directing the picture, you would use them. But I do not like them. As I am directing the picture, I shan't use them!'

End of conversation. Beginning of antagonism which was evident throughout the shooting and, at least with Paul Newman, has not abated: '*Exodus*!' Joanne Woodward said to a British television interviewer years later, 'Paul can't bear to talk about it or even think about it!' For *Exodus* read 'Preminger'.

Preminger hardly noticed. When he is absorbed in his work, he forgets the insults and affronts he doles out and is surprised if the anger of those at the receiving end does not subside as quickly. He is liable to assume that a friendly pat on the back makes up for the most offensive remark.

XIX

Preminger's 'Matso Opera'

It was not all work. Anxious as he was to start on schedule, Otto Preminger was just as impatient to get married. He and Hope were in a hurry to regularise their position. They wanted children. They were only waiting for the formal divorce papers to arrive from California. At long last the lawyers cabled that he was a free man. The official document reached Israel a few days before the first scene was due to be shot. Let Meyer Weisgal take up the story which he relates with great tact.

'For some reason Otto was determined to wed in the Holy Land and gave not a second thought to the fact that marriages between Jews and non-Jews in Israel, while not completely unknown, are almost impossible. But to Preminger nothing is impossible. He corralled into the service of this ambition a trio consisting of Abba Khoushy, the late Mayor of Haifa (where he was doing much of the shooting), Khoushy's secretary Milka (who was also appearing in the film) and me as co-ordinator. We had to convince the rabbinate of the urgency of the marriage without revealing too many unnecessary details about Hope's ancestry. The rabbinate proved amenable and understanding and the wedding took place. Mazel Tov!'

'We were married at the Hotel Zion in Haifa the day before shooting started,' Hope Preminger told me in New York in the summer of 1971, recalling my own visit to Haifa a few weeks after the big day in her life. 'I was told that there was not such a thing as a civil marriage in Israel and we had to wait for a tribunal to give permission. All that was required was proof of divorce. They may have assumed that I was Jewish.'

The rabbi came to Preminger's suite to perform the

ceremony. Says Hope: 'It was all in Hebrew . . . I didn't understand a word.' Did she adopt the Jewish faith? 'I did not – not that I would have minded.'

Since the only marriages legally valid in Israel are between members of the Jewish faith, she was not really married, I suggested. Hope found the thought amusing: 'Well, that's quite fashionable nowadays, isn't it?' she laughed. I asked Otto about it: 'We went to the American Consulate,' he said, 'and made it legal.'

When Meyer Weisgal's memoirs were published by Weidenfeld and Nicolson late in 1971, the passage about Preminger's marriage caused an angry reaction in Israel. Rabbis asked for an investigation into the circumstances. The storm broke over Otto's head while he was in London. In the presence of his usual audience of old friends and associates – Martin Schute and Eva Monley happened to be there – Otto telephoned Weisgal and upbraided him about his revelations.

His next call was to New York: 'Hopsie,' he told his wife, 'there is a row in Israel about Weisgal's account of our wedding . . .' A few minutes later the ever-alert *Daily Express* was on to him about the reports from Israel: 'It doesn't matter,' Otto told the reporter. 'When we got back to the United States we were legally married!' Nobody asked him to produce his wedding certificate but, with or without official Israeli sanction, no two people could be more married than Otto and Hope Preminger.

There was certainly no doubt about the validity of the marriage in the mind of Israel's Prime Minister David Ben Gurion when he invited Otto to his house in Tel Aviv. Leaving Hope behind at the Dan Hotel, Preminger went to see the Premier. While he was there, the telephone rang at the hotel. Hope answered. 'Have you ever heard the name of Paula Ben Gurion?' the lady at the other end asked. Hope was taken aback. Of course she knew the name of the Prime Minister's wife.

'What are you doing?' was Paula Ben Gurion's next question.

'I am in the bathtub.'

'I am sending the car . . .' Paula said, and half an hour later Hope joined her husband in the house of the Ben Gurions.

Through Teddy Kollek, his right-hand man – now Mayor of Jerusalem – the Prime Minister was well informed about the progress of *Exodus*. A Viennese by birth, Kollek took a personal interest in the production and visited the Premingers at the Hotel Zion in Haifa. I joined them at dinner but only Teddy knew that, a few hundred yards from where we were, Adolf Eichmann, the mass murderer of the Jews, having been captured by Israeli commandos in the Argentine, was just then being interrogated in the greatest secrecy. A poignant coincidence – while Preminger was re-creating the birth of Israel, justice caught up with the man who had tried his damnedest to exterminate the Jewish race.

To be in Israel meant rejoicing with the Jewish people that fate had frustrated Hitler's genocidal plans and to admire the vigour and strength of the survivors from the Furor Teutonicus. In the person of Otto Preminger we saw something of the Furor Judaicus. Like shock waves preceding an earthquake, minor outbrusts escalated into bigger upheavals.

'In private life Otto is totally different,' says Hope Preminger. 'When we were first married there was not so much difference between him as a public and a private person but he has since become progressively more private and the contrast has grown. He still enjoys the image of a big blustering bully. It's a game with him – he has great fun!'

Others speak of the 'method in his madness' and have analysed the style, technique and purpose of his outbursts. They are not always pretty to watch. There was one scene in *Exodus* with a dozen Israeli tiny tots, none older than six, expecting an Arab attack on their house in the children's village of Ben Gafra. Preminger wanted them to look frightened and to cry.

'Tell them to cry!' he instructed the Israeli interpreter.

'Cry!' the Israeli repeated the request. Not a tear. 'Cry!' he demanded once more. Nothing.

'Cry, you little monsters!' Preminger shouted. To no effect.

Preminger ordered the children's parents who had been watching the proceedings from the wings to be sent away. The children looked tired and unhappy but they still would not cry. It was time for the man himself to take over. With a menacing expression equalling his finest performance as a Nazi, he turned to the children: 'Do you know where your mothers are?' he barked. 'They have left you and they will not come back. Never!'

The children burst into tears and cried their little hearts out. With a happy smile, Preminger signalled the cameraman: 'Action!'

Everything stopped – or moved – on Preminger's instructions. He was in Haifa dockyards shooting the emotional scene in which the refugees are shown at the end of their perilous voyage from Cyprus setting foot on the blessed soil of Israel. After half a day's intricate preparations, the camera began to roll when, smack in the middle of the view, the outline of a modern passenger liner appeared on the horizon. It was the 22,000-ton SS *Jerusalem* arriving from the United States with a full complement of passengers.

Steaming towards the harbour, she was too big and distant for Preminger's stentorian voice to reach her. The captain obviously did not notice him waving her furiously away. Relentlessly she sailed towards the spot on which the camera was focused. Nothing could have been more out of place in the context of the period Preminger was recording.

'Almost any other director,' says Martin Schute, 'would have resigned himself to the unwelcome interference, would have postponed the scene and lost a day.' Not Preminger. He instructed Schute to telephone the Israeli Minister of Trade and Industry and tell him to get that vessel out of shot.

Using 'Preminger' as a password – none better in Israel in these days – Schute was soon talking to the Minister. It would cost a lot of money to set the scene up a second time, he explained. It would disrupt the whole schedule. After a brief resistance the Minister suggested a compromise. By the grace of Preminger, the passengers were allowed to disembark quickly but the ship was ordered to leave the harbour and steam out to sea again without unloading the baggage. It took three and a half hours to complete the scene and another hour or so before the *Jerusalem* could return and the passengers were reunited with their luggage.

The Haifa sequences completed, lorry-loads of generators, cameras, and lights, coaches of technicians and extras, a cavalcade of cars carrying stars and production teams rumbled towards Jerusalem. Someone commented that the expedition was big enough to frighten the Arab armies on Israel's border and start another war.

Jerusalem. For the scene depicting the proud moment when the new State of Israel is proclaimed, a big square would have to be filled with people – five thousand, ten thousand, fifteen thousand. How to get such a large number of unpaid crowd actors together? 'It was decided to arrange a raffle with big prizes and issue thousands of tickets,' said Martin Schute, 'the draw and the announcement of the results to coincide with the climax of the big scene.' Would they come? And how many? Only the day would bring the answer.

Before the day dawned Preminger had to deal with another problem. There was no sign of Meyer Weisgal who was scheduled to appear as Ben Gurion on a balcony to face the big crowd with the other Israeli leaders: 'Where is Meyer' Preminger demanded. Weisgal was traced to London where he was attending a conference of scientists.

Once more Preminger's voice reached him across thousands of miles: 'Meyer, this is Otto – we have an agreement, remember?' He was needed in Jerusalem within the week – for the balcony scene: 'Impossible!' Weisgal said. 'No appearance, no million dollars!' Otto answered with menacing finality.

Weisgal packed his bags, returned to Israel and, 'like a good actor', reported for duty. The script required him to embrace Golda Meir who was being played by Milka, the secretary of the Mayor of Haifa. About his part in the affair, Weisgal says: 'I didn't think it was too great a sacrifice for a million dollars, and I was by far the highest paid actor in that production.'

The response to Preminger's raffle was phenomenal. As Weisgal joined the stars on the balcony, forty thousand people from all over Israel filled the big square below. As the result of the raffle was announced a tremendous cheer went up. As far as *Exodus* was concerned, the cheers were, of course, for the proclamation of the State of Israel.

The central figure of the scene was that accomplished American character actor Lee J. Cobb who was about to make a long and difficult oration. Perched on top of a crane at the other side of the square, Preminger was shouting instructions. Cobb could not hear Preminger. Preminger could not hear Cobb. An inquest on what followed did not produce a clear-cut picture of the incident.

Preminger was unhappy because Cobb apparently could not remember his lines. Cobb was even more unhappy because he was forced to do the scene over and over again, altogether ten times. Instead of doing it an eleventh time, as Preminger demanded, he delivered himself of a speech which was not part of the script and certainly not in the festive spirit of the occasion. Preminger would not allow Cobb or anyone else to outshout him and shouted back, his voice reverberating across the square: 'You're an idiot!' Cobb did not take kindly to the insult. It was a miracle that the scene was completed at all.

Going off to the King David Hotel for a meal, Preminger

was heard to mutter: 'That son of a bitch! I pay him 75,000 dollars and he doesn't even know his lines!' As far as he was concerned, Cobb was finished. He cancelled the actor's accommodation at the hotel, his way of sending his star packing. The well-meaning Meyer Weisgal assumed that there was a reconciliation but Preminger and Cobb have, in fact, not talked to each other since.

Though the balcony scene brought the film to an end and was the last sequence to be shot in Israel, it was by no means the end of the production. In time-honoured practice, the beginning of the picture remained to be shot. It was set in Cyprus which made it necessary to move the whole circus from Israel to the big island in the eastern Mediterranean. At the King David Hotel, on that Friday morning, Otto walked over to Martin Schute and shook him by the hand: 'See you in Cyprus on Monday morning,' he said. 'We start shooting at Nicosia at 9 a.m.'

'I slept briefly on Friday night,' Martin Schute says, 'and not again until Monday night.' As Otto flew on ahead, Schute was left to shift the unit of a hundred and fifteen, technicians and actors, a merchant ship carrying thirteen generators and the whole lighting equipment plus a fleet of cars and lorries from Israel to Cyprus: 'We also had to take the three hundred and fifty Israeli passengers of the illegal immigrant ship *Exodus* . . .'

In Cyprus, in the meantime, Eva Monley was preparing the ground for the early Monday morning start. The base was Famagusta but the first scene, involving Eva Maria Saint and a local guide, was set at Nicosia's castle, Ivory Towers. Unbelievably, everything was ready and in position. Shooting started on Monday at 9 a.m. and continued according to schedule. Confounding the doubters, Preminger completed the whole picture in just under fourteen weeks. It was cut and edited in London and printed (in 'Superpanavision') in the United States.

The crew praised Preminger's professionalism. Martin

Schute said: 'Carl Foreman started shooting *The Guns of Navarone* before work on *Exodus* began and was still shooting when Preminger delivered the final print of *Exodus* to United Artists. The cost of *Exodus* was one third of the cost of *The Guns* . . ., a remarkable achievement. *Exodus* grossed thirteen million dollars, *The Guns* . . . twenty-five million!'

Long before *Exodus* was released, there were political objections. Moderate Israelis felt that it gave too much prominence to the terrorists and asked for changes ('You do not want to rewrite the script,' Preminger retorted, 'you want to rewrite history!'). The terrorists complained that they were not given enough credit, Cairo radio denounced *Exodus* as a 'Jewish imperialist plot'.

Others were worried by what they regarded as excessive emphasis on violence, the bombings, the blowing up of Acre Prison. Preminger, as so often, took refuge in philosophical arguments. It was essential to show the violence, he said, because the State of Israel would not have come into being without violence: 'Every revolution needs some kind of terror or violence,' he opined. Naturally, he did not approve of violence and terror.

As with so many Hollywood operators, the illusion he created on celluloid developed into a delusion of grandeur. Super-producer seeing himself as super-politician, he said somewhat grandiloquently: 'I would be willing to defend my film of *Exodus* against some really big enemy of Israel, like Nasser. I would be willing to sit down with him and let him tell me why he felt this picture is unfair.'

The critics did not take kindly to the picture. Many thought it ponderous and, though the extremely difficult continuous shots added considerably to the tension, complained that there were only words where action was expected. Preminger was blamed for Paul Newman's big scene falling flat. 'Lack of feeling,' they diagnosed – Preminger's not Newman's. Some critics, as critics are wont to do, only sharpened their wits. About the big escape sequence, one wrote: 'There are more doors in *Exodus* than in the Waldorf Astoria.' *Exodus* was dubbed a 'Jewish Western' and Preminger's 'Matso Opera'.

In spite of the critics, it made a big impact all over the world and earned Preminger well over a million dollars before tax. Jill Haworth was a source of additional income. She was booked for two more appearances under his aegis after which, in another highly profitable transaction in Hollywood's human cattle market, he sold her contract to Columbia.

Altogether, the arrangement guaranteed her a quarter of a million dollars over the next seven years. Her moving love affair with Sal Mineo in *Exodus*, which was cut short by her screen death, blossomed on for some time in real life. Jill became an established star on screen and stage and, when I last saw her, was just ending a three years' run on Broadway in *Cabaret*. Stage and film producers were offering her big parts. The one she accepted was playing opposite a monster in a horror film.

By the time the Premingers left Israel, Hope was pregnant. For Otto to become a father at the age of fifty-five seemed, as he confessed later, like a miracle. Gratifying, but still requiring readjustment. After a restless life in search of an anchor, marriage alone – if experience was anything to go by – might not have steadied his roving eye. Fatherhood was a different matter – this, mind, was some years before he discovered Erik, Gypsy's son and his own.

For a couple of months he and Hope continued their perigrinations: 'We stayed at the Dorchester in London,' Hope said, 'then flew to New York and moved into Otto's old apartment.' With Hope's baby due in the not too distant future, it seemed best to stay put now. So as not to be idle, Otto agreed to direct Ira Levin's *Critics Choice* on Broadway. It opened the same day as *Exodus*.

Then things began to happen. The prospective father was advised that he could expect not one but two babies – Hopsie was about to present him with a double feature. The twins were born at the Doctors Hospital in New York on 3 October 1960: 'They were premature,' Hope said. Though they had to spend their first days in an incubator, they were splendid babies, a boy and a girl, with good features (like their father's at birth) and, after the precarious early days, healthy and quickly gaining in weight and strength.

Otto's apartment was too small for his new family. They moved into a suite at the Sherry Netherland Hotel which was the twins' first home. The boy was named Mark, after Preminger senior, and the girl Victoria or Vicky. She was still small when she acquired the nickname 'Missie' and has been Missie ever since.

Mark resembled his father's family while Missie, with a rounder face and wider eyes, promised to grow up as beautiful as her mother, a fortuitous arrangement of their natural heritage. Hope looked for a nurse and, after the usual tribulations, engaged a Scottish Nannie who remained with the children for years.

About her role as Otto Preminger's wife, Hope had definite views: 'We did not like the idea of a showbiz marriage,' she explained to me. 'But Otto is so totally involved – I did not want to be left out. You cannot lead two separate lives. That is why I decided to go on working – with him. Working together, we can talk whenever he has a free moment and it doesn't matter if he is too tired when he gets home at the end of a hard day.'

To Otto, the mother of his children was even more precious than a mere wife. The young harpies who used to count on diverting evening excursions with the famous producer and parading in his company in public places telephoned in vain: 'I would not want Hopsie to be upset by the kind of rumours which spread whenever I am seen with a woman,' he said to me. The search was over. Otto was home for good.

He had not thought of owning a house since he surrendered

his Hollywood mansion to the demands of the tax collectors
– they were still demanding but received their huge share
promptly. Now he wanted to strike roots. He looked for a
town house and soon found a suitable one at 129 East 64th.
Accustomed to create his own scene, he brought a big
production team together, architects, technicians, interior
decorators, lighting experts.

The producer-director was building his most striking set–
no better way of describing the spirit in which he tackled the
project. Master of his own budget, he was not skimping. His
plans provided for the old house to be reconstructed from
top to bottom, and, since he had no intention of climbing the
stairs from bottom to top, for a lift.

When, on my first visit two years later, the lift deposited
me on the first floor the effect was startling. The drawing-
room, one vast area from front to back. The décor in stark
black and white. Like stars dotted across the whole length of
the ceiling, the lighting (by the designer of the Kennedy
Airport illuminations) was variable from dim to brilliant.
The twelve-foot-plus couch under the outsize Miro fitted
easily into the big expanse. The aluminium leather-topped
easy chairs were of ultra-modern design.

Flanking the front window two desks with white marble
tops facing each other – his and hers. Behind a movable
Modigliani, the concealed bar. On the terrace behind the
wide plate-glass window, a tall gaunt Gacometti sculpture
and in the garden beyond, his prized Henry Moore ('Seated
Woman'). Paintings everywhere – Picasso, Braque, Matisse
– the fruits of thirty motion pictures, shrewd investment,
good taste and a predilection for modern paintings: 'One
must have the courage to live in one's own period,' he says.
(When he lent his Matisse for an exhibition, Pierre Matisse
sent him another to take its place temporarily.)

A dining-room of Spartan elegance; round marble table
with a crystal bowl, a square table for the overflow, black
leather chairs covered with cellophane, not a piece of useless

furniture. Two Chagalls, a Raoul Dufy, a Klee a Roualt and a Bissier. Upstairs, adjoining the bedrooms, a bathroom to humble Cecil B. de Mille and delight a Roman emperor, with two sunken baths in smooth red brick – his and hers. A rest room with an adjustable couch to fit the body at six different levels.

Another couple of years and Preminger's private set had grown taller. The three-storey house had sprouted a fourth and a fifth floor. The fourth with servants' quarters, a new nursery, a sauna bath and a gymnasium – one great sight was Otto in his blue trunks cycling away on the motorised exercise machine for all he was worth, his pallor darkened by the effort and the sun lamp. The crowning glory on the fifth floor was a fully automated screening-room with panavision-size screen, which we shall visit before long.

XX

Mr P. Goes to Washington

It's amazing that the American government permits a
picture like this to be made. This film proved to me that,
in spite of all the beefs you hear, this is really the only free
country where you have free expression.
       Otto Preminger in an interview with *On Film*

Hospitable as ever and anxious to make my visit to New
York a rewarding one, Otto Preminger asked: 'Will you and
your wife come with us to see *Advise and Consent* tonight?'

Fresh from Europe, I had to be enlightened about the
history of the Broadway hit. Distilled from the massive novel
of that name by Allen Drury, its theme is a clash between
the President of the United States and the Senate over the
appointment of a highly controversial Secretary of State. It
shines a rude torchlight on the American system of government, rattles skeletons in many cupboards and offers a view
of political passion and sex, hetero and homo, dishonesty and
ambition. The novel headed the best-seller list for forty-six
weeks, won the Pulitzer Prize and, eventually, went into
several paperback editions . . .

We had an enjoyable and instructive evening. Otto and
Hope Preminger had seen the Broadway production before,
but followed it with intense concentration. The implication
was obvious. After its successful transition, from page to
stage, Allen Drury's lurid political thriller was due for the
ultimate reward of literary enterprise – a movie version.
Producer and director: Otto Preminger. (The purchase price
of the film rights included a bonus for every week the novel
graced the best-seller list.)

And so, fresh from his conquest of Israel, Preminger
prepared to march on the Capitol. With the propaganda

drums beating and the trumpets blasting away, there was not the slightest doubt that the walls of Washington would come tumbling down as surely as Jericho's.

Realism was top priority. With the script envisaging, not without logic, a black senator from Georgia, Preminger proposed to give the part to an outstanding Negro leader. There were several intriguing choices and he arrived at the most striking of them – none other than Dr Martin Luther King. Within a week Preminger felt able to announce that Martin Luther King had agreed to play, his pay of 5000 dollars to go to charity.

'It is a short role,' Preminger said, 'and, while I know people will think of it as a publicity gimmick, it is nothing of the sort. Dr King was sought for the role and he accepted it simply because his appearance will make a positive statement for this country here and abroad. It should indicate that it is possible for a Negro to be elected to the United States Senate at any time, now or in the future.'

This may well be so. But in the event, the sensational off-beat casting having generated as much publicity as could be crammed into twenty-four hours, Dr King accepted some good advice and withdrew his consent on the grounds that some Southerners might be inflamed by the appearance of a Negro as Georgia senator. Besides, he said, the role was not of any significance in advancing civil rights. He added that he had not formally accepted or signed any agreement personally. The interlude ended with a few angry shouts of 'Bad taste! Bad taste!' in the direction of Preminger. *Time* chipped in with a rebuke for 'cynical backlighting'.

Preminger ploughed on. He decided to nominate to Congress some of the great romantic stars of yesteryear, now grey of temple and mature enough to represent their fans as senators – Henry Fonda as the controversial candidate for Secretary of State, Lew Ayres, Walter Pidgeon, Burgess Meredith. The President of the United States was Franchot Tone.

The ingenious impresario of the Washington scene still had a trick or two up his sleeve. Preminger cast Peter Lawford, restored from the eastern Mediterranean to the Potomac, as a particularly obstreperous senator. Did President Kennedy – the real President – mind his brother-in-law casting aspersions on the Presidency? 'We have been given all facilities in Washington,' Preminger replied, 'proof that the President has no objections!'

Casting, casting, casting! Although he denies it – lest the occasional flicker of humanity distorted the image of a heartless bully – personal considerations frequently influence Preminger's choice of a star. This time it was Gene Tierney, after years under the shadow of a mental breakdown, anxious to resume her career. Nine out of ten producers, sensing complications, would have kept well clear. Preminger jumped at the chance of performing another resurrection. As lovely as of yore, Gene, the *Laura* of his first major success, was cast in the key role of a prominent Washington hostess.

The personable Don Murray took a part in the centre of the conflict, and Paul Ford (*Sergeant Bilko*'s comic TV colonel) was allocated another seat on the Senate benches. The Senator from Georgia changed colour – and accent. In a most idiosyncratic piece of casting, the part went to the great Charles Laughton who diligently acquired a southern drawl. Mort Sahl, much in vogue at the time, was taken on.

Still on realism. The question of how deep the cameras would be allowed to penetrate into the recesses of the administration's tabernacles was quickly answered – nothing barred except the Senate Chamber and the White House. As background for the social shenanigans, Preminger scouts picked the Tregaron estate of Joseph E. (*Mission to Moscow*) Davies, and the problem of a typical Washington party was solved by inviting Washington socialites to play themselves for a 'fee' of twenty-five dollars per head to go to charity. For four hundred – the upper four hundred – Preminger paid 10,000 dollars.

Famous hostesses fell over themselves to be in on the gag. Politicians and administrators came with their wives decked out in their finest gowns. The party went with a bang, a Preminger bang. Arriving dutifully at 7 p.m. the eager socialites were in for a shock – drinks were strictly non-alcoholic. They soon realised that this was no conventional get-together for them to circulate and mingle as they pleased. Once the doors closed, they were under the director's orders. Giant lights glared down raising the temperature.

After the fifth take, one chap near the camera lit a cigarette: 'You, there!' came Preminger's voice, magnified by his megaphone. 'You did not smoke in the previous take, so put that cigarette out!' Another was rebuked for his 'sloppy appearance', yet another for wearing green socks. One guest moved in the wrong direction: 'Out!' Preminger shouted. 'But I'm from *Look*,' the man protested. '*You* look!' Preminger hit back, visibly pleased with his own joke.

A party of journalists flown in from Europe at great cost arrived at the wrong moment: 'Out!' Preminger screamed – a strange welcome. They withdrew terror-stricken from the line of shooting. 'The last Prussian of Hollywood,' one of the Germans commented. By midnight the fun was wearing thin. Tired guests made for the doors: 'We are not finished yet!' the Voice ordered them back. Only a few managed to escape before the party was over. It was 2 a.m.

In another major scene in which 'President' Franchot Tone was due to address a gathering, I was one of the unpaid extras in the audience. Our job was to listen attentively to Mort Sahl making an amusing warm-up speech. Overcome by the boredom of several repetitive takes, we were quietly dozing when Preminger roused us: 'That was supposed to be funny! So – Laugh!' Pause. 'When I tell you it is funny – Laugh!'

I felt the lights upon me and, out of the corner of my eye, saw the camera veering in my direction before it returned to focus on Mort Sahl. Our moment of glory! Alas, neither Mort Sahl nor I appeared in the movie. The scene was cut.

Realism took one knock at a genuine party for the cast which was attended by several senators. Two of the guests were seen in deep conversation, one with a noble profile and an interesting mane of hair, the other with rather nondescript, commonplace features: 'Who are they?' somebody asked. 'One is a senator, the other an actor who portrays a senator – guess who is who?' Need I quote the answer? The real senator, alas, was the gentleman who did not look like one.

For some people, though, *Advise and Consent* looked too real to be good for America's reputation. In a pointed reference to Preminger's picture of Washington, Ed Murrow – Edward R. Murrow, television star-turned-official – said that Hollywood should create a favourable 'film image' of Americans to show foreigners.

Preminger gave his answer to reporters: 'I am frankly surprised,' he said, 'knowing Mr Murrow and his past and his fight for freedom of expression, that he should now, having a job in the government, try to restrict freedom of expression of the screen . . .' He, Preminger, was sure new countries which have a choice between Russian propaganda and American truth would decide 'for our way of life'. Audiences should be left to draw their own conclusions. Naturally, he was against censorship but very much for voluntary, individual classification leaving responsibility to producers whether or not to label a film 'adult'.

Still, I found the finished movie entertaining and stimulating, if not quite up to one comment in a movie magazine which said that '*Advise and Consent* finally reveals Preminger as one of the cinema's great moralists.'

The Washington interlude over, Preminger took up where he left off in Israel. After the Jews, the Catholics. After the Holy Land, the Holy City. Following his foray into Jerusalem, he was bound to move on Rome sooner or later – and take in the Catholic citadels of Boston, Mass., and Vienna, Austria, on the way.

Remember all the pillars of Austria's Catholic establishment, including Cardinal Innitzer, attending Preminger's Viennese swan-song, the stage production of Emmet Lavery's *The First Legion* way back in 1935? Well, almost thirty years later, Cardinal Innitzer made another appearance for Preminger, this time posthumously and as a stage figure in his film, *The Cardinal*. Innitzer's reappearance and the return of Otto Preminger to Vienna caused considerable commotion.

Neither of them should have been there at all. Vienna did not figure in Henry Morton Robinson's novel about a Catholic priest's turbulent rise to the purple. Preminger first read the novel when it was published in 1950. By the time he recalled it a dozen years later it had been translated into several languages and sold twenty-five million copies. He thought it would make a monumental movie and acquired the film rights. It also seemed to offer an opportunity to kick dear old Vienna where it really hurts. There was no other explanation. With the authority which showbiz confers on its high priests, Otto simply decided to revamp the subject and introduce a passage with the background of pre-war Vienna.

So as to stir up as much trouble as possible, he chose the tragedy of Cardinal Innitzer who was duped by Hitler into welcoming the Wehrmacht in exchange, as he piously hoped, for Nazi concessions to Austria's Catholics: Innitzer foolishly signed a letter with the 'Heil Hitler' which was Nazi etiquette. It did not stop the Nazis from storming his palace and murdering his secretary or from persecuting the Catholics almost as viciously as the Jews. Innitzer, who died in 1955, went down in history as the 'Heil Hitler Cardinal'.

As a highly emotional incident, the Innitzer episode fitted well into the story of Robinson's Cardinal who wades through the morass of emotional tribulations to reach the top. Abortion, and whether a mother's life should be sacrificed rather than a pregnancy terminated; whether a priest should consort with his former girl-friend; whether he should stop a Klu-Klux-Klan flogging, whether he should give sanctuary to the ex-girl-friend who is married to a half-Jew are some of the dramatic questions the story poses.

With sure Preminger touch, a suicide was modelled on the death of the brilliant Austrian writer Egon Friedell who flung himself from a window to escape arrest by the Gestapo in March 1938 – and was enacted virtually in the authentic spot. (The scene was shot twelve times; twelve times the actor had to jump out of a fourth-floor window on to a precarious parapet: 'Usually, I am not superstitious,' he said, wiping his brow, 'but I doubt whether I would have jumped a thirteenth time!')

To do justice to these ingredients which 'one of the cinema's great moralists' was anxious to project, he chose a scriptwriter who (even long before *Myra Breckinridge*) was not above raising a few scandalous topics of his own, to wit Gore Vidal. The Gore Vidal ploy misfired. His script did not please Preminger, who rejected it. The two parted company and decided not to remain friends. Robert Dozier took over and concocted the final version.

When Preminger's new project was announced there was another spot of bother, though not of his making. Already in 1950 it had been suspected that Henry Morton Robinson's Cardinal was modelled in one respect on an episode in Cardinal Spellman's life and had created a good deal of ill-feeling. Not surprisingly, Cardinal Spellman was not too pleased to have the old story revived with all its implications, true or false.

Discreetly he asked the Catholic hierarchy in the United States not to co-operate with Preminger: 'Spellman has no influence,' Preminger said contemptuously and, in the event, the Catholics were no less co-operative than the Jews before them.

With the Vidal and Spellman row safely behind him, Otto Preminger set out for Vienna on the crest of a giant publicity wave – and towards new and even bigger rows. It was, of course, sheer coincidence but did not escape the alert Viennese that Hitler's 1938 invasion of Austria was launched under the code name of 'Operation Otto' (in memory of Otto Planetta, the Nazi who had assassinated the Austrian Chancellor Dollfuss four years earlier). Now the second 'Operation Otto' was under way. Followed by his crack unit of some fifty aides and technicians, Otto Preminger returned to the city of his early triumphs.

The Premingers – Otto, Hope, Mark, Vicky and Nannie – moved into the royal, or rather imperial, suite of the exquisite Hotel Imperial which Hitler occupied in 1938. This is the story that was put about but it was not quite correct. It was not true when it was said about Khrushchev at the time he met President Kennedy in Vienna, and it was not true about Preminger. The hotel was rebuilt after the war and the old Number One suite disappeared. Neither Khrushchev nor Preminger slept in Hitler's bed.

The suite was not less inviting for that because the Imperial is one of the most sumptuously elegant and comfortable hotels in the world. From his enviable command post, Preminger devised the strategy of his operation which required many historic places to be occupied by his unit.

Top of the list – the archbishop's palace, naturally, followed by St. Stephen's Cathedral, whose Gothic spire is a symbol of Vienna, and, for old times sake, the National Library where the boy Preminger cut his theatrical teeth. To smooth his path and establish contacts, he had the help of Ernst Häussermann, Vienna's leading theatrical figure who was his Austrian Meyer Weisgal. Though the Austrians welcomed one of Hollywood's big spenders with open arms, Häussermann had his work cut out to keep the peace between his protégé and his compatriots.

Trouble started as soon as details of the script became

known. Why, the Austrians asked, should a historical figure like Cardinal Innitzer be arbitrarily introduced into a piece of fiction? And why Innitzer? In the face of hostile questions, Preminger – nobody ordinarily more loquacious in confrontations with the press – was curt and uncommunicative: 'For such things, I am accountable to no one,' he said. 'It was done for private reasons!'

In an interview with the current Cardinal-Archbishop of Vienna, Dr Franz Koenig, strongly tipped as the next Pope, he was a little more accommodating: 'I have no intention of offending the Catholic church,' he assured the prelate, 'nor my former homeland.' All he wanted was to show how futile it was to strike deals with tyrants like Hitler. He would make it quite clear that Cardinal Innitzer as soon as he recognised his error, exhorted his flock from the pulpit to oppose Hitler.

Like most movie tycoons who can command an audience for anything they say, however trivial, Preminger delivered himself of his views about the Church of Rome: 'I think the Catholic Church is a political institution – forget religion!' he declared. The Church was not totalitarian, and the Pope never acted like Adolf Hitler: 'It's an interesting mixture of totalitarianism and, perhaps, not democracy but individual autonomy' – whatever that was supposed to mean.

New fuel was added to the Innitzer controversy when Preminger's publicity handouts revealed that the character would be played by Curt Jurgens, a fine figure of a man and a popular actor. Austria's Catholics objected because Jurgens had been married four times and had figured in almost as many public rows as the great Preminger himself. Utterly unsuitable to portray a cardinal!

Preminger stormed that he would not be dictated to but everybody's face was saved when Jurgens conveniently refused to abandon the highly successful play in which he was starring in Paris. A more acceptable Austrian actor was engaged in his place. Fulminating against all attempts to 'censor' him, Preminger still made a few minor changes in the script to appease the opposition.

A new altercation was already brewing up. It erupted over the handsome Austro-German star Romy Schneider, Alain Delon's highly publicised paramour, who was cast as the Cardinal's girl-friend. The Viennese were screaming for her blood because, it appeared, Romy had only recently told an Austrian reporter: 'I shall be coming to Vienna with a big American production, and shall soon show those *Teppen* that I can act . . .!' (*'Teppen'* is Viennese slang for idiots.)

'*Teppen?*' The reporter did not trust his ears.

'Yes, you write *Teppen* even if they are cross!'

At a press lunch to introduce Romy, Preminger spotted the offending reporter: 'Apologise to Miss Schneider!' he demanded. The reporter refused. Romy Schneider forcefully seconded her director-producer and weighed in to the reporter: 'You are no gentleman,' she shouted, 'and you will never be one! Get lost!'

Preminger treated the Austrian press with condescension amounting to contempt, an attitude towards Austrians which is adopted by many Jews when they return to the country from which they were driven by the Nazis. Apart from humbling the reporters, Preminger had the added satisfaction that his behaviour made the headlines beyond the frontiers of Austria.

When it came to arranging locations, St Stephen's opened its portals to Preminger, but his plan to hoist the swastika flag from one of the spires was too much to swallow. Next he applied for permission to shoot a scene in the National Library but Education Minister Dr Drimmel refused point-blank: 'At long last,' he said, giving vent to feelings that were pretty general, 'the grass has grown over the evils of 1938, and now there comes this camel and gobbles it up!'

Better at doling out insults than suffering them, Preminger reacted violently. He attacked the Minister in public and private, and has kept his grudge burning fiercely ever since.

Dr Drimmel occupies a permanent place in the Preminger shooting gallery and is spattered with verbal bullets on every possible and impossible occasion.

Only when the dust of all these battles settled was it possible to look at other aspects of the production. Preminger's casting ran along familiar lines. He found a part for Rudolf Forster whose pre-war moonlight flit from the New York rehearsals for *Margin for Error* gave Preminger his chance to prove himself the most hateful stage Nazi in the business. Jill Haworth was still under contract and duly squeezed into the cast. Maggie MacNamara who (very much like Gene Tierney) had been in the doldrums ever since *The Moon is Blue* was resurrected but Preminger's hope that this would launch her on a second career was disappointed.

The legendary Dorothy Gish was disinterred for the occasion, Burgess Meredith resumed his place among the Preminger regulars and the talented, sexy little Carol Lynley became the Cardinal's troublesome sister.

The part of the Bishop of Boston (not in the Vienna episode) went to fellow director John Huston in his first major film role: 'It's very good for the soul of a director,' he said, 'once in a while to be on the other side of the camera.' Huston who is a model of politeness but, according to agent Paul Kohner, 'can take people apart like a prosecuting attorney', was treated with great deference by Preminger. There was mutual respect between the two. In lieu of payment Huston accepted a de Stael painting.

With the name part of the Cardinal, Preminger took his biggest gamble. He gave it to Tom Tryon, an ex-cowboy of limited acting range but a physical stature attractive enough to disguise his deficiencies. It turned out to be a mistake and, as with Jean Seberg, the actor was made to suffer for it.

In an early scene Tom did so badly that Preminger blew his top, turned his back on him and told an assistant brusquely: 'Fire him!' That same evening Tom was rehired. 'Otto fired so many people,' said Eva Monley, 'I can't recall

all their names.' The incident created tensions which lingered. Tom Tryon seemed to be on the verge of a nervous breakdown. I was in Vienna with the Preminger production but did not see a lot of Tom. Nobody did. Whenever he came off the set, he hid himself away like a wounded beast.

In another scene, though I did not see it myself, he was said to have had such violent shakes that his arms had to be taped to the chair. A couple of days' later he was under doctor's orders. His body broke out in a rash: 'I did not have a nervous breakdown the way some people think,' he said later. 'I was in such a run-down condition that I was hospitalised with hepatitis. *The Cardinal* was such a terrible experience that I lost the urge to act after that . . .' Not quite! Tom Tryon worked for Preminger on another picture, did a few television shows, was for four years under analysis after that and emerged as a highly successful writer.

Once more Preminger's terror produced as much publicity as his artistry. One English reporter wrote about his 'reputation for wringing performances out of actors as if they were dirty washing', and a friend who wants to remain anonymous said: 'He is vicious, sadistic, cynical, ruthless and heartless – but he is charming.' Charming!

Away from the set he was – well, charming. Nostalgic or bloody-minded about Vienna – he insisted on taking his gentile aides to a Jewish restaurant and initiate them into the delights of *gefilte* fish. He visited the Café Landmann where an old waiter showed him his late father's regular table. At the National Gallery he relived his boyhood acting exercises – and worked up more steam against Dr Drimmel. Actors who used to work for him at the Josefstadt in the early thirties came to pay their respects and he seemed to forgive those who, after the annexation of Austria, revealed themselves as keen Nazis.

Vienna soon forgot the squabbles and proudly adopted him as one of their own – 'local boy who made good in America' sort-of-thing. They put his name on the list of distinguished Viennese to be honoured on all suitable dates, hence their letters to congratulate him on his sixtieth and sixty-fifth birthdays to which he would not even reply. What could he have said? Only 'You've got it wrong; I was not even born in Vienna.'

The logistics of the *Cardinal* operation were as complicated as the *Exodus* tactics, requiring as much ingenuity and organisation. From Vienna, crew and cast transferred to Rome. The papal authorities were most co-operative, thanks to Signore Mario Burgognini, a prominent lawyer and Vatican expert who advised and liaised. The Pope received Otto and Hope in audience and permitted his summer residence to be used as backcloth for several episodes.

Rome was where Preminger fired the one member of his staff who was regarded as totally secure. The problem arose over the robes of priests. It appears that Pope Pius XII modernised the styles his clergy wore. The period covered by the film – 1917, 1922, 1926, 1929 – necessitated intricate juggling with the costumes in the context of each episode's date. Even with two eminent ecclesiastical fashion advisers, slip-ups were unavoidable.

Otto complained bitterly. The costume co-ordinator tried to explain that he was asking the impossible: 'It can't be done!' she protested. 'Then get out,' Otto shouted, 'and don't do it! You're fired!' The costume co-ordinator was, of course, Hope Preminger. 'He has fired me three times altogether,' Hope told me. 'Luckily, he re-engaged me every time!'

After Rome and Boston came Hollywood. Some scenes, like the Nazi vandalism in the archbishop's palace, were shot in the studio – Preminger could not very well break up the real place. *The Cardinal* was finished off in Hollywood and the generous producer-director, by way of saying 'Thank you', invited some of his loyal staff to California although they were no longer required.

The film's reception was mixed. Preminger's reputation

as a bully, actors' scourge and general hell-raiser, obviously affected some critics who no longer judged his work on its merits, a publicity backlash which he had not anticipated. There was no middle way – either they liked Preminger or they loathed him. For those who liked him he could do no wrong. For those who loathed him, he could do no right.

XXI

Ships, Cops, Blows

It is not done well; but you are surprised to find it done
at all.

SAMUEL JOHNSON

At the new offices of Sigma Productions on the top floor of
the Columbia Building, 711 Fifth Avenue, New York, the
head of the firm and star of the show Otto Preminger, fresh
from his battle with *The Cardinal*, sits behind the big desk,
his finger, like that of a quiz show competitor, on the button
of the telephone loudspeaker, ready to pounce. Deep in
thought, he leaves idly through sheaves of papers and docu-
ments before him. Secretaries, accountants, clerks enter,
whisper, report, withdraw again. The only ones who linger
are his right-hand man Bill Barnes and Jack-of-all-trades
Nat Rudich.

Preminger's eyes wander along the paintings on the walls
before returning to a bulky document on his desk. Though
he knows every paragraph by heart, he flips through the
pages with an air of satisfaction. It is a new contract which
endorses his standing in the movie industry. A contract for
five Preminger films under the protective, gilt-edged
umbrella of Paramount.

The total amount involved is around fifteen million
dollars, his share of the loot over the next few years a solid
fifteen per cent plus participation in the profit. Few independent producers can boast such a long-term vote of confidence
from financiers and distributors. Sooner or later, Preminger
must make one more picture for Columbia guaranteeing him
an additional two hundred thousand dollars.

Presently the scene shifts to Hawaii where Preminger sets
up shop to produce his version of Pearl Harbor (7 December

1941), based on James Bassett's best-selling novel *In Harm's Way* ('I wish to have no connection with any ship that does not sail fast, for I intend to go in harm's way' – John Paul Jones).

When Preminger's advance guard, headed by Eva Monley first arrived at Ilikai, Waikiki Beach, Honolulu, the new hotel was still a-building: 'We shall want forty-five rooms,' she told the manager. 'They must be ready in five weeks' time!' Prodded by Eva, the manager went to work: 'We closed the underground garage and turned it into offices,' she recalls.

It was like setting up a military command post for the combined services, army, navy and air force, with married quarters, every top brass of the forties (represented by a Hollywood star) present and correct to help depict the grimmest chapter in America's recent history. Commander-in-Chief Otto Preminger, his wife and twins, John Wayne, wife and two children, Patricia Neal, husband Roald Dahl and six-month-old baby, Kirk Douglas, wife and two sons, installed themselves in a rented house for the duration.

Recalled by Otto, the whole old gang reported for duty: Burgess Meredith, Franchot Tone, Dana Andrews, Henry Fonda, Jill Haworth, Tom Tryon, whatever the gossips said, fit and well enough to take this place. At General Preminger's personal invitation, technicians brought their wives. 'One of his human sides,' says Eva Monley. It added up to a cosy military film colony.

'What good troopers John Wayne and Kirk Douglas are!' Preminger enthuses in retrospect. Arriving, so to speak, with sealed orders, they were ready for anything the boss demanded: 'I did not even show them the script, just told them the story and they came,' he says proudly. 'I don't welcome advice from actors, they are here to act,' he adds, and recalls how he showed Paul Newman where to get off. 'He never shouted at John Wayne,' Eva Monley remembers. 'Perhaps he felt he could not.'

He did not shout at the US Defence Department either, and had no need to. The military sensed how much he, who has never worn uniform in his life, enjoyed playing at soldiers, and were most co-operative. They provided everything the director needed to re-create the Japanese attack, even gave permission for him to film at the US Pacific Command HQ. But there were limits. No C-47 and B-25 aircraft – they no longer existed. No importation of explosives into operational bases and no laying mines in Pearl Harbor by civilians. Instead, dummies were rigged up on vacant lots and wired with gas and oil for controlled fires. Still, experts guaranteed most realistic bangs – when it came to explosions, Preminger had a reputation to defend.

Most things he had previously done were larger than life. This time he controlled a fleet authentic in every detail but scaled down to three-quarters of an inch to the foot. Every destroyer carried the correct number of guns. To organise the order of battle before shooting started – shooting by his cameras – one of the sights at Pearl Harbor was Preminger in slacks, shirt-sleeves and big straw hat, standing astride the bow of one of his miniature destroyers, or in a small motorboat with the model of a US warship in tow.

Even after all those years Pearl Harbor was still a little nervous about big bangs. Arrangements were made for Honolulu radio to broadcast reassuring messages that bombardments, fire, smoke and all other war-like activity was strictly *ersatz*, made by Preminger. Everything was geared to the big moment and, to get down to brass tacks, word went out that the attack, occupying five minutes of screening time, was costing one million dollars.

Somewhere in the turmoil of war was a story line but it was not important. For Preminger, War was the star of the show: 'After all these anti-war films which seem to have been more defeatist than pacifist,' he said, 'the Navy needs a film like this!'

*　　*　　*

What does a war lord do on the eve of battle? On the night before El Alamein, Montgomery slept the sleep of the just. All his plans laid for D-Day, Eisenhower did likewise. And Preminger, while the clouds of war once more gathered over Pearl Harbor? 'Otto is impatient,' says Martin Schute, who knows the master's *modus operandi* better than most. 'The development of a story is the main fascination for him . . . His mind races ahead, and by the time he gets to shooting a picture he is already bored with it and preoccupied with the next.'

Never more so than in Hawaii. Cables went back and forth between Waikiki and London. Preminger was busy setting up the production of *Bunny Lake is Missing* (from the novel by Evelyn Piper), his next picture which was to be shot in London. Having acquired the rights some time ago, he started thinking about it while working on *The Cardinal*, now thought of little else.

A treatment – the outline of the film version – was available but the first script did not find favour with Preminger. He commissioned a second writer to try his hand – no good; and a third – no good either. 'He has this habit of having scripts done by several people,' says Schute. 'He has a tremendous sense of story construction.' Few writers live up to his expectation. Someone once said to him: 'Your construction is so good, why don't you write your own scripts?' In a mellow mood, he answered: 'How can I write scripts in English when I can't even speak it?'

He next asked the eminent London writing couple John and Penelope Mortimer to tackle *Bunny Lake*. Penelope introduced a character which was not in the book, setting Preminger a new problem. It exercised his mind and the whole Pearl Harbor business began to take second place. 'Fly the Mortimers to Honolulu,' he cabled Martin Schute. 'Come with them and bring your wife . . .'

Five dozen people were getting the big attack on Pearl Harbor under way. For ten hours every day Preminger lorded it over cast and crew. While the others relaxed of an evening and recuperated from the day's hard labour in the barmy atmosphere of Hawaii, Preminger was closeted with the Mortimers: 'He has this incredible energy,' says Schute. 'Astonishing how he switches from work on one picture to talk about the characters in another,' John Mortimer marvels. The following day he gave his guests a grandstand view of the bombing which went according to plan. Long before the smoke had settled, Preminger was back with the Mortimers and *Bunny Lake*.

Once 'In Harm's Way' was in the can, Preminger invested as much effort in promoting the movie as he had put into making it. The unveiling of his grand naval epic inaugurated the Cannes Film Festival of 1965: 'You can't force a critic to like a film,' wrote Leonard Mosley, film expert of the *Daily Express*, of the occasion, 'but you can try to create the conditions that might make him well disposed.'

To make Mosley and a hundred fellow critics well disposed, Preminger chartered an aircraft, gathered them up in London, flew them to the South of France, where they were lodged in a luxury hotel, plied with caviar and champagne at his expense – approximate cost 25,000 dollars. A marvellous time was had by all.

Only Mosley struck a sour note with his public exposure of the traditional softening-up process to which producers subject critics, none more lavishly than Preminger. The host reacted angrily: 'Mosley accepts my hospitality,' he stormed, 'then attacks me!' Leonard Mosley, it so happened, was not his guest. The *Daily Express* does not permit its correspondents to accept such inducements, always pays their fares and expenses.

The little altercation did not destroy the euphoria of Cannes. To add lustre to the occasion, Preminger imported the glamorous Diahann Carroll to entertain the critics. It was heady stuff but the reviews were on the sober side.

* * *

In London not much later Otto, surrounded by friends and acolytes, monopolised the conversation with his booming voice and an undertone which threatened: 'We have ways of making you listen!' The topic of the conversation was *Bunny Lake is Missing* which Preminger's London company 'Wheel Productions' was making for Columbia, the last of the series. It was the story – departing from the novel in several details – of a mother who loses her little girl in the confusion of moving house – did she have a daughter or was it a phantom child? – and her brother who sets out to save her sanity and murder the child.

The mid-Atlantic cast included two American stars among the cream of English acting talent – Keir Dullea, handsome, temperamental, recent winner of a Best Actor award; and Carol Lynley, dainty and glamorous even in her drab outfit which gave little scope to Otto's 'costume co-ordinator' Hope Preminger.

The backdrop to a key scene was an apartment in Carlton Mews, near Trafalgar Square where the two English principals faced each other: Noël Coward, playwright, actor, chansonnier, promoter of musical mirth and English humour, elegant, self-assured with sparkling eyes and a superior smile; and Laurence Olivier – Sir Laurence Olivier, now Lord Olivier – prince of English stage and screen, star of innumerable classics, this time playing Detective-Inspector Newhouse who investigates the Bunny Lake mystery . . .

Oblivious of lights, crew, cameras – and Preminger waiting for them to go into their routine – Coward and Olivier were enjoying themselves, chatting, giggling, laughing, their shoulders shaking as they slapped their thighs: 'Do you remember . . .?' Bursts of laughter. Forty-five years ago, in *Private Lives*, Noel Coward gave Olivier his first break on the London stage . . . Great joke! It seemed to go on for ever and ever.

Better attuned to performers who are cowed and terrified of him, Preminger watched in amazement, obviously puzzled by the private hilarity of his star performers. Feeling shut out, he shook his head in utter bewilderment, tried to get in on the act but failed miserably.

Impatient to start the scene, he looked as if he were about to explode in time-honoured fashion but thought better of it. Apart from recognising the folly of taking on the powerful Coward-Olivier combination, he was conscious of the still photographer at work, Lord Snowdon, Princess Margaret's hard-working husband, who was covering the production for the *Sunday Times*, which promised excellent publicity. Impotent and resigned for once, Preminger waited for the laughing cavaliers to stop laughing and get on with the job. Their private interlude over, the two promptly responded to his direction and completed the scene without much ado.

Leaving them to resume their nostalgic exchanges, Preminger turned to the next scene, his strictures echoing through the apartment. Now it was Olivier's turn to be bewildered. Shaking his head in disbelief, he was heard muttering: 'Does he always scream like this?'

For another scene the production moved to the casualty ward of the West London Hospital. In a gloomy corridor crowded with film equipment, Preminger watched from behind the camera which was focused on Keir Dullea who is no Tom Tryon and showed no nerves. But the tension between star and director was evident: 'You are not doing what I want . . .!' the director shouted in exasperation and stopped the fourth take. He started to splutter and his unintelligible screams sounded insulting. Keir Dullea was getting very angry. Restraining himself as long as he could, he finally burst out: 'Why don't you let me play the f . . . . . . scene as I f . . . . . . well want to play it? You are driving me f . . . . . . mad!'

Preminger had found his match, just managed to hiss: 'Once more . . . Action!' Keir regained his cool, repeated the scene, bubbling below the surface. 'Cut!' Preminger exclaimed, 'Marvellous! Marvellous! Just what I wanted!'

and proudly claimed another success for his screaming tactics.

Noel Coward came to take his leave: 'I say, Otto, let's do a play together. Soon.'

Preminger: 'I'd love to do a Coward play, but most of them have been done.'

Coward: 'I'd like you to direct something of mine because I've thoroughly enjoyed my brief encounter with you on the screen.'

Preminger: 'Speaking of brief encounters, I once directed three one-act plays on television and one of them, I think, was *Brief Encounter*.'

Coward: 'Who was playing? Ginger?'

Preminger: 'Ginger Rogers and that wonderful English actor, Trevor Howard.'

Coward: 'He played the original on the screen . . .'

They were off on the wings of memory.

Bunny Lake is Missing earned no laurels, least of all from Otto Preminger: 'A small story,' he says. 'Not a successful film.'

On the top floor of Preminger's New York house on East 64 Street, Otto, Hope, Mark and Vicky were watching Batman and Robin triumphing over evil on the television screen, the twins shrieking with delight and horror. 'Daddy,' Mark asked with a small voice, 'could you be Batman?'

'I could try,' Daddy answered.

The birth of an idea. Without much difficulty, Otto arranged to insinuate himself into a 'Batman' episode playing 'Mr Freeze', George Sanders's old part. Otto-Freeze thrives on temperatures fifty below and lower and tries to freeze all others. A congenial part. It culminated in a confrontation with Batman and Robin who trip Otto up in the end, but do not kill him: 'They never do,' Preminger explains knowledgeably. 'They might want to use the character again. Perhaps Alfred Hitchcock next time!'

'Papa' Preminger will do anything for the twins: 'He takes

Mark to watch baseball,' Hope told me. It is a sacrifice. Otto is not interested in sport, does not understand baseball but suffers gladly for Mark's sake. Not much later he took Mark to join his first summer camp, very American. Mark did not enjoy it and Otto began to have doubts. Not many more camps for Mark whose forte is brain not brawn.

After a pleasant meal, Otto and Hope were about to leave the Twenty-One Club. Squeezing by agent Irving Lazar's table, Otto glowered. Lazar, through whom Preminger had hoped to buy the mòvie rights in Truman Capote's *In Cold Blood*, a gilt-edged proposition, had sold to Director Richard Brooks instead – for half a million dollars. Otto seemed to raise his hand and little Lazar looked terrified, later swore he thought Otto was about to hit him. Jumping up, he picked up a glass goblet and smashed it over Preminger's bald head.

Blood pouring from a long, deep, jagged cut, Preminger slumped. Hope comforted her husband, hustled him out of the club and drove him to an emergency ward where his head was stitched up. 'Fifty stitches' the news flashed round the world.

Friends telephoned from the four corners of the world to express sympathy, among them Bill Batchelor from London: 'I am sorry to read in the papers that you've been hurt. How are you feeling?'

'Fine!'

'You feel fine with fifty stitches?'

'You are incorrect. Fifty-one stitches!'

The assault left no visible scar on Otto's forehead and no other impact either.

XXII

Baton Rouge and other Battles

With three and a half million dollars in the kitty for his next project, Preminger quickly seized on another controversial subject. His spies informed him that Burt and Katia Gilden had just completed a novel set in rural Georgia, a Deep South drama of racial conflict in the post-war years of 1946–1947, prospective title: *Hurry Sundown*.

When shown the manuscript, Preminger was enthusiastic and certain that this was another *Gone With the Wind*. To nip competition in the bud, he offered 200,000 dollars for the film rights which clinched the deal (in the event, *Hurry Sundown* sold 300,000 copies, not bad but not sensational either.)

Preminger's idea was to shoot the film in the novel's original setting. The reaction was violent. Georgia would have nothing, nothing at all to do with a movie showing 'niggers gettin' the better of whites' or 'noble blacks scoring off white trash'. He next tried Atlanta but the answer was as dusty: 'Not here!'

Otto's friend Gene Callihan, Hollywood art director and stage designer with two Oscars to his credit, suggested Baton Rouge, Louisiana, some seventy miles up the Mississippi from New Orleans: 'Louisiana', said Callihan, who was born in Baton Rouge, 'looks better in colour than Georgia.'

He visited the city of his birth, inspected suitable locations and produced an impressive report. When Preminger went to see for himself, he immediately put a scheme in hand to 'improve' the landscape and engaged a large work force to carry it out. To lend verisimilitude to a big flood scene, they built a big dam and a reservoir holding seventeen and a half million gallons of water. Cornfields were planted and sharecroppers' cabins erected.

Though greedy for crumbs from the producer's well-endowed exchequer, Baton Rouge was yet tardy with co-operation. Shooting in the church – the Elders said: 'No!' In the courthouse – the judge objected. In the general store – out of the question. Weary of the constant battles and in utter desperation, Eva Monley summoned Preminger from New York: 'He came and schmalzed everybody into compliance,' she says, as always full of admiration. All except the store owner. No problem. Preminger built a store of his own.

Crew and cast were accommodated in the colonial-style Bellemont Motor Hotel, second biggest motel in the United States but there was no question of just putting Preminger into the best of the available rooms. Knowing her boss, Eva Monley had one apartment specially rebuilt: 'I had a couple of walls removed and the place redecorated for him,' she says.

On 1 June the big man himself arrived with the script, a tight chronicle of pride, passion and plunder. The temperature was in the upper nineties when Otto with Hope, twins and Nanny reached the apartment. Entering, he collided with a solid wall of hot air: 'Phew! Put the air conditioning on!' he demanded. 'No air conditioning,' Eva said with a small voice. Otto looked uncomprehending. 'Sabotage!' she whispered. Otto could not understand: 'What have you been doing here for weeks?' he bellowed. Eva was resigned to this sort of thing: 'He made me feel it was all my fault,' she recalls.

The one solitary coat-hanger dangling in the wardrobe caught his eye. He could hardly contain himself: 'One coat-hanger?' His dozen suits, Hope's clothes, the children's, the Nanny's: 'One coat-hanger! Go out and buy two dozen!' Eva was glad to get away.

He had hardly settled in when the telephone rang. It was an anonymous call, the first of many. The post brought a dozen threatening letters and they kept coming. The Ku-Klux-Klan put it about that the whole Preminger outfit would go up in flames and the locals were terrified. A call from the producer secured a promise of support from the authorities. With so much money at stake for the city, state troopers were despatched to guard the Bellemont.

Inside the cast was settling down and making the best of a bad job – little Jane Fonda, pouting feline; Michael Caine (*Alfie*, *The Ipcress File*), another Englishman converted into a Southerner by Preminger and collecting 20,000 dollars a week for his efforts; John Philip Law, almost too handsome to be true; Burgess Meredith, of course; Faye Dunaway, the exciting young newcomer, signed up for a string of films (not tightly enough, it turned out); blonde, seductive starlet Donna Danton; and three black stars, Robert Hooks, Rex Ingram and the delectable Diahann Carroll.

The state troopers were alert but powerless against the enemy within. Preminger was not. When Diahann, Robert and Rex wanted to cool off in one of the Bellemont's three swimming pools, they were advised to go away – no mixed bathing, no mixing of races. Preminger exploded: 'Get me the manager!' He threatened to move his whole outfit out lock, stock and barrel unless . . . The manager collapsed. The swimming pools were integrated.

Preminger's day started at 8 a.m. with a dip in the pool, followed by breakfast with Hope and the twins. The blistering heat soon crumpled his splendidly laundered shirt and slacks, brought pearls of perspiration to his face. His shaven head glistened in the sun. The atmosphere was oppressive, but it was the Ku-Klux-Klan, not Preminger, who created the terror. The unit was under constant guard: 'An aura of fear hangs over this place,' someone said.

Police outriders flanked Preminger's car as he drove to the location and, on sound advice, he changed drivers and routes every day. But before long snobbery and celebrity-worship triumphed. The State's Democratic Governor John Mac-

Keithen invited Preminger to address the Legislature. It was a splendid performance. Rising to the occasion, Preminger exclaimed: 'Bless the people of Louisiana! Bless America!' His reward was a standing ovation. On television he thanked the people of Louisiana for being so broadminded and allowing his film to be made in their State. Speaking in his wake, Alabama Governor George Wallace was not so broadminded.

'Governor and Mrs MacKeithen would like to entertain Mr and Mrs Preminger at dinner . . .' The suggestion was offered informally with a discreet hint that the Governor and his Lady expected their guests to bring the movie's stars along – the white ones, that is. 'Either all my stars are invited or I should have to decline,' was Preminger's blunt answer. No formal invitation was issued. Blandly, Preminger invited the Governor to attend his dinner for visiting French pressmen. The Governor was delighted to accept. Preminger was a genial host but none of his stars attended the dinner, no black stars, no white stars.

But even Preminger's ardour dampened in the heat and life under constant threat of violence and sabotage. Almost as good as its threats, the KKK was active at Francisville where the unit was shooting: 'Be out of here by 8 p.m.!' the Klan warned. Hurrying uncharacteristically, Preminger managed to get cast and technicians away in time. Still, he never lost his rough sense of humour. When one of his production assistants in search of a 'White Only' sign boarded a Mississippi barge while Preminger watched from the bank, the crew threatened to throw the terrified young man into the river: 'What's the matter with you,' Preminger shouted across to him, 'can't you swim?'

Some thought he was beginning to feel the strain. Not really. He simply reverted to type, dismissed a cameraman and a girl secretary, the daughter of the Mayor of Baton Rouge and sent scriptwriter Tom Ryan packing. So many people got the sack that 'heavy breathing' filled the Bellemont's corridors and the crew renamed Preminger's Sigma Productions 'Asthma Productions'.

Insults flew as usual. As often before, Preminger followed a pattern of his own in selecting his principal victims, was insufferably beastly with John Philip Law and Donna Danton – Preminger watchers swear that handsome young actors and actresses are his favourite targets – but was impeccably polite to Jane Fonda and Michael Caine with whom he formed a close friendship: 'I like him,' Caine told me later.

For the press, Preminger's behaviour was grist to their mills. Reporters described him as 'the most hated man in the movie industry', and one of them called him 'The monster who knows how to draw attention to himself.' Words like 'exhibitionist' and 'sadist' were bandied about. His technique came under fire: 'He handles a camera like a meat cleaver,' wrote Rex Reed who, like Preminger, knows how to hit where it hurts most. When he tried to be nice Preminger did not fare much better: 'A compound of flattery, schmalz and heavy-footed mittel-European humour,' was how his lighter mood was described.

The subtlety which went into one scene was enough to belie Reed's verdict. It showed Jane Fonda sitting at the feet of Michael Caine blowing seductively into a saxophone, a typical example of Preminger's knack of creating images in people's minds, sexy, suggestive, releasing inhibitions . . . When the publicity boys selected the scene to advertise the film, not without his prompting, the London censor stepped in: 'We had some trouble over the saxophone scene,' says John Trevelyan. 'I did not want it advertised. I gave the film an "A" certificate – any child could go. It stopped the distributors publicising this kind of scene!'

Threats, difficulties, danger – to have the picture shot on location seemed to make it all worth while. The church scene with the local congregation singing their own hymns was not only realistic, it was real: 'Could not be done in Hollywood,'

Preminger crowed. Painstakingly, day after day, he put his three, four, five minutes screening time on film, a total of 174 minutes. It was excruciatingly boring work to all not immediately employed on the set – and to many of them as well. The repetitiveness, the routine, the tyranny in the interest of perfection as he saw it suited Preminger's temperament.

Alas, *Hurry Sundown* was not a success. Not with the critics, not with the public. Preminger's greatest accolade was the badge of a Sheriff of Baton Rouge, ceremonially conferred on him.

From racial conflict to unruly youth, from Baton Rouge, Louisiana, to San Francisco, California. Otto Preminger in hippieland was hoping to come to terms with the new generation, very much like an ox trying to mate with a butterfly. Suddenly he found himself saddled with a subject into which he had slithered by accident, and in spite of his highly professional show of enthusiasm and involvement wished he hadn't.

While working on a screen version of John Hershey's, *Too Far to Walk* which seemed too deep to screen – at least for him – and going through the routine of gobbling up scriptwriters by the score, Preminger came across a screenplay by Dorian Wm. Cannon which instantly struck a chord. An ageing square, Otto had only recently discovered his natural son Erik who had told him about his life as a drop-out and a couple of bad 'trips' in Greenwich Village . . .

That's what Bill Cannon's screenplay was all about except that it was set in San Francisco, cradle of hippie culture. Since the Hershey project was clearly not on, Otto turned to the hippie saga: 'It's a comedy,' he said, 'and I haven't done a comedy in a long time.' Not since *The Moon is Blue*. 'A comedy like this,' he went on, 'a far-out, wild farce comedy is meaningless if explained . . .' It could also be meaningless if screened.

By way of preparation Preminger went to see Dr Sidney Cohen, expert on hallucinatory drugs, under whose supervision he took a 'trip', much like young Austrian archdukes at the beginning of the century took their first conducted tours into the mystery of sex. Preminger did not get very high, did not jump out of a window, but felt the experience had taught him enough about the subject to discuss it with the hippies of San Francisco and work on the script with the author of the 'original screenplay' and with Elliott Baker whom he called in to supply the final polish.

For the production, in spite of all he ever said, Preminger returned to a Hollywood studio. 'It's a tricky set,' he claimed. Anyway, he had never said he was against shooting in a studio. So there! His stars were not exactly of the hippie generation – George Raft, Groucho Marx, Burgess Meredith, Peter Lawford, Carol Channing. Jackie Gleason was the one who had to act out what Preminger felt during his 'trip'.

The inclusion of John Philip Law, of *Hurry Sundown* memory, in the cast was fortuitous because his younger brother happened to be a drop-out living with a hippie community in the mountains. Finding Hollywood professionals impersonating hippies much too stagey, Preminger invited the two hundred inhabitants of the hippie colony down from the hills, put them on the payroll to play themselves in the comedy which he called *Skidoo*.

With his sense of humour questionable at the best of times, his *rapport* with the hippies was, to say the least, imperfect. Fergus Cashin, the English film writer, was one of the few who extracted some fun from the situation. Visiting the Preminger outfit on the coast, the first thing he saw was Jackie Gleason in a giant trash can suspended from a balloon crash-landing on the deck of a yacht (John Wayne's, hired for the occasion). It was the highlight of a trash can ballet. 'Cut!' yelled Otto Preminger. 'Go cut your throat!' the hippies and actors echoed in chorus.

Groucho Marx, cigar stuck in the corner of his mouth, was looking out of a porthole: 'How the hell did you get here?' snarled George Raft. 'Yer walk on the water or something?'

'We didn't see your signal, Otto,' Jackie Gleason complained. 'May I ask you, please, why?' Preminger countered. 'Because your bald head was shining in our eyes!'

Said Carol Channing: 'This is wild. Someone should shoot Otto directing this film . . .' Groucho Marx: 'Someone should shoot Otto – period!'

If only the script had been as amusing as the impromptu exchanges. Instead, the whole thing was a disaster. Said *Time* Magazine: 'Ostensibly a comedy, *Skidoo* was produced and directed by Otto Preminger, who has also unleashed on an unwary public such titbits as *Hurry Sundown* and *In Harm's Way*. He is funnier when he is serious.'

Preminger between pictures – never! Plans overlap. Private life is virtually non-existent. The occasional dinner party at home, coffee and brandy in the top-floor private cinema where he screens the latest, sometimes as yet unreleased, movies. On other evenings, he is out to restaurants, new shows, film premiéres, functions (like the opening gala of the Kennedy Center), old and new night-clubs.

'Otto works at a high level of tension,' says Nat Rudich. 'Something has to happen all the time. It's a twenty-four hour job.'

Rudich is one of the associates with whom he lunches at Twenty-One or Côte Basque, President Nixon's favourite New York restaurant, on the ground floor of 711 Fifth Avenue.

'Have some fruit!' Preminger hospitably invites Nat Rudich.

'Strawberries, please!'

'Why strawberries?' Otto counters with a tinge of irritation. 'Why not blueberries like me?' Then dictatorially:

'Have blueberries!' Rudich has blueberries: 'It's easier to do as he says than to argue,' he sighs in an aside.

Back at the office: 'What about the plumber? Has the plumber been to the house? If he does not come before three, the maid will have gone and he can't get in. Rudich! Check when the plumber is coming. Call the house and see that the maid stays!'

The problem which keeps the office humming is little Mark's new bathroom. Elaborate design, new layout, made to size, a major plumbing job. Mark's voice comes over the loudspeaker:

'Hello, Daddy . . .'

'Mark, how are you? . . . Goodbye. I love you!'

'Goodbye, Daddy. I love you!'

It's the turn of Mark's sister next: 'Hello, Missie . . . I love you!'

'Hello, Daddy . . . Goodbye. I love you!'

It's a family game. Otto beams.

The secretary is on the inter-com: 'Mr Preminger, your brother . . .'

'Hello, Ingo . . .'

Ingo is quitting agency work: 'I am making a movie . . .' He tells Otto all about it.

'I was fed up putting deals together for others,' Ingo tells me, 'watching other people do it, like a voyeur. I knew I could do it myself.'

After thirty years as an agent acting for clients, he has acquired the film rights in a novel called $M \cdot A \cdot S \cdot H$ for himself: 'A juxtaposition of laughter and love, a good mixture. I was sure it would be either a complete flop or an enormous success!' Ingo sent the book to Dick Zanuck, Darryl's son and successor (at the time) and made his deal with Twentieth Century Fox inside a week, engaged Ring Lardner junior to write the script, Robert Altman to direct. The 'nice Preminger' is content to sign as producer.

Big Brother Otto, in the meantime, was off on another

off-beat venture. He has read a novel called *Tell Me That You Love Me, Junie Moon*: 'It fascinated me,' he says. 'The three characters, their courage, the idea of three disabled people deciding to pool their disabilities and make a life for themselves, not to depend on charity or pity.'

Having set up the deal in brisk negotiations, he has got Liza Minnelli to take the part of a girl who has acid thrown in her face ('Acid in the wrong face!' the anti-Preminger brigade quips predictably), shacks up with a paraplegic homosexual and a stuttering epileptic: 'It's not epilepsy,' Preminger declared gravely, 'but an undiagnosed disease.'

Before showing the film in London, Preminger decided to consult John Trevelyan, the British film censor, seeking his personal view and official sanction. Together they watched the film in a private cinema in London. Trevelyan told me he was aghast at the scene in which acid is thrown into Liza Minnelli's face and she writhes in agony on the floor: 'This scene must be cut out!' he told Preminger.

'You are a butcher!' Otto protested.

'And you are a sadist!' Trevelyan countered.

The reaction to the picture was devastating: 'Tell Me Why You Do It, Otto Preminger,' one critic asked and added: 'His record for debasing the popular to the vulgar is unblemished.'

'Don't you think critics and public did you an injustice when they rejected your film?' Pem, film expert and old friend, asked Preminger: 'I don't understand you,' Preminger retorted: 'I don't make movies for my own pleasure. If press and audience reject a film of mine, I am, of course, wrong!'

Otto Preminger's *Junie Moon* was shown at the Cannes Film Festival at the same time as Ingo Preminger's *M·A·S·H*. *M·A·S·H* ran away with all the honours, *Junie Moon* was nowhere: 'I was not really in competition with my brother,' the nice Preminger said good-naturedly. 'The movie with which *M·A·S·H* was competing was *Catch 22*.'

'Ingo had a tremendous success,' says Otto.

Preminger's prestige was low and he was desperate for
another success, another *Exodus*, perhaps. Washington journalist Dan Kurzman has written the perfect sequel, *Genesis,
1948*, the painful birth of the State of Israel, the late British
Foreign Secretary Ernest Bevin's anti-Jewish policy, the
Labour government's machinations to prevent peace between Jews and Arabs in 1949. Dirty work behind the scenes
of Whitehall. King Abdullah of Jordan crying out: 'Only
the British are to blame! Only the British!'

Preminger worked hard to put a deal together, tried hard
to rope in British Jews, New York associates, Hollywood
companies and the perennial Meyer Weisgal. It was not
easy. For once, he seemed rattled. To curry favour with the
Jews he accepted an invitation to attend the World Conference on Soviet Jewry in Brussels and lent his name to
stimulate interest.

On 5 March 1971 with the World Conference smug in
the after-glow of the previous week's impressive show of
unity, Preminger, an honoured guest, took his seat among
delegates from all over the world. That day, Rabbi Meir
Kahane, the vocal, charismatic leader of the militant Jewish
Defence League of New York, tried to gatecrash the conference. Afraid lest he preach activism and violence and
harden Soviet attitudes, the organisers refused his admit-
tance. The result was dispute across the conference hall and
uproar.

Preminger, unable to contain himself, erupted with a
typical outburst: 'This conference, by barring Rabbi
Kahane, is reacting in the same contemptible way as the
Nazis and the Russian Communists!' was his ill-chosen
protest. Reporters' typewriters clattered. Preminger made
headlines all right for the World Conference. One of the
extremists who supported him was Menachem Begin, Israeli
politician and ex-leader of the violent Irgun underground.

The bulk of the conference was stunned and hurt by Preminger's uninhibited attack. This was not the way to obtain Jewish goodwill. Totally lacking in political judgment, he had no idea what he had done, no notion of the difference between liberty and licence. Rabbi Kahane was expelled from Belgium. Preminger was forced to retract his remarks. *Genesis, 1948* would have to wait for another day.

XXIII

Cut! Print! Very Good!

> Stars no longer exist because the director no longer
> exists in a supporting capacity; he has himself become
> the star, his style unmistakable and his performers
> interchangeable as likely as not green newcomers.
> Hildegard Knef in *The Gift Horse*

Coloured lights flash wildly as Otto Preminger manipulates
the instrument panel below the marble table. One button
closes the shutters across the wide window, another releases
a big silvery screen which covers the whole length of the
wall, a third gives the projectionist the go-ahead.

In his own comfortable screening-room with Hope,
cameraman and cutter in attendance he is watching rushes
of the previous day's shooting of his latest film, *Such Good
Friends*, based on Lois Gould's best-selling novel – 'the most
intimate novel a woman ever wrote'.

A key scene is going across the screen. Cal Whiting, played
by Ken Howard, a Preminger stalwart, is perched on top
of the lusciously sexy Julie Messinger – Dyan Cannon,
America's latest film find and in private life the divorced
wife of Cary Grant and mother of his pretty five-year-old
daughter.

Although only faces and bare shoulders of the combatants
on the carpet are showing – in outsize close-ups and glittering
technicolour – the motions and the accompanying dialogue
leave nothing to the imagination.

Julie: 'Many men lose their erection when they attempt
intercourse for the first time with a new woman.'

Cal: 'Well, I don't. For years I had intercourse with new
women only, Goddamit.'

Julie: 'I would say this isn't working out well.'

Cal: 'Goddamit, Julie, I'm going to lay you if it takes me all night.'

Adept at handling titivating situations in life and on screen, Preminger casts an expert eye on his handiwork. The action is preceded – and interrupted – by studio noises and his own voice ('Action!' . . . 'Stop!' . . . 'Action!' . . . 'Cut, print, very good!') but there is no question about the impact of the uninhibited cameo.

For Preminger this is a critical time. *Such Good Friends* is the fifth and, so far, last of his five contracted films for Paramount. None of the preceding four was an outstanding success. *Such Good Friends* is the crunch – success or failure might determine whether Preminger and Paramount would remain such good friends.

This particular operation started a year or so earlier while *Junie Moon* was still in the editing stage. Everywhere Preminger scouts were on the qui vive. In publishing houses up and down the United States, in England, France and Germany they had their ears to the ground. They knew that, as always, Preminger was looking for a potential best-seller. The important thing for him was to get his hands on a useful property before publication and before another greedy producer could snap it up.

Within a week or so a whisper reached his office. An exciting project was in the making, a new novel by a woman author which had been written and rewritten and turned out extremely well. The massive Preminger juggernaut rumbled into action to secure the rights. Combining gentle persuasion with a tempting, if tentative, offer, Preminger's adopted son Erik, his story scout and casting director, obtained a copy of the manuscript for Otto Preminger to read. Otto's wife Hope read it, Erik read it, Nat Rudich read it. There was a good deal of discussion among them.

The book had the basic ingredients of success. Human drama, sex, humour, fantasy, set in a milieu which Preminger thoroughly understands. A story of tangled relations in New

York's intellectual belt in the permissive age. Preminger bought it on the spot. He sent a copy to Paramount whose OK was needed to set the finance machinery in motion but did not wait for a reaction before putting the deal through. If it was good – and he was convinced it was – it was worth paying for. He offered a generous price, and guaranteed the author a bonus for every week the book appeared in the *New York Times* Best-seller List.

'It's a woman's story which needs a woman scriptwriter!' Preminger decided. He was thinking of Elaine May but she was involved in a project of her own, writing, directing and acting, and could not make time. He engaged Joan Silver to work with him on the script but her part in the proceedings lasted only two weeks. No other suitable woman writer came to mind. Preminger remembered the fictionalised story about *Playboy* Heffner by David Slavitt, took him on but their association was also short-lived.

In the summer of 1970 the Premingers moved from New York to Los Angeles. A husband-and-wife team, novelist Joan Didion and John Dunne took up where the other writers had left off. They worked with Otto through the summer but when he returned to New York they refused to move East. End of another chapter in the scripting of *Such Good Friends*.

Assigned to comb the literary scene for writer Number Six, Erik Preminger came up with David Shaver, author of short stories and television features, a bright young man who ought to have brought a fresh mind to bear on the subject. It did not work out.

It was nearly a year since Preminger first thought of Elaine May. When approached once more, she was free and willing. With telephone calls and visitors barred, she and Otto completed the script, working at his house or at the office on and off for the next ten weeks.

Dissecting the finished manuscript, Preminger decided to allocate ten weeks to the shooting – all on location in New York – preceded by three weeks rehearsal. Contracts would be drawn up for ten weeks which would seem to give performers a higher pay rate than if made out to include rehearsals – movie people are prone to this kind of self-deception and pretence which fools no one in the trade.

Imagination might carry one away with a glamourised notion of the next stage in the proceedings – the producer in his office making generous use of the casting couch, intimate dinners in night-clubs so that director and star might get to know each other better.

Instead we have Nat Rudich trotting up to the Sixth Avenue HQ of IATSE (International Alliance of Theatrical and Stage Employees) to negotiate conditions of work – 'They are different in New York from any other part of the US' – haggling with union bosses, co-ordinating pay scales and timetables with those of the Teamsters who also represent members of the film's work force.

A skilled backseat driver, Preminger issued instructions to Rudich: 'I want to work to West Coast rules!' He may not like the Hollywood label, but labour out there was more alive to the needs of movie makers. When does a working day begin? At 8 a.m. or when shooting starts? Each union has its own rules. How many working hours before meal-times? Six for one union, five for another. In England, it is said, 'everything stops for tea', but at least everybody stops at the same time!

No sooner were satisfactory agreements reached when there was a major upheaval. Unions started demanding – and negotiating – new working rules for the whole industry. For the Preminger team, caught in the switch-over, it meant re-negotiating their agreements. Preminger insisted on a no-strike clause and had his way.

Casting was now a matter of urgency. Watching the highly successful film *Bob and Carol and Ted and Alice*, Preminger was impressed by Dyan Cannon in the part which earned her the New York Film Critics Award. She looked handsome and sexy, very much as he visualised the Julie Messinger of

Such Good Friends, intellectual, Bohemian, Jewish – Dyan is, in fact, half Jewish.

Preminger wanted to make doubly sure. One night, in the pouring rain, he, Erik and Nat Rudich drove to Long Island to watch a sneak preview of *The Anderson Tapes* which was still being edited and at least six months away from release. Again, he liked Dyan Cannon in her small part. Next, the Preminger brains trust went to see the Columbia-Mike Frankovich film *Doctors' Wives* with Dyan Cannon. Otto's mind was made up: 'She looks right!' he decided.

Dyan Cannon was in California and Erik, who was going there on personal business anyway, met her and gave her the script. She was about to take off for Europe on holiday – with a two-hour stop-over in New York. Otto met her at Kennedy Airport; they talked, discussed the script. She agreed she was right for the part.

Her agent made it clear that Dyan was not going cheap but Preminger signed her just the same. Next he took up his option on Ken Howard with whom he had worked well on *Junie Moon* and who seemed perfect for the part of Cal Whiting. The usual off-beat casting was Jimmy Coco, comfortable and rotund, another *Junie Moon* veteran, unlikely victim of Julie's seductive urge. And there was Burgess Meredith.

As he watched the 9.30 a.m. television show, 'Men Only', one of the three women panellists caught Preminger's eye. Nina Foch had the voice, appearance, manner for the part of Dyan Cannon's film mother. 'Celebrity Service' gave Erik the name of her agent – she was free and happy to oblige. Other parts were quickly filled.

Production designer Rouben Ter-Arutunian (*The Loved One*) investigated locations. Long sequences are set in hospital – for a consideration of not much below 50,000 dollars, at an educated guess, facilities were arranged with a Fifth Avenue clinic. The Guggenheim Museum agreed to two scenes being shot in the galleries. Bonwit Teller permitted the heroine to chose her bridal gown in the authentic setting of the store's wedding department. The Shakespeare Festival Theatre in Central Park provided the background for another episode.

For the multiple motor crash which figures in the script the New York police department willingly promised to close a street near the Lincoln Arts Center for a day or more – inconceivable that any American authority or institution should refuse to accommodate a film producer, however great the disruption or inconvenience to others.

Photographing on water is intricate at the best of times, and one scene set in a yacht caused a lot of headaches. It could not be done without hiring a captain, and not even Preminger could expect to control the tide. He transferred the scene to a roof garden with a fine view of the New York skyline.

With the beginning of the production only weeks away, negotiations for the use of an apartment for several important scenes were hanging fire. The managers of a well-known Manhattan co-operative apartment building were willing but some of the owners objected. With time running out – and known to be running out – the managers of another building hitched the price higher and higher, expecting Preminger to give in under time pressure. They ought to have known better: 'I will not be held to ransom,' he thundered. Ingo's daughter came to the rescue and arranged for the use of an apartment in her block on Central Park, West.

Recalling some splendid photographic work by cameraman Gayne Rescher in *Rachel, Rachel*, Preminger went to see another film photographed by him, *John and Mary* (with Dustin Hoffman). Then he remembered Rescher way back refusing a job as stand-by cameraman and insisting with Preminger-like obstinacy: 'I don't stand by, I shoot!' Here was a man after his own heart. Though free from February, Rescher agreed to wait without pay for work on *Such Good*

Friends to start in July and was engaged as Director of Photography.

Production manager Roger Rothstein started out with high hopes but was soon disillusioned – or perhaps Preminger was disillusioned with him. Rowdy exchanges culminating in a final clash – and Rothstein's departure on the third day of shooting. The able Nat Rudich, all things to Preminger stepped into the breach as Associate Producer (Production Manager).

The second Associate Producer (Casting Director) listed in the credits: Erik Preminger. Costume Co-ordinator: Hope Preminger. Nothing if not loyal to his own, Otto made sure that a fair slice of his payroll stayed in the family.

Orson Welles may pooh-pooh the mystique surrounding a movie director ('Anyone can direct') but Hildegard Knef is closer to the truth when she describes the director as the star. It is certainly true of Otto Preminger. He leaves his actors in no doubt about what he wants and discourages individual notions or interpretations. After three weeks of rehearsals he expects the stars to be word perfect and to know their place in every sense.

By the time I join the operation in August 1971, more than half the film is securely in the can and half the cast and crew at loggerheads with Otto Preminger. When not actually before the cameras, Dyan Cannon keeps as far away from him as possible. No private word passes between director and star. As his friend, I am separated from Miss Cannon by an invisible dividing line which is never crossed.

The brooding silence between the two adversaries is only broken by a noisy row which ensues when Otto instructs Dyan to strip for a key scene: 'Absolutely No!' she declares. Otto pleads with uncharacteristic sweetness but the answer is still 'No!' He threatens – without effect. 'Perhaps she does not like her own body,' he quips. But he is very sore. The break is complete.

Otto will not be frustrated. Since his script requires Julie Messinger to be seen in the nude in a photograph, Preminger has a picture taken of another nude girl – she happens to be Erik's girl-friend – and Dyan Cannon's head superimposed. Dyan is livid, prowls the set like an angry lioness waiting to pounce at the first opportunity.

In the meantime, Preminger and his unit are taking over the third-floor apartment in Central Park, West. Cables loom up from a mobile generator in the street and link up with the spot-lights grouped like a battery of heavy guns around the bulky camera. Sharp, angry rays flash aggressively. The whole paraphernalia of technical equipment concentrates ominously on the spot where the principal characters will step into view.

Passage, kitchen, servants' quarters are fit to burst with people. The unit hogs the drawing-room, bedroom, dressing-room, soon spills over into another flat a few floors up. Some sixty people await Preminger's appearance. He arrives at 8.30 a.m., surveys the extraordinary but familiar scene with a jaundiced early morning eye. No reaction.

A young lady who turns out to be the owner of the apartment clutches her tiny lap-dog to her bosom and tries desperately to keep him quiet and herself out of camera range, is driven out of her own bedroom, the lights, the camera, the technicians in hot pursuit. Lost in a deep armchair, Erik Preminger quietly reads the script of another film. Buddy Rosenthal, press and publicity man, settles next to a young freelance journalist with a tape recorder and a three-hundred-dollar retainer from the *New York Times Magazine* for an article on Preminger – if accepted, the fee to be a thousand dollars.

Designer Ter-Arutunian tries to conduct a conversation with Hope Preminger who is attended by her handsome bearded deputy, the spitting image of Ken Howard. A man with a record under his arm ('Everything You Always Wanted to Know about News') and looking like a song-plugger happens to be the composer of the background music; he joins Pierre Sauvage, erudite, young French-American film enthusiast who helped to prepare a season of Preminger films in France and graduated to the job of Erik Preminger's assistant (which he has since given up).

Least aggressive man present is the stunt expert waiting to discuss the street accident scene he is hired to direct. Preminger's attention is riveted on a handsome young blonde, Dyan Cannon's stand-in, who is gripping the rails of the drawing-room cocktail bar and stretching her slim legs: 'What are you doing?' his voice explodes in her face like an anti-personnel grenade. 'You are ruining the furniture! It's not civilised!' (A favourite expression.) The girl blushes, shrugs her shoulders with the resignation of one not in the position to answer back and disappears, presumably to contemplate the nature of civilised behaviour.

A man nails 'No Smoking' signs on doors which fail to persuade the half-dozen smokers to stub out their cigarettes. Scene shifters and electricians put the final touches on a corner of the room. Shown a lamp which will be in shot, Preminger nods silent approval. He prides himself on personally attending to the smallest detail.

In a cluster around the camera, first assistant director, assistant to production manager, property master and 'gaffer' (with the German aristocratic name of Willy Meyerhoff) co-ordinate proceedings with Jack Priestley, operating cameraman. Gayne Rescher and Preminger give the go-ahead.

Dyan Cannon peels away from the crowd, followed by dresser and hairdresser, and takes up position *vis-a-vis* 'family doctor' Jimmy Coco. The lights come on. An ear-shattering 'Quiet Please!' echoes and re-echoes half a dozen times down the line, followed by Preminger's final command:

'Action!' With a wicked smile around her full lips and dia-
bolical determination in her eyes, Dyan Cannon proceeds to
open Jimmy Coco's fly . . .

From early morning a section of Sixty-Third Street is
closed to traffic. Some ten or twelve vehicles including several
cabs are lined up for the multiple crash. A big camera with
a lever which raises the platform carrying cameraman and
director hovers over the street.

On the platform Preminger high above the small army of
assistants, technicians and actors – no wonder a movie
director, as he surveys the little earth-bound creatures below
feels like God.

The scene involves Dyan Cannon diving recklessly into the
traffic to hail a cab, and Ken Howard running after her and
just managing to save her from being run over. Though
skilled drivers man the cars, stars must not be exposed to the
slightest risk. Dyan Cannon's double is standing by to take
her place at the critical moment when she is grabbed, pulled
out of danger and ends up sprawling in the street. Ken
Howard's double, a stuntman with identical beard and blond
hair (skilful make-up) is waiting to step in for the 'dangerous'
bit.

Dyan Cannon watches from a table in the corner café
which is crowded with Preminger auxiliaries. She looks lively
and well after a day's indisposition which has held up shooting. In old trooper tradition she has Jenifer, her little
daughter, with her, attended by a black nurse and perfectly
at ease among show people.

What goes on in a star's mind during the interminable
waiting for her cue? Dyan's poker face gives no hint of
concern about her impending court battle with Cary Grant,
who wants his ex-wife to comply with a court order giving
him custody of Jenifer for one month a year. No hint – except
for sudden surges of possessive affection when she hugs the
child.

With the stunt expert's help, Preminger's no-nonsense direction ploughs through the tricky scene well inside the allotted time. One of the stuntmen car drivers jars his ribs in the final crash but the stars are intact. The scene is, of course, a big fake such as is perpetrated in every movie because most film stars cannot ride, wrestle, run or do anything much out of the ordinary; nor dream of exposing themselves to danger.

Audiences like nothing better than to be deceived and applaud the fakes which are part and parcel of the movie business. Which says a lot about movie mentality and movie morality. Risk ceases to be risk, false pretence becomes negotiable currency, substitutes are the real thing and make-believe is doubly compounded. The Gods of Hollywood making the world in their own image.

My work on this chronicle comes to an end as *Such Good Friends* makes its début in New York with Elaine May's name, at her request, omitted from the credits. The *New York Times*, rightly, assumes that the film will offend a lot of people, but adds that 'it should dispel the notion that most of the director's energies go into publicising his films. This one can stand on its own.'

Dyan Cannon's performance wins her rave notices: 'She gives a performance light years above the script,' according to the *Los Angeles Times*.

'No thanks to Preminger,' is her caustic comment. Then she lets fly. 'How can a director who has no feeling make a movie about a feeling woman?' she tells all who want to listen. 'The discord and mayhem on his set sent me reeling. I would never make another film rather than work with Preminger again. I don't think he could direct his little nephew to the bathroom.'

Accustomed to this kind of reaction from his stars, Preminger replies with a savage grin: 'Imagine how good her performance will be in her next film if her performance in this one was so brilliant with a bad director . . . Anyway, I didn't hire her to praise me; I hired her to give a good performance. And she did.'

The lively exchange makes the headlines which is what film producers hope for but Preminger is already absorbed with his next project, the film about the Rosenberg spy couple. He has decided on a title which could also be a verdict on his own life, work and future.

It is 'Open Question'.

Bibliography

ALPERT, HOLLIS: *The Barrymores* (W. H. Allen, 1965)

BAREA, ILSA: *Vienna* (Secker & Warburg, 1966)

BASSETT, JAMES: *In Harm's Way* (World Publishing Co., New York, 1962)

COURTENEY, MARGUERITE: *Laurette* (Reinhart, New York, 1955)

DRURY, ALLEN: *Advise and Consent* (Collins, 1963)

GUSSOW, MEL: *Don't Say Yes Until I Finish Talking* – a life of Darryl Zanuck (Doubleday & Co., New York, 1971)

HABE, HANS: *Ich Stelle Mich* (Kurt Desch, Munich, 1954)

HOTCHNER, A. E.: *Papa Hemingway* (Weidenfeld & Nicolson, 1955)

KELLOGG, MARJORIE: *Tell Me That You Love Me, Junie Moon* (Secker & Warburg, 1969)

KNEF, HILDEGARD: *The Gift Horse* (André Deutsch, 1971)

LEE, GYPSY ROSE: *Gypsy* (André Deutsch, 1957)

LOURCELLES, JACQUES: *Otto Preminger* (Editions Seghers, Paris, 1965)

MILNE, TOM: *Mamoulian* (Thames & Hudson, 1969)

NIVEN, DAVID: *The Moon's a Balloon* (Hamish Hamilton, 1971)

PREMINGER, MARION MILL: *All I Want is Everything* (Mac-Faden, New York, 1957)

REED, REX: *Do You Sleep in the Nude?* (New American Library, New York, 1969)

ROBINSON, HENRY MORTON: *The Cardinal* (Simon & Schuster, New York, 1950)

THOMAS, BOB: *King Cohn* (Barrie & Rockcliffe, 1967)

URIS, LEON: *Exodus* (Allan Wingate, 1959)

WEISGAL, MEYER: *So Far* ... (Weidenfeld & Nicolson, 1971)

WILK, MAX: *The Wit and Wisdom of Hollywood* (Atheneum, New York, 1971)

THE PLAYS
AND FILMS
OF
OTTO PREMINGER

Plays Directed by Otto Preminger

(Plays directed by Otto Preminger at the Theater in der Josefstadt, Vienna)

1925
Kreidekreis (The Chalk Circle) by Klabund

1931
Voruntersuchung (Preliminary Inquiry) by Max Alsberg and Otto Ernst Hesse
Reporter (Front Page) by Ben Hecht and Charles McArthur (with Marion Mill as Peggy Malloy)

1933
Die Liebe Des Jungen Nosty (The Love of Young Nosty) by Koloman von Mikszath
Markart by Duschinski

1934
Mehr Als Liebe (More Than Love) by L. Bus Fekete
Christiano Zwischen Himmel und Hölle (Christiano between Heaven and Hell) by Hans Jaray
Macbeth by William Shakespeare
Die Princessin auf der Leiter (The Princes on the Ladder) (also known as *Meine Schwester und Ich:* My Sister and I) by Louis Verneuil
Sensationsprozess (Libel) by Edward Wooll
Einen Jux Will er Sich Machen (He's Going to Have Fun) by Johannes Nepomuk Nestroy
Menschen in Weiss (Men in White) by Sidney S. Kingsley

1935
Adrienne Ambrosat by Georg Kaiser
Eine Frau Luegt (A Woman Lies) by Fodor
Der Koenig Mit Dem Regenschirm (The King with the Umbrella) by Ralph Benatzky
Kleines Bezirksgericht (The Little District Court) by Otto Bielen
Die Erste Legion (The First Legion) ,by Emmett Lavery

(Directed by Otto Preminger in the United States)

Libel by Edward Wooll (N.Y. 1935)
PRODUCER: Gilbert Miller. CAST: Charles Francis (William Bale), Ernest Lawford (Sir Wilfred Kelling, K.C., M.P.), Frederick Leister (Hon. Sir Arthur Tuttingon), Wilfrid Lawson (Thomas Foxley, K.C.), Colin Clive (Sir Mark Loddon), Joan Marion (Lady Enid Loddon), Helen Goss (Sarah Carleton), Colin Hunter (George Hemsby).

Outward Bound by Sutton Vane (N.Y. 1938)
CAST: Morgan Farley (Scrubby), Helen Chandler (Ann), Alexander Kirkwood (Henry), Bramwell Fletcher (Mr Prior), Florence Reed (Mrs Clivedon Banks), Vincent Price (Rev. William Duke), Laurette Taylor (Mrs Midgit), Louis Hector (Mr Lingley), Thomas Chalmers (Rev. Frank Thomson).

Margin for Error by Clare Boothe (N.Y. 1939)
PRODUCERS: Richard Aldrich and Richard Myers. CAST: Bramwell Fletcher (Baron Max von Alvenstor), Sam Levene (Officer Finkelstein), Evelyn Whale (Frieda), Bert Lytell (Dr Jennings), Elspeth Eric (Sophie Baumer), Otto L. Preminger (Karl Baumer), Matt Briggs (Otto Horst), Leif Erickson (Thomas Denny), Edward McNamara (Capt. Mulrooney).

My Dear Children by Catherine Turney and Jerry Horwin (N.Y. 1940)
PRODUCERS: Richard Aldrich and Richard Myers. CAST: Arnold Korff (Kleinbach), Otto Hulett (Reed Hanson), Dorothy McGuire (Portia Trent), George Reynolds (Titcomb), Tala Birell (Felice, Comtesse de Britonne), John Barrymore (Alan Manville), Roland Hogue (Albert), Loi Hall (Miranda Burton) Doris Dudley (Cordelia Clark), Lloyd Gough (Lee Stevenson), Philip Reed (Willard Nelson), Stiano Braggiotti (Jacques Korbi), Leo Chalzel (Ernst van Berke).

Beverly Hills by Lynn Starling and Howard J. Green (N.Y. 1940)
PRODUCER: Lawrence Schwalb and Otto Preminger. CAST: Helen Claire (Lois Strickland), Enid Markey (Della), Peter Goo Chong (Jose), Robert Shayne (Art Browder), Frank Chew (Pedro), Doro Merande (Miss White), Clinton Sundberg (Leonard Strickland), Ilka Chase (Jean Harding), Violet Heming (May Flowers), William J. Kelly (A. Trumbull Eastmore).

Cue For Passion by Edward Chodorov and H. S. Kraft (N.Y. 1940)

PRODUCERS: Richard Aldrich and Richard Myers. CAST: Doris Nolan (Vivienne Ames), George Coulouris (John Elliott), Clare Sanders (Elsie), Bert Conway (bellboy), Thomas Coley (Dave Herrick), Claire Neilson (Ann Bailey), Fred Sears, Melchior Ferrer, John Neilan, Ellen Love (Reporters), Philip Faversham, Leonard Keith (Photographers), Gale Sondergaard (Frances Chapman), Oscar Karlweis (Paul Albert Keppler), Wilton Graff (General Escobar), Ralph Locke (Clifford Gates), Lauren Gilbert (Herbert Lee Philips), Roland Hogue (maître d'hôtel).

The More The Merrier by Frank Gabrielson and Irvin Pincus (N.Y. 1941)
PRODUCERS: Otto Preminger and Norman Pincus. CAST: Dorrit Kelton (Miss Craig), Louis Hector (Harvey Royal), J. C. Nugent (Senator Broderick), Herbert Duffy (Jackson), Robert Gray (Crivers), Frank Albertson (Daniel Finch), Grace McDonald (Bug Saunders), Keenan Wynn (Joseph Dolma), John McKee (Mr Cartwright), Mrs Priestley Morrison (Mrs Cartwright).

In Time To Come, a prologue and seven scenes by John Huston and Howard Koch (N.Y. 1941)
PRODUCER: Otto Preminger. CAST: Richard Gaines (Woodrow Wilson), Nedda Harrigan (Edna Bolling Wilson), Randolph Preston (Captain Stanley), William Harrigan (Tumulty), Russell Collins (Colonel House), Bernard Randall (Judge Brandeis), James Gregory (Dillan), Harold S. Kennedy (Terry) Philip Coolidge (Smith), Edgar Mason (Price), Robert Gray (Gordon), Alexander Clark (Dr Cary Grayson), John M. Kline (Henry White).

Four Twelves Are 48 by Joseph Kesselring (N.Y. 1951)
PRODUCERS: Richard Aldrich and Richard Myers, Julius Fleischmann and Otto Preminger. CAST: Rosetta Le Noire (Rose Bolton), Pat Crowley (Dorothy Bawke), Billy James (Jerry), Jane Du Frayne (Philippa Bawke), Joshua Shelley (Mischa Cogn), Ludwig Donath (Anton), Mrs Priestley Morrison (Mrs Kelly), Ernest Truex (Uncle Snake Tooth), Anne Revere (Nellie Hawke), Eulabelle Moore (Calendula Watkins), Ruth Taylor (Mary Bawke), Hiram Sherman (Philip Dupre), Doro Merando (Jane Dupre), Royal Dano (Joe Hungry Horse).

A Modern Primitive by Herman Wouk (Hartford, Conn. 1951)
(Preminger asked Wouk to rewrite certain scenes, Wouk refused and Preminger did not take the play to New York.)

The Moon is Blue by F. Hugh Herbert (N.Y. 1951)
PRODUCERS: Richard Aldrich, Richard Myers, Julius Fleisch-
mann. CAST: Barbara Bel Geddes (Patty O'Neill), Barry Nelson
(Donald Gresham), Donald Cook (David Slater), Ralph Dunn
(Michael O'Neill).

The Trial based on 'The Trial' by Franz Kafka. Opera by
Gottfried von Einem (N.Y. 1953)
CAST: John Druary (Joseph K.), Norman Treigle (Franz), Emile
Renan (Willem), Lawrence Winters (the Inspector), Edith Evans
(Frau Grubach), Phyllis Curtin (Fraulein Burstner).

This is Goggle by B. Plagemann (U.S.A. 1958)
PRODUCER: Otto Preminger. No showing on Broadway.

Critic's Choice by Ira Levin (N.Y. 1960)
PRODUCER: Otto Preminger. CAST: Henry Fonda (Parker Ballan-
tine), Georgann Johnson (Angela Ballantine), Eddie Hodges
(John Ballantine), Murray Hamilton (Dion Kapakos), Billie
Allen (Esse), Mildred Natwick (Charlotte Orr), Virginia
Gilmore (Ivy London).

Filmography

Die Grosse Liebe (Vienna 1931)
SCREENPLAY: Siegfried Bernfeld, Arthur Berger. CAMERA: Hans
Theyer. MUSIC: Walter Landauer, Frank Fox. RELEASE: Allianz
Film, Vienna, E.M.L.K. Weissman Tonfilm. CAST: Hansi Niese
(The Mother), Attila Hörbiger (Franz), Betty Bird (Anni
Huber), Hugo Thimig (Chief of Police), Ferdinand Maierhofer
(Herr Huber), Maria Waldner (Frau Huber), Hans Olden (Dr
Steinlechner), Adrienne Gessner (Rosa).
DIRECTOR: Otto Preminger.

Under Your Spell (Hollywood 1936)
SCREENPLAY: Frances Hyland, Saul Elkins. CAMERA: Sidney
Wagner. EDITOR: Fred Allen. MUSIC and LYRICS: Arthur Schwartz,
Howard Dietz. MUSICAL DIRECTOR: Arthur Lange. RELEASE: 20th
Century Fox. CAST: Lawrence Tibbett (Anthony Allen), Gregory
Ratoff (Petroff), Wendy Barrie (Cynthia Drexel), Arthur
Treacher (Botts), Gregory Gaye (Count Paul of Rienne), Berton
Churchill (The Judge).
DIRECTOR: Otto Preminger.

Danger, Love at Work (Hollywood 1937)
SCREENPLAY: James Edward Grant, Ben Markson. CAMERA:
Virgil Miller. MUSIC: David Buttolph. LYRICS: Mack Gordon,
Harry Revel. RELEASE: 20th Century-Fox. CAST: Ann Southern
(Toni Pemberton), Jack Haley (Henry Mac Morrow), Edward
Everett Horton (Howard Rogers), Mary Boland (Alice Pember-
ton), Bennie Bartlett (Pemberton Jr), Walter Catlett (Uncle
Alan), John Carradine (Herbert Pemberton), Etienne Girardot
(Albert Pemberton), Maurice Cass (Uncle Goliath), Alan
Dinehart (Allan Duncan), E. E. Clive (Wilbur), Margaret
McWade (Aunt Patty), Margaret Seddon (Aunt Pitty), Elisha
Cook Jr (Druggist).
DIRECTOR: Otto Preminger.

Margin for Error (Hollywood 1943)
SCREENPLAY: Lillie Hayward. Based on a play by Claire Boothe
Luce. CAMERA: Edward Cronjager. ART DIRECTORS: Richard

Day, Lewis Creber. EDITOR: Louis Loeffler. MUSICAL DIRECTOR: Emil Newman. WARDROBE DESIGNER: Earl Luick. RELEASE: 20th Century Fox. CAST: Joan Bennett (Sophie Baumer), Milton Berle (Moe Finkelstein), Otto Preminger (Karl Baumer), Carl Esmond (Baron Max von Alvenstor), Howard Freeman (Otto Hurst), Poldy Dur (Frieda), Clyde Fillmore (Dr Jennings), Joe Kirk (Salomon), Hans von Twardowski (Fritz), Ted North, Elmer Jack Semple, J. Norton Dunn (The Saboteurs), Hans Schumm (Kurt Moeller), Ed McNamara (Captain Mulrooney), Selmer Jackson (Coroner).
PRODUCER: Ralph Dietrich; DIRECTOR: Otto Preminger.

In the Meantime, Darling (Hollywood 1944)
SCREENPLAY: Arthur Kober, Michael Uris. CAMERA: Joe Mac-Donald. EDITOR: Louis R. Loeffler. MUSIC: David Buttolph. MUSICAL DIRECTOR: Emil Newman. WARDROBE DESIGNER: Bonnie Cashin. CHOREOGRAPHY: Geneva Sawyer. RELEASE: 20th Century Fox. CAST: Jeanne Crain (Maggie Preston), Frank Latimore (Lt Daniel Ferguson), Mary Nash (Mrs Preston), Eugene Pallette (H. B. Preston), Stanley Prager (Lt Philip 'Red' Pianatowski), Gale Robbins (Shirley Pianatowski), Jane Randolph (Jerry Armstrong), Doris Merrick (Mrs MacAndrews), Cara Williams (Mrs Sayre), Anne Corcoran (Mrs Bennett), Reed Hadley (Major Phillips), Heather Angel (Mrs Nelson), Bonnie Bannon (Mrs Farnum), William Colby (Lt Farnum), Cliff Clark (Colonel Corkery), Elisabeth Risdon (Mrs Corkery), Marjorie Masson (Mrs Cook).
PRODUCER and DIRECTOR: Otto Preminger.

Laura (Hollywood 1944)
SCREENPLAY: Jay Dratler, Samuel Hoffenstein, Betty Reinhardt. CAMERA: Joseph La Shelle. ART DIRECTORS: Lyle R. Wheeler, Leland Fuller. EDITOR: Louis R. Loeffler. MUSIC: David Raksin. MUSICAL DIRECTOR: Emil Newman. WARDROBE DESIGNER: Bonnie Cashin. RELEASE: 20th Century Fox. CAST: Gene Tierney (Laura Hunt), Dana Andrews (Mark McPherson), Clifton Webb (Waldo Lydecker), Vincent Price (Shelby Carpenter), Judith Anderson (Anne Treadwell), Dorothy Adams (Bessie Clary), James Flavin (McAvity), Clyde Fillmore (Bullitt), Ralph Dunn (Fred Callahan), Grant Mitchell (Corey), Kathleen Howard (Louise).
PRODUCER and DIRECTOR: Otto Preminger.

Royal Scandal (British title: *Czarina*) (Hollywood 1945)
SCREENPLAY: Edwin Justus Mayer. ADAPTED BY: Bruna Frank
from the play 'Czarina' by Lajos Biro, Melchior Lengyel.
CAMERA: Arthur Miller. ART DIRECTORS: Lyle R. Wheeler, Mark
Lee Kirk. EDITOR: Dorothy Spencer. MUSIC: Alfred Newman with
orchestration by: Edward Powell. WARDROBE DESIGNER: René
Hubert. RELEASE: 20th Century Fox. CAST: Tallulah Bankhead
(Catherine II), Charles Coburn (Chancellor Nicolai Ilyitch),
Anne Baxter (Countess Anna Jaschikoff), William Eythe (Lt
Alexis Chernoff), Vincent Price (Marquis de Fleury), Sig Ruman
(Genery Ronsky), Mischa Auer (Captain Sukov), Vladimir
Sokoloff (Malakoff), Mikhail Rasumny (Drunken General),
Grady Sutton (Boris), Don Douglas (Variatinsky), Egon Brecher
(Wassilikov), Eva Gabor (Countess Demidow).
PRODUCER: Ernst Lubitsch; DIRECTOR: Otto Preminger.

Fallen Angel (Hollywood 1945)
SCREENPLAY: Harry Kleiner. Based on a novel by Marty Holland.
CAMERA: Joseph La Shelle. ART DIRECTORS: Lyle R. Wheeler,
Leland Fuller. EDITOR: Harry Reynolds. MUSIC: David Raksin.
MUSICAL DIRECTOR: Emil Newman. WARDROBE DESIGNER: Bonnie
Cashin. RELEASE: 20th Century Fox. CAST: Dana Andrews (Eric
Stanton), Alice Faye (June Mills), Linda Darnell (Stella),
Charles Bickford (Mark Judd), Anne Revere (Clara Mills),
Bruce Cabot (Dave Atkins), John Carradine (Professor Madley),
Percy Kilbride (Pop), Olin Howlin (Joe Ellis), Jimmy Conlin
(Receptionist).
PRODUCER and DIRECTOR: Otto Preminger.

Centennial Summer (Hollywood 1946)
SCREENPLAY: Michael Kanin. Based on the novel by Albert E.
Idell. CAMERA: Ernest Palmer. ART DIRECTORS: Lyle R. Wheeler.
Leland Fuller. EDITOR: Harry Reynolds. MUSIC: Jerome Kern,
MUSICAL DIRECTOR: Alfred Newman. SONGS AND MUSIC BY: Jerome
Kern, Leo Robin, E. Y. Harburg. LYRICS BY: Oscar Hammer-
stein II. WARDROBE DESIGNER: René Hubert. RELEASE: 20th
Century Fox. CAST: Linda Darnell (Edith Rogers), Jeanne Crain
(Julia Rogers), Cornel Wilde (Philippe Lascalles), William Eythe
(Benjamin Franklin Phelps), Walter Brennan (Jesse Rogers),
Constance Bennett (Zenia Lascalles), Dorothy Gish (Harriet
Rogers), Barbara Whiting (Susanna Rogers), Larry Stevens
(Richard Lewis), Kathleen Howard (Deborah), Buddy Swan

(Dudley Rogers), Charles Dingle (Snodgrass), Gavin Gordon (Trowbridge).
PRODUCER and DIRECTOR: Otto Preminger.

Forever Amber (Hollywood 1947)
SCREENPLAY: Philip Dunne, Ring Lardner Jr. ADAPTED BY: Jerome Cady from the novel by Kathleen Winsor. CAMERA: Leon Shamroy. ART DIRECTOR: Lyle R. Wheeler. EDITOR: Louis R. Loeffler. MUSIC: David Raksin. MUSICAL DIRECTOR: Alfred Newman with orchestration by Maurice De Packh, Herbert Spencer. TECHNICOLOR ADVISERS: Natalie Kalmus, Richard Mueller. WARDROBE DESIGNERS: Charles Le Maire, René Hubert. CAST: Linda Darnell (Amber St Clair), Cornel Wilde (Bruce Carlton), Richard Greene (Lord Almsbury), George Sanders (Charles II), Glenn Langan (Captain Rex Morgan), Richard Haydn (Lord Radcliffe), John Russell (Black Jack Mallard), Jane Ball (Corinne Carlton), Leo G. Carroll (Matt Goodgroome), Jessica Tandy (Nan Britton), Anne Revere (Mother Red Cap), Robert Coote (Sir Thomas Dudley), Natalie Draper (Countess of Castelmaine), Margaret Wycherley (Mrs Spong), Alma Kruger (Lady Redmond), Edmond Breon (Lord Redmond), Alan Napier (Landale).
PRODUCER: William Perlberg; DIRECTOR: Otto Preminger.

Daisy Kenyon (Hollywood 1947)
SCREENPLAY: David Hertz. Based on the novel by Elizabeth Janeway. CAMERA: Leon Shamroy. ART DIRECTORS: Lyle R. Wheeler, George Davis. EDITOR: Louis Loeffler. MUSIC: David Raksin. MUSICAL DIRECTOR: Alfred Newman with orchestration by Herbert Spencer. WARDROBE DESIGNER: Charles Le Maire. RELEASE: 20th Century Fox. CAST: Joan Crawford (Daisy Kenyon), Dana Andrews (Dan O'Mara), Henry Fonda (Peter Lapham), Ruth Warrick (Lucille O'Mara), Peggy Ann Garner (Rosamund O'Mara), Connie Marshall (Mariette O'Mara), Martha Stewart (Mary Angelus), Nicholas Joy (Coverly), Art Baker (Lucille's lawyer), Robert Karnes (Lawyer), John Davidson (Mervyn), Charles Meredith (Judge), Roy Roberts (Dan's lawyer), Griff Barnett (Thompson), Tito Vuolo (Dino), Victoria Horne (Marsha), George E. Stone (Waiter), Walter Winchell, Leonard Lyons, John Garfield, Fernando Lamas (Stork Club Patrons).
PRODUCER and DIRECTOR: Otto Preminger.

That Lady in Ermine (Hollywood 1948)
SCREENPLAY: Samson Raphaelson. Based on an operette by Rudolph Schanzer and E. Welisch. CAMERA: Leon Shamroy. ART DIRECTORS: Lyle R. Wheeler, J. Russell Spencer. EDITOR: Dorothy Spencer. MUSIC and LYRICS: Leo Robin and Frederick Hollander. MUSICAL DIRECTOR: Alfred Newman with orchestrations by Edward Powell, Herbert Spencer, Maurice De Packh. WARDROBE DESIGNER: René Hubert. CAST: Betty Grable (Angelina and Francesca), Douglas Fairbanks Jr (Colonel Ladislas Karolyi Teglash and the Duke), Virginia Campbell (Theresa), Cesar Romero (Mario), Walter Abel (Major Horvath and Benvenuto), Reginald Gardiner (Alberto), Harry Davenport (Luigi), Whit Bissell (Guilio), Edmund MacDonald (Captain Novak), David Bond (Gabor).
PRODUCER: Ernst Lubitsch; DIRECTOR: Otto Preminger.

The Fan (British title: *Lady Windermere's Fan*) (Hollywood 1949)
SCREENPLAY: Walter Reisch, Dorothy Parker, Ross Evans. Based on the play 'Lady Windermere's Fan' by Oscar Wilde. CAMERA: Joseph La Shelle. ART DIRECTORS: Lyle R. Wheeler, Leland Fuller. EDITOR: Louis R. Loeffler. MUSIC: Daniele Amfitheatrof. MUSIC DIRECTOR: Alfred Newman with orchestration by Edward Powell, Maurice de Packh. WARDROBE DESIGNERS: Charles Le Maire, René Hubert. RELEASE: 20th Century Fox. CAST: Jeanne Crain (Lady Windermere), Madeleine Carroll (Mrs Erlynne), George Sanders (Lord Darlington), Richard Greene (Lord Windermere), Martita Hunt (Duchess of Berwick), John Sutton (Cecil Graham), Hugh Dempster (Lord Augustus Lorton), Richard Ney (Mr Hopper), Virginia McDowell (Lady Agatha), Hugh Murray (Dawson), Frank Elliott (The Jeweller), John Burton (Hoskins), Trevor Ward (The Auctioneer).
PRODUCER and DIRECTOR: Otto Preminger.

Whirlpool (Hollywood 1949)
SCREENPLAY: Ben Hecht (under the pseudonym Lester Bartow), Andrew Solt. Based on a novel by Guy Endore. CAMERA: Arthur Miller. ART DIRECTORS: Lyle R. Wheeler, Leland Fuller. EDITOR: Louis R. Loeffler. MUSIC: David Raksin. MUSICAL DIRECTOR: Alfred Newman with orchestration by Edward Powell. WARD-ROBE DESIGNERS: Charles Le Maire, Oleg Cassini (for Gene Tierney). RELEASE: 20th Century Fox. CAST: Gene Tierney (Ann Sutton), Richard Conte (Dr William Sutton), José Ferrer (David Korvo), Chalres Bickford (Lt Colton), Barbara O'Neil (Theresa

Randolph), Eduard Franz (Martin Avery), Constance Collier (Tina Cosgrove), Fortunio Bonanova (Ferruccio di Ravallo). Ruth Lee (Miss Hall), Ian MacDonald (Detective Hogan), Bruce Hamilton (Lt Jeffreys), Alex Gerry (Dr Peter Duval), Larry Keating (Mr Simms), Mauritz Hugo (Hotel Employee), John Trebach (Freddie), Myrtle Anderson (Agnes), Larry Dobkin (Surgeon Wayne), Jan Van Duser (Miss Andrews), Nancy Valentine (Taffy Lou), Clancy Cooper (Eddie Dunn). PRODUCER and DIRECTOR: Otto Preminger.

Where The Sidewalk Ends (Hollywood 1950)
SCREENPLAY: Rex Conner. Based on an adaptation by Victor Trivas, Frank P. Rosenberg, Robert E. Kent of a novel by William L. Stuart. CAMERA: Joseph La Shelle. ART DIRECTORS: Lyle R. Wheeler, J. Russell Spencer. EDITOR: Louis Loeffler. MUSIC: Cyril Mockridge. MUSICAL DIRECTOR: Lionel Newman with orchestration by Edward Powell. WARDROBE DESIGNERS: Charles Le Maire, Oleg Cassini (for Gene Tierney). RELEASE: 20th Century Fox. CAST: Dana Andrews (Mark Dixon), Gene Tierney (Morgan Taylor), Gay Merrill (Scalise), Bert Freed (Paul Klein), Tom Tully (Jiggs Taylor), Karl Malden (Lt Bill Thomas), Ruth Donnelly (Martha), Craig Stevens (Ken Payne), Robert F. Simon (Inspector Nicholas Foley), Harry von Zell (Ted Morrison), Don Appell (Willie), Neville Brand (Steve), Grace Mills (Mrs Tribaum), Lou Krugman (Mike Williams), David McMahon (Harrington), David Wolfe (Sid Kramer), Steve Roberts (Gilruth), Phil Tully (Tod Benson), Ian MacDonald (Casey), John Close (Hanson), John McGuire (Gertessen), Lou Nova (Ernie), Ralph Peters (Counterman), Oleg Cassini (Mayer), Louise Lorimer (Mrs Jackson), Lester Sharpe (Friedman), Chili Williams (Teddy), Robert Foulk (Feeney), Eda Reiss Merin (Mrs Klein). PRODUCER and DIRECTOR: Otto Preminger.

The Thirteenth Letter (Hollywood 1950)
SCREENPLAY: Howard Koch. Based on a script by Louis Chavance for Le Corbeau (H. G. Clouzot, 1943). CAMERA: Joseph La Shelle. ART DIRECTORS: Lyle R. Wheeler, Maurice Ransford. EDITOR: Louis Loeffler. MUSIC: Alex North. MUSICAL DIRECTOR: Lionel Newman with orchestration by Maurice De Packh. WARDROBE DESIGNERS: Charles Le Maire, Edward Stevenson. RELEASE: 20th Century Fox (Exteriors, Quebec, Canada). CAST:

260

Linda Darnell (Denise Tourneur), Charles Boyer (Dr Paul Laurent), Michael Rennie (Dr Pearson), Constance Smith (Cora Laurent), Françoise Rosay (Mrs Simms), Judith Evelyn (Sister Mary), Guy Sorel (Robert Helier), June Hedin (Rochelle),Paul Guevremont (Postman), George Alexander (Dr Fletcher), J. Leo Cagnon (Dr Helier), Ovila Legare (The Mayor), Camille Ducharme (Fredette). PRODUCER and DIRECTOR: Otto Preminger.

Angel Face (Hollywood 1952)
SCREENPLAY: Frank Nugent and Oscar Millard. Based on a story by Chester Erskine. CAMERA: Harry Stradling. ART DIRECTORS: Albert S. D'Agostino, Carroll Clark. MUSIC: Dimitri Tiomkin. MUSICAL DIRECTOR: Constantin Bakaleinikoff. WARDROBE DESIGNER: Michael Woulke. RELEASE: RKO. CAST: Robert Mitchum (Frank Jessup), Jean Simmons (Diane Tremayne), Mona Freeman (Mary Wilton), Herbert Marshall (Mr Charles Tremayne), Leon Ames (Fred Barrett), Barbara O'Neill (Mrs Catherine Tremayne), Kenneth Robey (Bill Crompton), Raymond Greenleaf (Arthur Vance), Griff Barnett (The Judge), Robert Gist (Miller), Jim Backus (Judson), Morgan Brown (Harry the Bartender), Morgan Farley (A Juror), Herbert Lytton (The Doctor). PRODUCER: Howard Hughes; DIRECTOR: Otto Preminger.

The Moon is Blue (Hollywood 1953)
SCREENPLAY: F. Hugh Herbert. Based on his play 'The Moon is Blue'. CAMERA: Ernest Laszlo. EDITORS: Louis R. Loeffler, Otto Ludwig. MUSIC: Herschel Burke Gilbert. LYRICS: Sylvia Fine. WARDROBE DESIGNER: Don Loper. RELEASE: United Artists. CAST: Maggie MacNamara (Patty O'Neill), William Holden (Don Gresham), David Niven (David Slater), Dawn Addams (Cynthia Slater), Gregory Ratoff (Taxi Driver), Fortunio Bonanova (Television Announcer), Hardy Krüger and Johanna Matz (A couple in the final scene). PRODUCERS: Otto Preminger and F. Hugh Herbert. DIRECTOR: Otto Preminger.

River of No Return (Canada 1954)
SCREENPLAY: Frank Fenton. Based on a story by Louis Lantz. CAMERA: Joseph La Shelle. ART DIRECTORS: Lyle Wheeler, Addison Hehr. EDITOR: Louis Loeffler. MUSIC: Cyril Mockridge and Lionel Newman. MUSICAL DIRECTOR: Lionel Newman with orchestration by Edward Powell. WARDRODE DESIGNERS: Charles

Le Maire, Travilla. RELEASE: 20th Century Fox. CAST: Robert Mitchum (Matt Calder), Marilyn Monroe (Kay Weston), Rory Calhoun (Harry Weston), Tommy Rettig (Mark Calder), Murvyn Vye (Dave Colby), Douglas Spencer (Sam Benson), Ed Winton (A Gambler), Don Beddoe (Ben), Claire André (Surrey Driver), Jack Mather (A Croupier), Edmund Cobb (A Barber), Will Wright (Merchant), Jarma Lewis (Dancer), Hal Baylor (A Drunken Cowboy), Arthur Shields (The Minister).
PRODUCER: Stanley Rubin; DIRECTOR: Otto Preminger.

Carmen Jones (Hollywood 1954)
SCREENPLAY: Harry Kleiner. Based on a musical comedy by Oscar Hammerstein II. CAMERA: Sam Leavitt and Albert Myers. ART DIRECTOR: Edward L. Ilou. EDITOR: Louis R. Loeffler. MUSIC: Herschel Burke Gilbert based on the music of Georges Bizet. WARDROBE DESIGNER: Mary Ann Nyberg. TITLES: Saul Bass. RELEASE: 20th Century Fox. CAST: Dorothy Dandridge (Carmen Jones), Harry Belafonte (Joe), Olga James (Cindy Lou), Pearl Bailey (Frankie), Diahann Carroll (Myrt), Roy Glenn (Rum), Nick Stewart (Dink), Joe Adams (Husky Miller), Brock Peters (Sgt Brown), Sandy Lewis (T-Bone), Maurie Lynn (Sally), DeForest Covan (Entertainer), Rubin Wilson (Husky's Opponent), Carmen De Lavallade and Archie Savage (Dance Soloists).
PRODUCER and DIRECTOR: Otto Preminger.

The Man with the Golden Arm (Hollywood 1955)
SCREENPLAY: Walter Newman, Lewis Meltzer. Based on the novel by Nelson Algren. CAMERA: Sam Leavitt. ART DIRECTOR: Joe Wright. EDITOR: Louis R. Loeffler. MUSIC: Elmer Bernstein. WARDROBE DESIGNERS: Joe King, Adele Parmenter, Mary Ann Nyberg. TITLES: Saul Bass. RELEASE: United Artists. CAST: Frank Sinatra (Frankie Machine), Kim Novak (Molly), Eleanor Parker (Zosch), Arnold Stang (Sparrow), Darren McGavin (Louis), Robert Strauss (Schwiefka), George Matthews (Williams), John Conte (Drunky), Doro Merande (Vi), George E. Stone (Sam Markette), Emil Meyer (Inspector Bednar), Himself (Shorty Rogers), Himself (Shelly Manne), Leonid Kinskey (Dr Dominowski), Frank Richards (Piggy), Ralph Neff (Chester), Ernest Raboff (Bird-Dog), Marth Wentworth (Vaugie), Jerry Barclay (Junkie), Leonard Bremen (Taxi Driver), Paul Burns (Suspenders), Charles Seel (Proprietor), Will Wright (Lane), Tommy

Hart (Kvorka), Frank Marlowe (Antek), Joe McTurk (Meter Reader).
PRODUCER and DIRECTOR: Otto Preminger.

The Court Martial of Billy Mitchell (British title: *One Man Mutiny*) (Hollywood 1955)
SCREENPLAY: Milton Sperling and Emmett Lavery. Based on a true story by General William Mitchell. CAMERA: Sam Leavitt. ART DIRECTOR: Malcolm Bert. EDITOR: Folmar Blangsted. MUSIC: Dimitri Tiomkin. WARDROBE DESIGNER: Howard Shoup. RELEASE: Warner Brothers. CAST: Gary Cooper (Brig.-General William Mitchell), Charles Bickford (General James Guthrie), Rod Steiger (Major Allen Gullion), Ralph Bellamy (Congressman Frank Reid), Elizabeth Montgomery (Margaret Lansdowne), Fred Clark (Colonel Moreland), James Daly (Colonel Herbert A. White), Darren McGavin (Russ Peters), Jack Lord (Zachary Lansdowne), Peter Graves (Captain Elliott), Robert F. Simon (Admiral Adam Gage), Charles Dingle (Senator Fullerton), Dayton Lummis (General Douglas MacArthur), Tom McKee (Captain Eddie Rickenbacker).
PRODUCER: Milton Sperling; DIRECTOR: Otto Preminger.

Saint Joan (London 1957)
SCREENPLAY: Graham Greene. Based on the play 'Saint Joan' by Bernard Shaw. CAMERA: Georges Perinal. MUSIC: Mischa Spolianski. TITLES: Saul Bass. RELEASE: United Artists. CAST: Jean Seberg (Saint Joan), Richard Widmark (Charles, The Dauphin), Richard Todd (Dunois), Anton Walbrook (Cauchon, Bishop of Beauvais), John Gielgud (Earl of Warwick), Felix Aylmer (The Inquisitor), Harry Andrews (John de Stogumber), Barry Jones (de Courcelles), Finlay Currie (Archbishop of Rheims), Bernard Miles (The Executioner), Patrick Barr (Captain La Hire), Kenneth Haigh (Brother Martin), Archie Duncan (Baudricourt), Margot Grahame (Duchess of la Trémouille), Francis de Wolfe (La Trémouille), Victor Maddern (An English soldier), David Oxley (Gilles de Rais, 'Bluebeard'), Sidney Bromley (Baudricourt's steward), David Langton (Captain of Warwick's Guard).
PRODUCER and DIRECTOR: Otto Preminger.

Bonjour Tristesse (South of France 1957)
SCREENPLAY: Arthur Laurents. Based on the novel by Françoise Sagan. CAMERA: Georges Périnal. EDITOR: Helga Cranston. MUSIC: Georges Auric. COSTUME CO-ORDINATION: Hope Bryce.

CREDITS: Saul Bass. RELEASE: Columbia. CAST: Deborah Kerr (Anne Larsen), David Niven (Raymond), Jean Seberg (Cécile), Mylene Demongeot (Elsa Mackenbourg), Geoffrey Horne (Philippe), Juliette Greco (Night Club singer), Walter Chiari (Pablo), Martita Hunt (Philippe's Mother), Roland Culver (Mr Lombard), Jean Kent (Mrs Lombard), David Oxley (Jacques), Elga Anderson (Denise), Jeremy Burnham (Hubert Duclos), Eveline Eyfel (The Maid), Tutte Lemkow (Pierre Schube). PRODUCER and DIRECTOR: Otto Preminger.

Porgy and Bess (Hollywood 1959)
SCREENPLAY: Richard Nash. Based on the stage operatta by George Gershwin from the novel 'Porgy' by DuBose and Dorothy Heyward. CAMERA: Leon Shamroy. ART DIRECTORS: Serge Krizman, Joseph Wright. EDITOR: Daniel Mandell. MUSIC: George Gershwin. MUSICAL DIRECTOR: André Prévin. WARDROBE DESIGNER: Irene Sharaff. RELEASE: Columbia. CAST: Sidney Poitier (Porgy), Dorothy Dandridge (Bess), Sammy Davis Jr (Sportin' Life), Pearl Bailey (Maria), Brock Peters (Crown), Leslie Scott (Jake), Diahann Carroll (Clara), Ruth Attaway (Serena), Clarence Muse (Peter), Everdinne Wilson (Annie), Joel Fluellen (Robbins). PRODUCER: Samuel Goldwyn; DIRECTOR: Otto Preminger.

Anatomy Of A Murder (USA 1959)
SCREENPLAY: Wendell Mayes. Based on the novel by Robert Traver. CAMERA: Sam Leavitt. EDITOR: Louis R. Loeffler. MUSIC: Duke Ellington. COSTUME SUPERVISION: Hope Bryce. TITLES: Saul Bass. RELEASE: Columbia. CAST: James Stewart (Paul Biegler), Lee Remick (Laura Manion), Ben Gazzara (Lt Frederick Manion), Joseph N. Welch (Judge Weaver), Kathryn Grant (Mary Pilant), Arthur O'Connell (Parnell McArthur), Eve Arden (Maida Rutledge), George C. Scott (Claude Dancer), Brooks West (Mitch Lodwick), Orson Bean (Dr Smith), John Qualen (Sulo, The Guard), Murray Hamilton (Alphonse Paquette), Russ Brown (Mr Lemon), Don Ross (Duane Miller), Jimmy Conlin (Clarence Madigan), Ned Weaver (Dr Roschid), Ken Lynch (Sgt. Duro), Duke Ellington (Pie-Eye), Mrs Welch (A Juror). PRODUCER and DIRECTOR: Otto Preminger.

Exodus (Israel 1960)
SCREENPLAY: Dalton Trumbo. Based on the novel 'Exodus' by Leon Uris. CAMERA: Sam Leavitt. EDITOR: Louis R. Loeffler.

MUSIC: Ernest Gold. WARDROBE DESIGNERS: Joe King, May Walding, Margo Slater, Rudi Gernreich (for Eva Marie Saint). COSTUME SUPERVISOR: Hope Bryce. GENERAL MANAGER: Martin Shute. PRODUCTION MANAGER: Eva Monley. RELEASE: United Artists. CAST: Paul Newman (Ari Ben Canaan), Eva Marie Saint (Kitty Fremont), Ralph Richardson (General Sutherland), Peter Lawford (Major Caldwell), Lee J. Cobb (Barak Ben Canaan), Sal Mineo (Dov Landau), Meyer Weisgal (Ben Gurion), John Derek (Taha), Hugh Griffith (Mandria), David Opatoshu (Akiva), Jill Haworth (Karen), Gregory Ratoff (Lakavitch), Felix Aylmer (Dr Lieberman), Marius Goring (Von Storch), Alexandra Stewart (Jordana), Michael Wager (David), Martin Benson (Mordekai), Paul Stevens (Reuben), Betty Walker (Sarah), Martin Miller (Odenheim), Victor Maddern (Sgt), Peter Madden (Dr Clement), Joseph Furst (Avidan). PRODUCER and DIRECTOR: Otto Preminger.

Advise and Consent (Washington 1962)
SCREENPLAY: Wendell Mayes. Based on the novel 'Advise and Consent' by Allen Drury. CAMERA: Sam Leavitt. EDITOR: Louis R. Leoffler. MUSIC: Jerry Fielding. TITLE SONG, LYRICS: Ned Washington. Sung by Frank Sinatra. TITLES: Saul Bass. WARDROBE DESIGNERS: Joe King, Adele Parmenter, Michael Harte, Bill Blass (for Gene Tierney). COSTUME CO-ORDINATOR: Hope Bryce. RELEASE: Columbia Pictures. CAST: Henry Fonda (Robert Leffingwell), Charles Laughton (Senator Seabright Cooley), Don Murray (Senator Brigham Anderson), Walter Pidgeon (Senator Bob Munson), Peter Lawford (Senator Lafe Smith), Gene Tierney (Dolly Harrison), Franchot Tone (The President), Lew Ayres (The Vice-President), Burgess Meredith (Herbert Gelman), Eddie Hodges (Johnny Leffingwell), Paul Ford (Senator Stanley Danta), George Grizzard (Senator Fred Van Ackerman). PRODUCER and DIRECTOR: Otto Preminger.

The Cardinal (Vienna, Rome, Boston, Hollywood 1963)
SCREENPLAY: Robert Dozier. Based on the novel by Henry Morton Robinston. CAMERA: Leon Shamory. EDITOR: Louis R. Loeffler. MUSIC: Jerome Moross. COSTUME CO-ORDINATOR: Hope Bryce. TITLES: Saul Bass. EXECUTIVE ASSISTANT TO THE PRODUCER: Nat Rudich. ASSOCIATE PRODUCER: Martin G. Shute. PRODUCTION MANAGERS: Harrison Starr, Eva Monley, Henry Weinberger, Paul Waldher. RELEASE: Columbia. CAST: Tom Tryon (Stephen

Fermoyle), Carol Lynley (Mona Fermoyle), Dorothy Gish (Celia), Maggie MacNamara (Florrie), Bill Hayes (Frank), Cameron Prud'Homme (Din), Cecil Kellaway (Monsignor Monaghan) Loring Smith (Cornelius J. Deegan), John Huston (Cardinal Glennon), Jose Duval (Ramon Gongaro), Pat Henning (Hercule Menton), Burgess Meredith (Father Ned Halley), Jill Haworth (Lalage Menton), Russ Brown (Dr Heller), Raf Vallone (Cardinal Quarenghi), Tullio Carminati (Cardinal Giacobbi), Ossie Davis (Father Gillis), Don Francesco Mancini of Veroli (M.C. at Ordination), Dino Di Luca (Italian Monsignor), Carol Lynley (Regina Fermoyle), Donald Hayne (Father Eberling), Chill Wills (Monsignor Whittle), Arthur Hunnicutt (Sheriff Dubrow), Romy Schneider (Annemarie), Peter Weck (Kurt von Hartman), Rudolf Forster (Drunk Man at the Ball), Josef Meinrad (Cardinal Innitzer), Dagmar Schmedes (Madame Walter), Eric Frey (Seyss-Inquart), Josef Krastel (Von Hartman's Butler), Wolfgang Preiss (S.S. Major).
PRODUCER and DIRECTOR: Otto Preminger.

In Harm's Way (Pearl Harbor 1964)
SCREENPLAY: Wendell Mayes. Based on the novel by James Bassett. CAMERA: Loyal Griggs, Philip Lathrop. EDITORS: George Tomasini, Hugh S. Fowler. MUSIC: Jerry Goldsmith. SPECIAL PHOTOGRAPHY: Farciot Edouart. TITLES: Saul Bass. COSTUME CO-ORDINATION: Hope Bryce. ASSISTANT TO THE PRODUCER: Nat Rudich. PRODUCTION MANAGERS: Eva Monley, Henry Weinberger, Stanley H. Goldsmith, James Henderling. RELEASE: Paramount Pictures. CAST: John Wayne (Captain Rockwell Torrey), Kirk Douglas (Cdr Paul Eddington), Patricia Neal (Lt Maggie Haynes), Tom Tryon (Lt William McConnel), Jill Haworth (Ens. Annalee Dorne), Dana Andrews (Admiral Broderick), Stanley Holloway (Clayton Canfil), Burgess Meredith (Cdr Powell), Franchot Tone (CINCPAC I Admiral), Henry Fonda (CINCPAC II Admiral).
PRODUCER and DIRECTOR: Otto Preminger.

Bunny Lake Is Missing (London 1965)
SCREENPLAY: John and Penelope Mortimer. Based on the novel by Evelyn Piper. CAMERA: Denys Coop. MUSIC: Paul Glass. TITLES: Saul Bass. COSTUME CO-ORDINATOR: Hope Bryce. ASSOCIATE PRODUCER: Martin C. Shute. ASSISTANT TO THE PRODUCER: Max Slater. RELEASE: Columbia Pictures. CAST: Keir Dullea (Stephen), Carol Lynley (Ann), Laurence Olivier (Newhouse),

Martita Hunt (Ada Ford), Noël Coward (Wilson), Lucie Mannheim (Cook), Adrienne Corri (Dorothy), Anna Massey (Elvira), Finlay Currie (Doll-maker), Clive Revill (Andrews), Jill Melford (Teacher), Kika Markham (Nurse), Delphi Lawrence (First mother at school), Suzanne Neve (Second mother at school), Richard Wattis (Clerk in shipping office), Victor Maddern (Taxi Driver), Fred Emney (Man in Soho), David Oxley (Doctor), Megs Jenkins (Hospital Sister).
PRODUCER and DIRECTOR: Otto Preminger.

Hurry Sundown (Louisiana 1966)
SCREENPLAY: Thomas C. Ryan, Horton Foote. Based on the novel by B. and K. Gilden. CAMERA: Milton Krasner, Loyal Griggs. EDITORS: Louis Loeffler, James D. Wells. MUSIC: Hugo Montenegro. WARDROBE DESIGNERS: Estevez. ASSISTANT TO PRODUCER: Nat Rudich. PRODUCTION MANAGERS: Stephen F. Kesten, Eva Monley. RELEASE: Paramount Pictures. CAST: Michael Caine (Henry Warren), Jane Fonda (Julie Ann Warren), John Phillip (Rad McDowell), Diahann Carroll (Vivian Thurlow), Robert Hooks (Reeve Scott), Faye Dunnaway (Lou McDowell), Burgess Meredith (Judge Purcell), Jim Backus (Carter Sillens), Robert Reed (Lars Finchley), Beah Richards (Rose Scott), Rex Ingram (Professor Thurlow), Madeleine Sherwood (Eula Purcell), Doro Merande (Ada Hemmings), George Kennedy (Sheriff Coombs), Frank Converse (Rev. Clem De Lavery), Loring Smith (Thomas Elwell), Donna Danton (Sukie Purcell), John Mark (Colie Warren), Luke Askey (Dolph Higginson), Peter Goff (Lipscomb), William Elder (Bishop), Steve Sanders (Charles McDowell), Dawn Barcelona (Ruby McDowell), David Sanders (Wyatt McDowell), Michael Henry Roth (Timmy McDowell), Gladys Newman (Mrs Coombs).
PRODUCER and DIRECTOR: Otto Preminger.

Skidoo (1968)
SCREENPLAY: Dorian Wm. Cannon. CAMERA: Leon Shamroy. ASSISTANT DIRECTOR: Eric von Stroheim Jr, Wally Jones, Al Murphey, Steven North. EDITOR: George Rohrs. MUSIC and LYRICS: Harry Nilsson. TITLES: Sandy Dvore. WARDROBE DESIGNER: Rudi Gernreich. ASSISTANT TO THE PRODUCER: Nat Rudich. RELEASE: Paramount Pictures. CAST: Jackie Gleason (Tony Banks), Carol Channing (Flo Banks), Groucho Marx ('God'), Frankie Avalon (Angie), Fred Clark (A Tower Guard), Michael Constantine (Leech), Frank Gorshin (The Man), John

Philip Law (Stash), Peter Lawford (The Senator), Burgess Meredith (The Warden), George Raft (Captain Garbaldo), Cesar Romero (Hechy), Mickey Rooney ('Blue Chips' Packard), Austin Pendleton (The Professor 'Fred'), Alexandra Hay (Darlene Banks), Luna ('God's' Mistress), Arnold Strang (Harry), Doro Merande (The Mayor).
PRODUCER and DIRECTOR: Otto Preminger.

Tell Me That You Love Me, Junie Moon (USA 1970)
SCREENPLAY: Marjorie Kellogg. Based on her novel. CAMERA: Boris Kaufman. MUSIC: Philip Springer. TITLES: Stanley Cortez. COSTUME CO-ORDINATOR: Hope Bryce. ASSOCIATE PRODUCER: Nat Rudich. ASSISTANT TO THE PRODUCER: Erik Kirkland. RELEASE: Paramount Pictures. CAST: Liza Minnelli (Junie Moon), Ken Howard (Arthur), Robert Moore (Warren), James Coco (Mario), Kay Thompson (Gregory), Fred Williamson (Beach Boy), Ben Piazza (Jesse), Emily Yancy (Solana), Leonard Frey (Guiles), Clarice Taylor (Minnie), James Beard (Sidney Wyner), Julie Bovasso (Romona), Gina Collins (Lila), Barbara Logan (Mother Moon), Nancy Marchand (Nurse Oxford), Lynn Milgrim (Nurse Holt), Ric O. Feldman (Joebee), James D. Pasternak (The Artist), Angelique Pettyjohn (Melissa).
PRODUCER and DIRECTOR: Otto Preminger.

Such Good Friends (New York 1971)
SCREENPLAY: Ester Dale. Based on the novel by Lois Gould. CAMERA: Gayne Rescher, A.S.C. (Jack Priestley). ASSOCIATE PRODUCERS: Nat Rudich, Erik Preminger. PRODUCTION DESIGNER: Rouben Ter-Arutunian. COSTUME DESIGNERS: Hope Preminger, Ron Talsky. MUSIC: Thomas Z. Shepard. RELEASE: Paramount Pictures. CAST: Dyan Cannon (Julie Messinger), James Coco (Dr Timmy Spector), Jennifer O'Neill (Miranda Graham), Ken Howard (Cal Whiting), Nina Foch (Mrs Wallman), Laurence Luckinbill (Richard Messinger), Burgess Meredith (Bernard Kalman), James Beard (Dr Mahler), Rita Gam (Doria Perkins), Nancy Guild (Molly Hastings), Elaine Joyce (Marian Spector), Sam Levene (Uncle Eddie), Nancy R. Pollock (Aunt Harriet), William Redfield (Barney Halstead), Doris Roberts (Mrs Gold), Lee Sabinson (Dr Bleiweiss), Richard B. Shull (Clarence Fitch), Clarice Taylor (Mrs McKay), Virginia Vestoff (Emily Lapham).
PRODUCER and DIRECTOR: Otto Preminger.

Index